Islamism

Islamism

Religion, Radicalization, and Resistance

ANDERS STRINDBERG and MATS WÄRN

polity

First published in 2011 by Polity Press

Polity Press
65 Bridge Street
Cambridge CB2 1UR, UK

Polity Press
350 Main Street
Malden, MA 02148, USA

ISBN-13: 978-0-7456-4061-7 (hardback)
ISBN-13: 978-0-7456-4062-4 (paperback)

A catalogue record for this book is available from the British Library.

Typeset in 11.25 on 13 pt Dante by Toppan Best-set Premedia Limited
Printed and bound in Great Britain by the MPG Books Group

The publisher has used its best endeavors to ensure that the URLs for external websites referred to in this book are correct and active at the time of going to press. However, the publisher has no responsibility for the websites and can make no guarantee that a site will remain live or that the content is or will remain appropriate.

Every effort has been made to trace all copyright holders, but if any have been inadvertently overlooked the publisher will be pleased to include any necessary credits in any subsequent reprint or edition.

For further information on Polity, visit our website: www.politybooks.com

Contents

Acknowledgments

Throughout the research for, and writing of this book, we have received much help and encouragement from many individuals and institutions. It is impossible to acknowledge all of them, and many must unfortunately remain anonymous for their own protection. However, some from among this collection of supportive colleagues, encouraging friends and cooperative research subjects not only can, but must be acknowledged. Each in his or her own way has helped us – either individually or as an authorial team – to think in new ways about the issues at hand, provided access to primary sources, or in some other way helped to improve the manuscript. They include: Ambassador Tommy Arwitz, Swedish Ministry of Foreign Affairs; Talal Atrissi, Lebanese University; Saqr Abu Fakhr, Institute of Palestine Studies, Beirut; David Brannan, Naval Postgraduate School, Center for Homeland Defense and Security; Linda Butler, Institute of Palestine Studies, Washington, DC; Ali Fayyad and his staff at the Consultative Center for Studies and Documentation, Beirut; Philip F. Esler, University of St Andrews; Tahsin Halabi, Palestinian Writers' Union, Syria; Raymond A. Hinnebusch, University of St Andrews; Bruce Hoffman, Georgetown University; Clive Jones, Leeds University; Haytham Muzahem; Nadim Shehadi, Chatham House; and Abdolkarim Soroush.

Anders would like to acknowledge the Naval Postgraduate School, Center for Homeland Defense and Security – and especially its Executive and Academic Directors, Ted Lewis and Chris Bellavita – for providing an uncommonly dynamic and exceptionally stimulating intellectual environment. He would like to dedicate his contribution to this volume to his wife Samantha, for her support, advice, and patience.

Mats would like to thank the Politics of Development Group at Stockholm University (PODSU) for support in terms of seminars, comments, comradeship and grants that made fieldwork possible. He would like to dedicate his contribution to this volume to Kumba, for her commitment, kindness, and support.

Monterey and Stockholm, June 2011

A Note on Transliteration

Throughout the narrative, we have followed commonly used, simplified forms for transliterating the original Arabic, rather than any of the standard systems. We have done so for reasons of readability.

1

Introduction: The Islamist Challenge

Verily, God does not change the condition of
a people until they change it themselves.

Quran 13: 11

Islam is the second largest religion in the world, and the fastest growing. Roughly one-quarter of the world's population is Muslim, and over one-third of all sovereign states are members of the Organization of the Islamic Conference, most of them in the so-called global South. In the course of its thirteen centuries of expansion and consolidation, Islam has infused, absorbed, supplanted, and dialogued with a wide range of local cultures and experiences. In the process, it has become not only a transnational, but also an intensely local source of identity to its adherents around the world. Yet in the modern era, it is only in the last three decades – coinciding with the failure of third worldism and advent of globalization – that Islam has been propelled from the sidelines of third world politics to a defining role on the global stage. Its political manifestations feed into, and are fed by real socioeconomic concerns around the globe; local injustices as well as regional and global imbalances, real or perceived. Its representatives have emerged as self-styled defenders of the downtrodden, restorers of local autonomy, and defenders against neo-colonial impositions. Grounded in the experiences and narratives of real communities, Islamic political leaders have come to champion a range of oftentimes contradictory parochial narratives. Framed by the universal claims of a common confession, they also constitute a global movement that encompasses and transcends any and all of its local manifestations.

This local–global dualism can be seen clearly by looking at the disparate and dispersed local events and processes that have marked Islam's rise to global political prominence; from the Islamic Revolution in Iran to educational reform in Indonesia; from discontentment and revolt in post-colonial Algeria, to the defeat of Soviet forces in Afghanistan at the hands of an international brigade of Islamic warriors; from patterns of immigration in

1

Europe to state manipulation of religious identities in Kashmir and Punjab; from empowerment of culturally marginalized peoples in the post-Soviet Caucasus to improvement of quality of life in West African villages; from the grinding struggles of Hezbollah in Lebanon and Hamas in Palestine, to the spectacular attacks by al-Qa'ida on September 11, 2001; from the writings of intellectuals in Egypt, India, and Morocco to the ongoing war in Iraq. Through the synergy of these and a myriad other processes, Islam has emerged as a sophisticated, multifaceted, fluid and modern discursive framework that provides a potent alternative way of thinking and speaking about politics; a series of locally grounded, yet globally connected critical discourses articulated by intellectuals and educators, all of which contain a challenge to the structures and ideals of modern secularism. Through the interconnectedness of these local challenges, Islam has come to frame a powerful counter-hegemonic challenge to the very structures of global politics within which it has emerged, to the interests those structures serve, and to the normative assumptions that sustain them. This simultaneously local and global sociopolitical challenge that inheres in, is framed by, and expressed through Islam is what this study understands as Islamism.

The 'fractured unity' of Islamism has been noted (Martin and Barzegar 2010: 2), but not yet adequately addressed by Western scholarship, notwithstanding an ever-distending scholarly corpus and the urgent, even existentially anguished tenor among those whose narratives frame the discourse. Western scholarship (with some stellar exceptions) appears to have barely begun a rigorous and systematic investigation into the local–global dynamic within Islamism. Indeed, Western academia appears to be a prisoner of its own post-Enlightenment discourse, systemically incapable of accepting and hence of adequately explaining the continued prevalence of religion as a sociopolitical organizing principle in the modern and post-modern age.

In all cases where research subjects operate in a context other than that of the researcher, it is inevitable that the issue of culture – in particular the cultural difference between the investigator and his or her subjects – assumes a critical significance. Our standard models for explaining Islam and Islamism are most commonly attempts to explain away more than they explain, often resulting in odd generalizations about the pre-modern politics of backward peoples, more or less uniformly defined by a monolithic and never-changing creed. In this context, political culture theorizing has been particularly problematic due to its close relationship with political science and international relations, the globalizing and universalizing tendencies of which have had two distinct effects. Either it has led to the idea of 'cultural spheres' on far too large a scale to be meaningful, or else it has essentialized the concept of culture based on deterministic assumptions about its nature and content.

Johannes Fabian (1983) has noted that conversation based on mutuality and respect is impossible within a cognitive model that fixes on difference and exoticism. To be sure, political culture theories have tended to homogenize and reify 'the Other' by creating stereotypes that reduce human agency and cogency to objects of inquiry. In most Western intellectual traditions, it is part of the definition of an object that it can neither speak, think, nor know; thus, the objectified cultural Other has had nothing to say. Dialogue between Etic (the researcher's perspective) and Emic (the research subject's perspective) is superfluous or impossible. Gabriel Ben-Dor (1977) noted that political culture theorizing became popular within Middle East and Islamic studies in the 1950s and 1960s due to the explanatory inadequacy of earlier structuralist approaches. Ben-Dor himself believed that the common Arab and Islamic heritage from Morocco to the Persian Gulf meant that the 'Islamic nation' was in fact a useful unit of analysis. By examining this unit, he suggested, scholars would be able to uncover its unchanging core political precepts – if only they would stop focusing on issues "temporary and particular rather than the lasting and general" (Ben-Dor 1977: 52). It is an illustration of the approach that Lisa Anderson (1995: 89) criticized when she noted that "the implicit (and sometimes explicit) assumption that attitudes and beliefs born in the desert in the era of the Prophet are timeless, unchanging, and overwhelmingly powerful . . . is a reflection of an inability to think critically about change."

Anderson is surely correct, and this inability remains a defining feature of the dominant Western narratives on Islam and Islamism. Samuel Huntington's hypothesis of an undifferentiated Arab–Islamic civilization stretching from Mauretania to Bahrain; Raphael Patai's understanding of an essential 'Arab mind'; Bernard Lewis' depiction of a Muslim civilization gone wrong; Fouad Ajami's reductionist fantasies about the Arab–Islamic psyche; and Paul Berman's notion of Islamism as a further installment in a timeless totalitarian struggle against the ideals of freedom are all highly influential cases in point: They are remarkable, not for their insight, but because they fly in the face of empirical realities in which not all Muslims have the same experience and think, act, and feel alike; in which Islamic states are as capable of rational and innovative agency as any Western state, and, importantly, in which Islamic political groups and movements pursue a vast range of strategic objectives, employing an equally vast range of tactical approaches.

The Western study of Islamism – counter-hegemonic challenges articulated on the basis of, and expressed through Islam – as distinct from the study of Islam itself, has yet to transcend its emergence as an exercise in power political threat assessment. In the late 1970s and early 1980s, a very specific series of events combined to stimulate Western interest in Islam as a political force – the assassination of Egyptian President Anwar Sadat, the Islamic revolution in Iran, and the emergence of hostile Islamist movements around the world, most notably the Palestinian Islamic Jihad and the Lebanese Hezbollah. Although the different groups and movements were geographically dispersed, grappling with different social realities, drawing on different theologies, and working towards a range of often conflicting political objectives, the emerging Islamist groups and movements nevertheless appeared to share a common ideological ideal encapsulated in the slogan of the Iranian revolution: "Neither East nor West – only Islam!" On the surface – beyond which very few scholars ventured for at least a decade – Islamists were therefore not only a new enemy, but one that was wholly other and entirely unlike us; a political creature from the black lagoon of exotic and alien religion. Importantly, the same series of events that kindled academic interest in Islamism also attracted the attention of Western security agencies and policy makers, and ever since, Western scholarship on Islamism has fused with foreign policy concerns and security political interests, creating a continuous political-academic feedback loop based on a common narrative of threat assessment. That the early interest within academia came to identify with the security concerns of government becomes apparent when one considers what fell, and what did not fall within scholars' foci of interest. The various jihad groups terrorizing the pro-Western regime in Egypt quickly became objects of intense interest, while the deeply fundamentalist, US-supported mujahedin fighting the Soviets in Afghanistan elicited only scant scholarly concern at the time. The self-styled 'revolutionary' and 'anti-imperialist' Islamic Republic of Iran engrossed scholarly imaginations, while the absolutist and fundamentalist ethics and practices of the religious–political establishment in Saudi Arabia merited much less interest. Hezbollah's operations in Lebanon – affecting American, Israeli, and other Western interests – was given ample attention, while the far more comprehensive campaign of violence waged against the Syrian government by the Syrian Muslim Brotherhood (MB) went virtually unnoticed in the corridors of academia.

As a result, the study of Islamism was immediately framed as the study of a dangerous enemy. Literature on 'political Islam' or 'Islamic fundamentalism' was packaged and sold as exotic threat assessment, often with direct recommendations for how governments could best combat the new scourge. Obviously, the point is not to indict scholars for failing to study all angles of all phenomena all the time, nor for containing suppositions about what is ultimately right and wrong. Rather, the problem is that the specific foci of scholarly interest in Islamic fundamentalism – especially within political science – demonstrated much less of a concern with Islamism as a multifaceted and contextual social phenomenon, than as an emergent one-dimensional global threat to Western interests and allies; the 'green menace' that slowly but decisively replaced the 'red peril' of the Cold War (Esposito 1995). Islamism became a geostrategic concern. For this reason, and to this day, the bulk of Western scholarship on Islamism contains virtually no account of its simultaneously local and transnational character, or – when it does recognize the importance of local context – fails to account for its transnational and global dimensions. The rule, which does admit of some very significant exceptions, has been to reduce Islamism to a one-dimensional enemy with a devotion to pre-modern ideas in a simplistic and context-less quest to erect an Islamic State, either locally or globally.

There is absolutely nothing wrong with scholars advising government – it may well be one of their primary functions as public intellectuals – but there is something profoundly troubling about scholarship taking its cues, frames of reference, research agendas, and objectives from practitioners, effectively becoming a research arm of the government. The literature suggests that many of those whose narratives define our current received wisdom on Islamism have been doing just that, resulting in serious scholarly deficiencies. When the interdisciplinary field of terrorism studies gradually devoured the study of Islamic fundamentalism, many of these scholars openly flaunted the standard practices of modern academia – which include, at a minimum, efforts to maximize detachment and minimize bias – opting instead to become self-styled counter-terrorism practitioners (Schmid and Jongman 1983). The general canons of Western post-Enlightenment scholarship were replaced by a "hermeneutic of crisis management" within which scholars developed "a communal self-perception of its being an adjunct to the various Western counterterrorism agencies," resulting in the research subject being reduced to "a research object, an enemy to be engaged in combat rather than a social phenomenon to be understood" (Brannan, Esler, and Strindberg 2001: 4). Dissection and explanation eclipsed dialogue and understanding, and an insistence by many terrorism experts on talking about, but almost never with the research subject, has resulted in a body of literature with little foundation in the reality it purports to describe.

The stream of scholarly commentary on Islamism that had begun following the Iranian Revolution two decades prior grew into a veritable torrent after Al-Qa'ida's attacks on US soil on September 11, 2001, yet quantity did by no means improve quality. Western academia was already trapped in its own discursive structures and, in a significant part of Western political consciousness and discourse, Islamists became synonymous with terrorists and one-dimensional 'evil doers,' ultimately symbolized and represented by Osama bin Laden, until he was killed on May 2, 2011, during a US raid on his compound in Pakistan. The post-9/11 academic feeding frenzy notwithstanding, very little seems to have been achieved. The study of Islamism has almost invariably taken place at the expense of Islamist perspectives; scholars have privileged their own 'objective' and 'scientific' frameworks of analysis over the subjective perspectives and self-understandings of the research subjects. There are some encouraging exceptions to this rule – which will be dealt with in the following chapters – but because the literature is cumulative, not only occasional insights, but also the habitual errors, misconception and prejudices attain considerable longevity. Indeed, much of Western scholarship remains focused on establishing to which positive Western values Islamism provides a negative corollary; how are 'they' not like 'us'? To this end, some have argued that the emergence of contemporary Islamism is part of an epic conflict between civilizations defined by religion (Lewis 2004; Ajami 2004). Others understand Islamism as an expression of a socio-cultural inability to deal with modernity and pluralism, making it a variation on the same theme as the violent and xenophobic spasms of fascism, Nazism, and the Emperor cult of Meiji Japan (Buruma and Margalit 2004). Others still claim that it as a dangerous perversion and corruption of a religion of peace, an internal hijack operation that threatens the liberty of 'real Muslims' as well as their neighbors (Albertini 2003). What makes this academic conversation and its various diagnoses of the Islamist illness highly significant is that it has become an integral element of an ongoing global conflict. As flawed anthropology once aided colonial expansion, flawed economics fed communist dictatorships, and flawed biology contributed to fascist reigns of terror, so now is flawed scholarship on Islam and Islamism actively entrenching a sociopolitical conflict of global dimensions.

The frequency and eloquence with which the generalities of Islam and Islamism are discussed are ultimately powerless to conceal the fact that diversity is also part of the norm. In this book, we will attempt to shed light on the nature of Islamism, examining the complex interplay of diversity and unity, while also critically re-examining the received view within Western scholarship. To this end, the book attempts to answer a core set of questions: What is the relationship of Islamist groups to the specific sociopolitical contexts from which they emerge, on the one hand, and simultaneously to a common ideological and theological core discourse, on the other? What factors determine groups' tactical and strategic choices, and how may they evolve over time? Is Islamism particularly prone to militancy and, if so, why? How does Islamism relate to non-Islamic ideologies? In answering these questions, the present volume takes an interdisciplinary approach, drawing on theoretical and methodological insights produced within the fields of sociology, social psychology, anthropology, and political science, as well as a series of case studies that are representative of at least some of the diversity within the global Islamist movement. To understand current and emerging events, not only do we need to know what Islam and Islamism are, but the many ways in which its local manifestations differ from and relate to each other. What makes a movement Islamist? What does it mean to call an act of violence 'Islamic terrorism'? Does our focus on the macro-contextual frame 'Islamic' add to or obscure our understanding of the micro-political realities that seed movements in Lebanon, Afghanistan, Indonesia or the Philippines? How does one fruitfully combine these different levels of analysis? This volume aims to answer such questions by focusing on the features of Islamism that makes it a generically human expression of grievances and aspirations, thereby disentangling it from the web of received wisdoms based on threat assessments and cultural exoticism. To be sure, almost all of the groups and movements examined in these cases studies are to some degree militant. There are two primary reasons for this selection. First, major militant groups such as Hezbollah, Hamas, al-Qa'ida have come to define Western imaginings of Islamism, especially in the wake of 9/11 and the 'global war on terror.' Supposed truths about these groups have become iconic for how we understand Islamism more generally. This not only warrants, but demands further critical examination. Second, precisely because of their iconic status, calling attention to the complex social dynamics, political nuances and widely divergent aspirations *even among these supposedly well known and thoroughly studied groups* has implications for the study of Islamism more generally: not even the groups and movements that have come to function as archetypes of Islamism within the dominant scholarly narratives of the West actually conform to the explanatory models supplied by those narratives. This, then, provides a powerful case for an effort to critically rethink our assumptions and models for the study of Islamism in general; to acknowledge the intellectual harm caused by neo-Orientalist scholarship, and the disservice it does to the communities it purports to study and to the government officials and policy makers who rely on its findings.

The purpose of this book can best be summarized as a rigorous attempt to understand where, how and why Islamism emerges within the wider framework of Islamic discourse, and what accounts for the often vastly different political agendas, tactical choices and strategic objectives of individual Islamist groups. While it may be obvious to many or most Westerners that 'the West' is not a monolithic entity advancing a single common narrative, or that the concept 'Christianity' covers a range of divergent and frequently incompatible interpretations of core doctrine (including, for that matter, what that core consists of), it often appears less clear that the same applies to 'the Islamic world.' Yet Islam is no less diverse in its many self-understandings than the West, and, as in the West, this self-understanding is very much a product of scholarship. In the Western hemisphere – after the collapse of the familiar enemies of the Cold War and against the background of increasing friction with enemies broadly identified as Islamic – academics were drafted to explain the nature of the new world order. On the other side, the leaders of Islamist struggles frequently have been, and are scholars, or else depend heavily on the work of scholars past and present and the intellectual coherence and legitimacy drawn from this foundation. Indeed, Islamic politics is in part defined by various understandings of *shari'ah*, Islamic law, and significantly impacted by an ongoing process of jurisprudential scholarship, *fiqh*. Numerous key Islamists are also historians, economists, social scientists, educators, and, of course, theologians who place their work in the service of their understanding of Islam, hoping thereby to impact the trajectory of their local community, the Islamic nation at large, or even the course of world history. Thus, Islamist groups and movements are as varied as the social, cultural and political contexts within which they emerge. In Palestine, the nationally focused Hamas movement won a landslide victory in the January 2006 parliamentary elections while, throughout South East Asia, the transnational Jemaah Islamiyah eschews democracy and engages in relentless terrorist attacks against tourists and Christians. The leaderships of al-Qa'ida and its affiliates have explicitly declared a war on the Christians and Jews, while the leaderships of numerous other Islamist groups argue for the possibility, or even necessity of coexistence based on intercultural dialog. In countries such as Syria, Algeria, and Egypt, repressive state structures have forced militant Islamist groups to reform themselves into democratic, civil society based organizations, while elsewhere, in countries such as Jordan and Indonesia, comparatively inclusive political structures are contributing to the growth of Islamist radicalism. Islamist discourse may often appear universal, but its interpretations, uses, and implications are numerous.

To say that jurisprudential scholarship defines Islamism does not imply that all these scholars come to the same conclusion, or even that they use the same sources. Nor does it negate the importance of non-intellectual influences, such as emotive action, local custom, and Islamicized folk beliefs, which frame and give reality to otherwise abstract concepts. As an ongoing intellectual process, different understandings of key concepts – such as war, force, modernity, and apostasy – produce different conclusions that contend with one another for the ability to impact the common narrative. In other words, it is precisely the different understandings and applications of common terms of reference that is able to produce a movement that is at the same time intensely local and thoroughly global.

When the so-called Arab Spring broke out in early 2011, this offered a challenge as well as an opportunity for the region's Islamist movements. The sociopolitical dynamics underlying this regional wave of revolutions and uprisings was certainly familiar to them. The Arab Spring may well have signified something 'new' in Arab politics but it was nevertheless triggered by the same 'old' order of autocracy, repression and humiliation that had once triggered, and then sustained, the region's various Islamist projects. Despotism, incompetence and corruption among local elites. Rulers more concerned with the flow of foreign capital than the needs of their peoples. A regional system molded and maintained by an international community paying lip service to the cause of democracy and human rights while safeguarding neo-colonial interests with an iron fist. The birth of the Muslim Brotherhood and Hezbollah, the Islamic revolution in Iran, and the formation of al-Qa'ida were all products of the same crippled and crippling political order as the Arab Spring. While not leading the charge in any of the region's uprisings, Islamists were quick to respond to the new environment. These responses, however, ranged from enthusiastic endorsement to efforts at co-opting and sabotaging the process, and thus laid bare the tactical, strategic and ideological divisions within the Islamist universe.

The intellectual context in which this book has been written is defined by the US-led war on terrorism and the seemingly self-fulfilling prophecy of a clash of civilizations. Regardless of one's understanding of the genesis of this conflict, it has pitted proponents of particular Western self-images against proponents of particular Islamic self-images. There is nothing monolithic about the positions of either side; not only are ideas of Western and Islamic civilizations simplifications, but even the conflicting self-images, when broken down by critical examination, reveal a range of positions, ideas, and ideals. One of the greatest obstacles to understanding the conflict is the insistence – by stakeholders on both sides – on cohesion, while glossing over plurality and diversity. It is the contention throughout the following pages that, although global in scale and implications, this conflict is not a clash of civilizations as is so often claimed, but a series of clashes within and across civilizations; internal struggles on both sides for the ability to define the key texts, symbols, and narratives, and ultimately the future of one's ingroup. The focus of our scholarship is turned on Islam and Islamism, and that focus in and of itself is part of the ongoing contest in the West. We cannot pretend to transcend, merely challenge the discursive boundaries that define our concerns.

Arab Spring - democratic uprisings that arose independently & spread accross the Arab world in 2011.

2

Definitions and Representations: The Legacy of Orientalism

The contemporary Western study of Islamism, and the many problems that bedevil it, must be understood within the context of the more mature study of Islam. While Western scholarship began to grapple with Islam as an explicitly political phenomenon only relatively recently, earlier research on Islam certainly chronicled its social and political impact. Writing about Wahhabi Islam as "a fanatical heresy," famed Arabist T. E. Lawrence (1997: 135) wrote that its adherents

> dashed themselves to pieces on the urban Semites, merchants, and concupiscent men of the world. About their comfortable possessions the new creeds ebbed and flowed like the tides or the changing seasons, each movement with the seeds of early death in its excess of rightness. Doubtless they must recur so long as the causes – sun, moon, wind, acting in the emptiness of open spaces – weigh without check on the unhurried and unencumbered minds of the desert dwellers.

Lawrence's talk of eternally recurrent behavior among "desert dwellers" whose "unencumbered minds" are passively determined by, and acted upon by environmental factors represents a particular imagining of Muslims. Bruce Lawrence (2010: 303) has noted that the study of Islam must recognize the "pitfalls of prejudgments" that bedevil it. To this, he observes, must be added "the divergence of two variant approaches, roughly schematized as Orientalist, with a view to the past and defining texts, and social scientists, with a gaze on the present and understanding communities. Neither suffices to meet the challenge that the study of Islam poses on the human mind, and above all to the mind engaged in academic labor." To these two variants, for the purposes of this volume, one must add a third: neo-Orientalism, a hybrid that combines the Orientalist focus on ancient text with the social science focus on explaining contemporary communities, resulting in static and sterile stereotypes that fail to do justice to either school of thought.

In his survey of what he labeled as Orientalism – producing particular types of perspectives and discourse that have sustained, and been sustained by colonial efforts at system maintenance – Edward Said suggests that there is a severe problem of representation in Western scholarship. That is to say, subaltern peoples in the peripheries of the world – in the colonies and dependencies – are seldom allowed to represent themselves, and their grievances, rage, and militancy are thought to be more coherently and adequately explained by experts and observers. Orientalism, which developed into the received view and defining framework of Near East studies, imagined the Arab Muslim, not so much as a dynamic human being engaged in an ongoing relationship with his surroundings, as a self-contained and static black box defined by the ancient past while tossed to and fro on the cresting waves of history. Said (1979) criticized the *ex cathedra* self-aggrandizement of Orientalist scholarship, its determinist explanations of native political activism and exoticizing claims of an essential dichotomy between 'Western civilization' and the 'backward Orient.' "The Oriental," Said suggested, "is imagined to feel his world threatened by a superior civilization; yet his motives are impelled, not by some positive desire for freedom, political independence, or cultural achievement on their own terms, but instead by rancor and jealous malice" (Said 1979: 249).

The idea of an immutable Muslim core, of a definable and essential 'native' mind is very much a product of nineteenth-century anthropology; a field of study that, at the time, stood at the service of European colonialism, creating and validating the racist stereotypes that justified the 'white man's burden' of political and economic exploitation. One might have thought that such instrumental stereotyping would have disappeared in the post-colonial era, yet it remains alive and well; not only in its original form, but also in a range of additional variants. For instance, within the field of terrorism studies (returned to below), the patterns of governmental patronage and academic service are as striking as they are entrenched, and serve to maintain the sort of ingroup-outgroup stereotyping that, in the words of Frantz Fanon (1988: 35), "allows no cultural confrontation. There is on the one hand a culture in which qualities of dynamism, of growth, of depth can be recognized. As against this, we find characteristics, curiosities, things, never a structure."

The Orientalist idea that Islam is a monolithic bloc stretching from Morocco to Kuwait, and that its core concepts are fixed and immutable are key elements of the political discourse of what has been referred to as neo-Orientalism. They are the result of a selective social scientific appropriation of older Orientalist scholarship, and in some cases a regression from actually useful ethnographic insights produced by the 'old school' Orientalists. Their romanticized exoticism notwithstanding, the early Orientalists rarely failed to recognize the kaleidoscopic nature of Islam. For instance, in the early twentieth century, in his seminal work on Sufism, Reynold A. Nicholson (1989: 5–6) notes how the early Islamic communities were intellectually and structurally impacted by the tension between religious and worldly ideas, and how this tension was intimately connected with geography, culture, and custom. He goes on to say:

> Hence arose the Murjites, who set faith above works and emphasized the divine love and goodness; the Qaddarites who affirmed, and the Jabarites who denied, that men are responsible for their actions; the Mu'tazilites, who built a theology on the basis of reason, rejecting the qualities of Allah as incompatible with His unity, and predestinarianism as contrary to His justice; and finally the Ash'arites, the scholastic theologians of Islam, who formulated the rigid metaphysical and doctrinal system that underlies the creed of orthodox Mohammedans at the present time. All these speculations, influenced as they were by Greek theology and philosophy, reacted powerfully upon Sufism. Early in the third century of the hegira – the ninth after Christ – we find manifest signs of the new leaven stirring within it.

The point is not the accuracy of Nicholson's typology, but his recognition of the early Islamic communities as complex and evolving social organisms that not only interact with, and are informed by, their environments and neighbors but engage in contest among themselves over the meaning of the texts and symbols that make up their shared Islamic heritage. Even the T. E. Lawrence quote that began this chapter recognized diversity and change, albeit superficially. However, much of that seems to have vanished in the narratives that are allowed to define our current understanding of Islam in general, and Islamism in particular. According to one influential publication (Ghosh 2008), "no contemporary writer has done more to inform Western perceptions of Islam than Bernard Lewis," while others (Boyd 1999: 719–20) have designated him "the most influential postwar historian of Islam and the Middle East." Yet his scholarly output contains a litany of subtle vilification and Orientalist generalization, hidden behind apparent recognition of various differentiating factors. As a prolific public intellectual and White House policy advisor in the aftermath of the 9/11 attacks, Lewis bears significant responsibility for resurrecting and perpetuating the Orientalist stereotype of 'the Eternal Muslim' within Western scholarship, as well as on the level of policy formulation. He has also been consistent in deploying his definitions of the Islamic essence and the Muslim mind to portray Islam as a virtually self-contained cultural unit; its choices and trajectories, including the emergence of Islamism, are portrayed as somehow *sui generis*. An important upshot of this is that the West is absolved of any and all responsibility for the current conflict. In *The Roots of Muslim Rage*, one of his most important articles, Lewis notes that Islamic "fundamentalism" is not the only Islamic tradition. Other, more tolerant traditions have contributed to the past achievements of Islamic civilization, he argues, and suggests that one "may hope that these other traditions will in time prevail." However, "before this issue is decided there will be a hard struggle, in which we of the West can do little or nothing. Even the attempt might do harm, for these are issues that Muslims must decide among themselves" (Lewis 2004: 330).

Lewis is of course correct in pointing to the existence within Islam of numerous and often contradictory understandings of what it means to be Muslim. He is also correct in noting that the task of determining that meaning lies within Islam itself, and in observing that the current 'fundamentalist' struggle primarily revolves around the ability to define Islam. Yet he misrepresents matters when he goes on to suggest that this struggle, even as it impinges on and is propelled by the social and political life of the Western world, is something that the West must stay out of. Not only does this imply that the West is not already deeply involved in defining the trajectory of the Muslim world – which is flatly false, especially given his own explanations of how Western political, economic, and military models brought poverty, tyranny and defeat to the Muslim world. More importantly, Lewis' language casts the West in the role of a passive bystander able to do nothing more than brace for impact; defending against the unpredictable vagaries of the Muslim mind, rather than critically examining policies past and present. As advisor to the George W. Bush administration – defined by a belief that Islamists 'hate our freedoms' and that US policy in no way can be held responsible for creating tensions in the Arab and Muslim world – Lewis' argument that Islamists ultimately struggle against secularism and modernism found fertile ground. While the struggle against secularism is conscious and explicit, Lewis contends, "the war against modernity" is generally subconscious and implicit, "directed against the whole process of change that has taken place in the Islamic world in the past century or more and has transformed the political, economic,

Secularism – Separation of Church + State.

social, and even cultural structures of Muslim countries." In this struggle, Islamism "has given an aim and a form to the otherwise aimless and form-less resentment and anger of the Muslim masses" towards the forces that have eroded traditional values and loyalties and "robbed them of their beliefs, their aspirations, their dignity, and to an increasing extent even their livelihood" (Lewis 2004: 330). Thus we are told that problems in the Muslim world are neither caused nor exacerbated by outsiders, merely blamed on them as part of an unconscious war against modernity, chan-neled by Islamic fundamentalism. Lewis' reductionist stereotypes have been accepted and developed by historians, political scientists, and policy makers eager for an explanation of current tensions that absolves the West and lays all blame for the current impasse at the doorstep of the Islamic world. However, these very notions of Islam as a defective, failed, and vengeful 'non-West' constitutes a significant obstacle for our ability to understand its complexity and diversity; its simultaneously global and local nature.

Distortion of native cultures and theories about their debilitating effects on individuals have always formed a crucial element in colonial and neo-colonial power play. As Amilcar Cabral (1973: 43, 39) observed, it is "within the culture that we find the seed of opposition" and "whatever the material aspects of [foreign] domination, it can be maintained only by the perma-nent, organized repression of the cultural life of the concerned people." For this reason, Fanon (2001: 32) noted, "the native is declared insensible to ethics; he represents not only the absence of values, but also the nega-tion of values. He is, let us dare to admit, the enemy of values, and in this sense he is the absolute evil." The dehumanizing and disempowering dis-course that Cabral and Fanon identified remains disturbingly prevalent, if often subtle, in the narratives of those prominent scholars who define Western imaginations of the Islamic and Arab worlds and underpin the war on terrorism, including Lewis, Ajami, and Huntington. Their images of the Muslim Arab as irrational, irresponsible, and belligerent, fanatically religious but prey to wicked passions, differ in degree, not in kind, from the anthropological treatises that once spoke of the 'childlike' or 'primitive Negro' in order to legitimize colonial hegemony in Africa under the guise of a *grande mission civilisatrice*. Osama bin Laden was a godsend to this tradition of stereotyping and vilification. Fiercely militant and zealously devout, he and his men dwelled in caves, sported turbans, kept their beards long, and appeared to shun the modern world. Their chilling rhetoric seemed ripped from the pages of an Orientalist textbook. Their spectacular and atrocious actions indicated no discernible program beyond a rejection of the West. After September 11, bin Laden's image within the neo-Orientalist narrative was elevated to the status of icon, empirical proof, explanatory matrix, trend indicator, and warning sign all rolled into one. Thus assisted by bin Laden, neo-Orientalist scholars succeeded, particularly in the United States, in defining and promoting the twenty-first-century version of the 'white man's burden': pacifying Middle Eastern terrorism; bringing secularism, democracy, and free market economics to the natives; making the region safe for that 'outpost of Western values,' Israel; and protecting the world at large from Islamic fundamentalism.

Such portrayals of contemporary Islamism would have one believe that the current conflicts and tensions in which Islamism is involved are simply products of the core concepts of Islamic theology and philosophy, or lingering infections following distant historical events, to the exclusion of contemporary sociopolitical discontent and aspirations. Yet the reality is that we are not faced with an either/or situation. The core concepts and beliefs of Islam matter intensely, as do the various ways in which the history of Islam is understood by Muslims, but these aspects are also intimately connected to ongoing sociopolitical efforts, serving as narrative frames and guidelines for action. It is important to realize that Islamic faith and Islamic concepts are not frozen in time. By virtue of their contemporary application, they continue to develop. Understanding the tenets of Islamic faith, views of history, and the real-life experiences of Muslims as a complex and dynamic web – as opposed to simple and static factoids – allows one to see specific meaning in the otherwise abstract; to ground in reality that which otherwise is purely theoretical. Yet the literature displays a strong reductionist and essentializing tendency, which appears to dovetail with a general trend within Western post-Enlightenment scholarship to separate – analytically, intellectually, and practically – religious belief from political practice. It has been noted that the currently dominant explanations of religion are "reductive, treating it as epiphenomenal to economic, political, or psychological realities." Moreover, within most Western intellectual traditions, the principle of separation of church and state has been understood as an "essential criterion of modernization and the measure of liberty. It leads scholars, journalists, and statesmen to assume that religion is an unequivocally private matter" (Almond, Appleby, and Sivan 2003: 4).

Against this tradition, it is important to emphasize the *constitutive* dimension of faith with respect to Islamist thinking, which goes beyond the structures and grievances of materialist worldviews. In the early 1980s, Kurshid Ahmad charged that the phenomenon of "awakening of faith" was often reduced by Western secular scholarship to "political and social rearrangements." This, he suggested, meant ignoring the ways in which religious convictions could recreate "the moral personality and character of the individual" and thus authorize "an upsurge of spirituality and idealism, generating a sense of direction and commitment to reconstruct their world, whatever the sacrifice" (Ahmad 1983: 227). Roxanne Euben (1999) also stresses how, to Islamists, materialist grievances and concerns are intertwined and mutually constituted with norms provided by faith and a belief in a transcendent reality. The gathering of hard data – like statistics related to unemployment and corruption, information on socio-economic inequalities, political repression, foreign interference, and so forth – may explain parts of these grievances, but not why the response should take a specifically Islamist character. While often rooted in materialist concerns, Islamist thought and mobilization cannot be reduced to only such concerns. Euben suggests that there is an identifiable and politically significant moral component to Islamism, embedded in the belief that Quranic revelation and the faith community that it gave rise to must permeate and sustain the Islamist project. While materialist concerns and structural opportunities may offer a *functional* account of Islamists, they cannot explain the *meaning* of Islamism, as understood by the Islamist themselves. By "deriving meaning from function," explanations of the Islamist phenomenon do not become more rational, in the sense of being more intelligible, as it tends to disassociate from the Islamists' "own understandings of the world" (Euben 1999: 154). Thus Euben suggests that we have to take seriously the ways in which Islamists view their own projects and objectives, that their self-understandings should be "central to the very standards of intelligibility," since such an Emic perspective may serve to counter the unfortunate but prolific approaches that define Islamists as either irrational fanatics or as mere agents for materialist betterment.

Much of contemporary scholarship continues unashamedly – sometimes perhaps inadvertently, out of habit – to proclaim what is and is not 'real Islam'; what are the components of its 'essence,' its immutable and eternal mechanics. Generalizations about the 'Muslim mindset' and 'how Muslims view the world' imply that Islam as a religion has a uniform impact on the sociopolitical commitments of its adherents. The resulting narratives are ones in which the entire Muslim world is a mobilizable army; a faceless mass, religiously programmed to think and act with single-mindedness of political purpose, once they discover the true content of their religion. Raphael Patai's *The Arab Mind* (2002) is a case in point. Patai's various stereotypes of Arab and Islamic cultural practices and their adverse effects on the development of the human person are works of fiction set within a framework of traditional, ethnocentric anthropology. As Patai goes about explaining anthropological idiosyncrasies – such as Islamic breast-feeding practices creating needy boys who grow up to be unbalanced adults, a general inability to articulate nuances, and so forth – he imagines these to be expressions of an Arab Islamic cultural identity (Patai 2002: 32–3, 166–7). Extrapolating from local data and anecdotes, Patai paints a panorama of an alien civilization teeming with various expressions of culturally contingent psychopathologies. After 9/11, the comfortable distance Patai places between Western and Arab–Islamic cultures along with its easy-to-understand racist stereotypes had significant appeal, and its pseudo-scholarly and political appropriations and applications have since been legion (Hersh 2005: 38–9; Whitaker 2004). For instance, Patai's work provides the foundation for psychologist Joan Lachkar's suggestion that suicide bombers suffer from borderline personality disorder and are, among other things, envious, dominated by shame for which they blame others, "impulsive, have poor reality testing, and impaired judgments…suffer from profound fears of abandonment and annihilation, as well as persecutory anxieties" (Lachkar 2002: 349–67). What is particularly interesting is that she goes on to trace these maladies to Islamic child-rearing practices, thus arguing that the 'condition' is in fact characteristic not only for suicide bombers, but for Muslims more generally; that is to say, it is a culturally induced mental illness. The fact that Patai's work was 'rediscovered' at a time when leading Western nations prepared for war with Muslim nations speaks volumes about its utility as a tool for dehumanizing and othering an enemy-subject, and suggests that Cabral and Fanon were prescient in their understanding of the political utility of academic discourse. When this sort of generalization is allowed to frame political science, the result is the neo-Orientalist image of Islamic politics as static and immutable; mechanics replace dynamics, there may be moving parts, but no growth or change. 'Facts about Islam' are posited as eternal essences, rather than as observations of a constantly renegotiated social phenomenon. Cultural distance may be a contributing factor – the nuances and dynamics that we are acutely aware of when we look at ourselves are less evident when we fix our gaze on peoples that are more distant. For instance, the idea that there is an immutable and essential French or German national genius has been almost entirely abandoned by Western scholars since the publication of Benedict Anderson's *Imagined Communities* (1993), which argued persuasively that communal identities are in constant flux.

One of the most commonly repeated 'facts' about Islam is that it makes no distinction between religion and politics; that it is a totalizing system within which all aspects of the individual's life, from personal piety to populist politics, are subsumed. Lewis writes that, "During Muhammad's lifetime, the Muslims became at once a political and religious community, with the prophet as head of state...the state that ruled them was that of Islam, and God's approval of their cause was made clear to them in the form of victory and empire in this world" (Lewis 2003: 6). But what does it actually mean that Muhammad at Medina "was at the same time a prophet, statesman, administrator and warrior" (Watt 1961: 229)? Or to say that Muslims consider Islam as "timeless and immutable" and imagine "an idealized Golden Age that consists of Muhammad's prophethood and his first four flawless successors" (Murawiec 2008: 169–70)? These are references to 'sacred history,' accounts compiled by Muslim historians for theological purposes, yet seemingly accepted by Orientalist and neo-Orientalist scholars as social and historical fact. In reality, such accounts are complex and contested sources of widely divergent readings, interpretations, and applications by actual Muslims. This sacred history provides intellectual frameworks that Muslims themselves fill with different, often contradictory content, based on their own specific context, challenges, agendas, and objectives. To be sure, the European post-Reformation distinction between 'the sword and the keys,' paving the way for to the post-Enlightenment ideal of separation of church and state, is not a defining feature in Islam. Yet Islam does contain competing interpretations of the early Muslim community, perhaps especially as it relates to the social organization at Medina, which in turn enables a range of Islamist attempts at giving that understanding contemporary meaning and function. As the Iranian Islamist intellectual Ali Shariati put it, "the only and sole society which throughout human history can be said to be...based upon this religion, not in the form of a historic reality in one age, but in the form of a symbol, a model, was the society of Madinah" (Shariati 2003: 49). To Shariati, however, Medina stands as inspirational symbol of the transient ascendancy of a truly Islamic liberation theology, "the religion of God and the deprived and oppressed people throughout history" (Shariati 2003: 48–9). To Shariati, the revolutionary theology of Medina contrasts with the unjust statist theology that eclipsed the Medina experiment almost immediately. Importantly, to Shariati, the Medina model accords precisely with his own revolutionary Shi'a agenda while the enemies of the Medina model were the very same reactionary and statist forces that opposed an Islamic revolution in Iran. That is to say, Medina served as a general model of just government that was given specific content by Shariati's social and political context.

If, to Shariati, Medina was the beginning and the end of truly revolutionary, egalitarian and liberation-oriented Islamic governance, other Islamist thinkers and intellectuals have also read into the Medina period their own ideas, ideals, and situations. Abu Musab al-Suri, one of the most influential intellectuals within al-Qa'ida, saw the Taliban emirate in Afghanistan as a reflection, or reproduction of Medina, even describing his own relocation from London to Kabul in 1998 as *hijrah*, the same word used for Muhammad's flight to Medina in AD 622, the beginning of the Islamic calendar (Lia 2008: 234). Meanwhile, Tariq Ramadan, an Islamic intellectual based in Switzerland and the United Kingdom, argues that disruption, rather than codification and enforcement of traditional roles and customs, lay at the heart of the Medina experience. "Medina meant new customs, new types of social relationships, a wholly different role for women (who were socially far more present than in Mecca) and more complex inter-tribe relations, as well as the influential presence of the Jewish and Christian communities, which was something new to Muslims" (Ramadan 2006). Working in exile on a continent where Muslims are a minority population, Ramadan draws from the Medina experience an example of exile and pluralism in which Muslims are nevertheless required "to remain faithful to the meaning of Islam's teachings in spite of the change of place, culture and memory" (Ramadan 2006).

Were it true that there is absolute and clear cut historical and textual authority for a particular political model, serving as example and rule for all subsequent generations of faithful, then debate about Medina would be redundant; there would be no problem establishing once and for all what Islamic politics is and how it functions. What may be common to Islamism is the understanding that, at Medina, the existential struggle of the Muslims as a community of faith gave rise to a sociopolitical organization dedicated to its survival as a community of faith. What certainly is not universally agreed is that the distinction between religion and politics was therefore erased in Muhammad's "communitystate," nor the contemporary implications of that experience (Esposito 1995: 17). This is an example of an important nuance that allows us to understand the diverse expressions of Islamic politics – from absolute monarchy to republican rule, from revolutionary to reactionary activism, from violence to pacifism – as products of different social and historical contexts, which have brought unique challenges and leverages to bear on interpretations of Muhammad's example. Reference to the same foundational or authoritative historical period does not make for sameness, but contest.

Another early source of differing political identification within Islam is the late seventh-century succession struggle that led to the division of Islam into Sunni and Shi'a schools of thought. This event is frequently described in the literature, but most commonly as a historical fact; only very rarely (Nasr 2007) is it understood as a contemporary reality lived by those whose sociopolitical heritage remains in part defined by the outcome of that struggle. Again, the basic historical components are straightforward. With one segment of the Muslim community insisting that Muhammad had created a hereditary caliphate and another maintaining that it should rather be a matter of electing the most capable person, the community–state split in two camps (which, importantly, suggests that not even the leaders of the original Islamic community–state understood it uniformly).The Shi'a – which is shorthand for *shi'at 'Ali*, the partisans of Ali – were defeated in the succession struggle but refused to relent and recant. Numerically inferior, they were subjected to harsh persecution by the Sunnis, and the foundation for an enduring enmity was thus laid. The sociopolitical implications of this differentiating event have been numerous, and far from limited to the enduring nature of the divide itself. As a persistently persecuted minority population, it was perhaps natural that the Shi'a would go on to develop, not only a stronger commitment to sociopolitical justice from the perspective of the oppressed, but also mechanisms for incorporating such themes into the common theology. Since the Islamic Revolution in Iran, some Western scholars have heaped scorn on its Islamist ideology because it builds, *inter alia*, on the adoption and development of elements of Marxism and other non-Islamic schools of thought. It has been portrayed as a perversion of real Islam. In the words of Murawiec, this "Islamo-Marxist hybrid" was "a monstrous laboratory experiment that was unleashed on the body of Iran"; an "ideologization" of Islam perpetrated by "clerical agents of . . . innovation" (Murawiec 2008: 286). Such claims are only possible if one assumes that there is an Islamic gold standard against which all things Islamic can and must be measured; that essential and unchangeable Islam of the seventh-century Arabian desert to which the researcher can refer in order to determine what is truly Islamic. This, however, amounts to discarding the ongoing real-life development of Islamic theology by simplistic appeal to tradition; it is new, therefore it cannot be genuine. This fallacy is based on a limited understanding of the nature of cultural and religious communities, seeing them as essential and static, rather than evolving and interactive organisms. Indeed, a significant element of contemporary Shi'a theology is there precisely because Islam is not immutable; because it is not closed to intellectual innovation, but developed and redefined through constant interaction with its sociopolitical environment. Importantly, if in Orientalist and neo-Orientalist analyses there is a purity standard against which to measure deviation, then one is also able to say something seemingly authoritative about efforts to return to or 'recapture' that purity. Groups within the Salafi movement do indeed understand their agenda in part as aimed at recreating or retrieving 'pure Islam.' It therefore becomes all the more important to reject Orientalist historiography and be cognizant of the fact that the Salafi vision of Medina is one of many competing visions, as illustrated above.

In a sense, as one grapples with contemporary social and political affairs, it does not matter what Muhammad's Medina was actually like. What matters are the various ways in which it is interpreted by those for whom it is an authoritative period. Moreover, it is simply not possible for any Muslim today to understand Islam as it was understood at Medina, and recapture it in its purity, whatever that might mean. This is so for the simple reason that today's Muslims are not seventh-century people, and do not live in the seventh century either socially, technologically, intellectually, or theologically. All that can be achieved, at best, is a twenty-first-century understanding of seventh-century Medina. It is impossible for any Muslim to think away the intervening fourteen centuries; in fact, the way in which the seventh century is imagined, as well as the impulse to 'return' to it, are products of social, political, economic, and cultural factors in the here and now. Moreover, this yearning for a lost golden era is a variant on a common theme. Efforts as varied as the Nazi 'return' to a mythical era of racial and cultural purity, Christian notions of recapturing the simplicity of the era of the apostles, and New Age adherents' attempts to recreate a pre-Christian cosmology are all examples of the same anachronistic impulse – ultimately futile because the cumulative experience of humanity does not have a reset button.

Statements about what Islam is and how Muslims think with reference to the Quran and Medina are made at the expense of the lived reality of Muslims today. They rest on the flawed notion that reappropriation and actualization of an Islamic essence is possible. Therefore they fail not only to capture the nuances of Islam in general, but also to properly conceptualize the dynamics of contemporary Islamism. Pointing to the teachings contained in the Quran and to Muhammad's rule in Medina obscures the fact that contemporary Islamism centers around twenty-first-century interpretations of the Quran and the Medina experience. Normative lessons are not necessarily the same just because the text, event, or period referred to is the same. Yet Orientalist and neo-Orientalist scholarship essentially underwrites the Salafi self-understanding, which is not helpful in understanding the diversity of Islamist opinion. The Salafi narrative is fiercely contested by other Islamists, and the Orientalist image of Islam as a static monolith shatters as soon as it is exposed to the reality it purports to describe. Even within Salafi Islam, there is more than one understanding of what the faith requires and forbids. The pacifist nature of the Indonesian manifestation of Salafi Islam is instructive, in that it has developed within an environment where not only the experience of European colonialism has been different from the Arabian Peninsula, but the underlying tribal and familial structures have differed (von der Mehden 2008). The impact of such differentiating factors on the hermeneutical process – the process of interpretation – through which the Quran and Medina are given contemporary real-life relevance belie ideas of immutability, purity and essence even within the very narrow Salafi subset of Islam. Again, as noted above, the cultural distance between researcher and research subject may be a factor contributing to these simplifications, compounded by the fact that most anthropologists and sociologists working on Islam are also area specialists. Those who work on Arab Islam seldom venture into South East Asian Islam, those whose focus is Central Asian Islam usually refrain from commenting on African Islam, and so forth. This compartmentalization in and of itself implies that academia does understand the importance of local context in shaping the various manifestations of Islam (and therefore by extension of Islamism), and that the insistence on treating Islamism as unified is in fact contradicted even by scholarly practice. Nevertheless, it also means that individual academics and their institutions are susceptible to assuming that their particular glimpse of Islam has a greater explanatory value than it actually does, and is somehow representative of the whole.

The importance of rejecting the simplistic notion that there is no difference between religion and politics in Islam is immediately apparent when one looks at one of the major rifts within contemporary Islamism, between what may be broadly termed third worldism, represented by locally entrenched and ideologically relatively inclusive groups such as Hezbollah and Hamas, and the neo-third worldism, or nativism, represented by al-Qa'ida and associated movements (AQAM) (Hadiz 2004; Strindberg and Wärn 2005). As chapter 6 demonstrates, Hezbollah's willingness and ability to work with and take seriously the thought of other groups and movements is predicated in part on its Khomeinist framework, which in turn is an outcome of the specifically Shi'a manner of engaging in *ijtihad*, reformulation of Islamic truths. The Sunni group Hamas, it will be shown, acquired its toleration for dissidence after coming into sustained contact with Hezbollah in 1993, while Palestinian Islamic Jihad (PIJ) has the unusual distinction of being a Sunni group that articulated its own emergence within the Shi'a intellectual framework established by Ayatollah Khomeini and the Islamic Revolution in Iran. Meanwhile, AQAM judges all of these groups to be errant and apostate precisely because of their willingness and ability to accept, adopt, and work within secular political structures. This distinction and comparison will be fully treated in depth in the following chapter. Suffice it for the moment to note that Cabral's statement quoted above – that national liberation movements are not exportable commodities, but products of the historical reality of each people – holds true also for Islamism, in part because its various constituent groups and movements see themselves as liberation movements.

The generalizing narrative of neo-Orientalism can survive only if removed from the local and specific; if differences are explained away, or used to construct an image of a homogenous whole. If one takes the local seriously, the monolith immediately fragments. Hezbollah, Hamas, and PIJ are engaged in struggles that are territorially based, against a specific enemy, and rooted in the needs and aspirations of specific peoples. The specific national projects of these movements aim at developing institutions and empowering their constituents; they stand accountable to those they represent; and they form part of, and cooperate within, a pluralistic spectrum of ideologies and creeds. In sharp contrast but with equal specificity, al-Qa'ida's struggle is rooted in Wahhabi theology, the tribal legacies of the Hijaz and the Najd, and the cumulative experiences of Afghanistan, the Balkans, Somalia, and other theaters of war. The movement stands accountable to no specific constituency because it limits its struggle to no specific territory; it seeks to create an alternative to the institutions and thought of modernity; and it rejects, other than on tactical grounds, political and religious pluralism as those outside the group are seen as *kuffar* (infidels) or *murtadun* (apostates). While Hezbollah, Hamas, and AQAM are all engaged in a resistance project, they are not engaged in the same resistance project. Conversely, while their political agendas and objectives are specifically their own, they share a political language that is broadly Islamic. In this context it is important to recall, in the words of one scholar, that understanding Islam as a discursive tradition capable of encompassing a range of local narratives can help make sense of its range of local political manifestations within a common frame of reference (Asad 1986: 14).

Jihad, sacred struggle, is a central concept for all the groups and movements treated in the case studies. Following on what has been argued above, however, the fact that jihad constitutes a common point of reference virtually guarantees that it is subject to a range of interpretations that are constituent parts of the Islamist diversity, as well as subject to constant negotiation. As with the various understandings of the relationship between religious and political authority, jihad is given meaning by local practice and exegesis. Rather than being unified by a common terminology, Islamist groups and movements are differentiated in part by their competing understandings of that terminology. Using the same words within a common discursive tradition does not produce sameness. Within the context of political economy, liberals and communists talk about 'productivity enhancers' without the implication that their agendas are one. Similarly, within the context of Christian theology, Roman Catholics and Calvinists both talk of 'predestination' but mean by this term vastly different things. It is not the articulation of the same words, but the often unarticulated assumptions and implications with which the words are loaded, that determine commonality or difference. Key symbols, texts, and events within Islam have the capacity to be at the same time centrifugal and centripetal, and different understandings of the same terminology are part and parcel of the processes of differentiation, opposition and conflict within Islam. Yet regardless of 1,300 years of debate, tension and outright conflict among theological schools, sects and groups, about the meanings and implications of key concepts, the fact that they use the same terminologies has somehow been misinterpreted as a sign of unity and cohesion. It is not, and as the case studies show, this conflict includes key concepts such as *ummah* ('community of believers'), *ijma'* ('consensus'), *khilafah* ('caliphate'), *bida'* ('innovation'), *murtad* ('apostasy'), and *fitnah* ('dissension') – and even the content and authority of *shari'ah* law and the meaning and implication of the *sunnah*, the example of the Prophet Muhammad and his companions. Attempts by Western scholarship to define any of these terms are relevant only as signposts to their actual implementation. It is important to remember that to the Islamists themselves, these are not abstract concepts, but sociopolitical instruments in constant use; they gain relevance from their application and are applied according to their relevance, in a feedback loop. As will be argued in chapter 4, the breakup of the Muslim Brotherhood as a regional movement was due in large measure to the fact that a unified regional agenda was unable to address the different needs of dispersed local constituencies. What was relevant and apposite in Egypt was not helpful in Palestine, Syria, or Jordan. Furthermore, common terminology is fragmented not only geographically, but socially, as demonstrated by studies examining the role of the concept of jihad in women's movements and youth culture (LeVine 2008; Wadud 2008).

The classical 'key concepts' of Islam constitute, in some sense, the basic building blocks of Islamic discourse precisely because their meanings and implications are sources of intense dispute and conflict. Against this background, it should not be a surprise that defining Islamism is fraught with difficulty. There are various ways in which scholars try to address this. One way may be to treat the term as too basic and self-evident to merit explicit definition, although the difficulties encountered by those who do attempt definitions suggest that this is not the case. For instance, Sheri Berman (2003: 257) argues that Islamism is "the belief that Islam should guide social and political as well as personal life." Olivier Roy (2006: 2) suggests that Islamism is "the building of an Islamic state" while Daniel Benjamin and Steven Simon (2002: 448, 449) define Islamism as "a religious ideology that insists on the application of *shari'ah* law by the state" after which they go on to define *shari'ah* as "Islamic law." Other definitional bids with more ambitious content include Efraim Karsh's (2006: 207) understanding of Islamists as "the political activists and ideologues" who in the first half of the twentieth century inherited the "Arab imperial dream" and "quest for Allah's empire" from failing monarchs. Less editorial are Carl Ernst's (2004: 68) definition of Islamism as an "anti-modernist ideology of reform in Muslim countries" and Guilain Denoeux's (2002: 61) suggestion that it is "a form of instrumentalization of Islam by individuals, groups and organizations that pursue political objectives," providing "political responses for today's societal challenges by imagining a future, the foundations for which rest on reappropriated, reinvented concepts borrowed from Islamic tradition." A common feature of all these definitions is that they point to other concepts that are left undefined, or the meanings of which are simply assumed. In each case, the definitional problem is merely transferred, begging the question – what then, do Islamists mean by 'Islam' and 'Islamic'? What is their understanding of Islamic law? What is an 'Islamic state'? As we have suggested above, there may be as many understandings of these concept as there are Islamist groups. In the words of one scholar (Browers 2005: 76–7), Islamism "does not exhaust the category of 'Islam.' But at the same time there is no 'Islam' that can be held apart from 'Islamism.' Hence, defining Islamism by merely pointing to Islam is a form of circularity."

A more serious problem is the instrumentalist focus common to many or most available definitions of Islamism. Achieving political domination by taking control, through elections or otherwise, of government is of course an important aspect of all politics (and not specific to Muslims), but exclusive focus on the instruments of political change ignores the context in which those instruments are formulated and put into action. What remains unanswered – because the question is rarely raised – is, *why this quest for an Islamic state in the first place, and why now?* Liberalism and social-ism could be defined instrumentally as 'post-Enlightenment ideologies whose adherents seek to gain control of the political system in order to affect social change in accordance with their ideologies.' It is easy to rec-ognize how such a definition, while correct, does not actually further our understanding of what it is that any given liberal or socialist actually wants, at least in part because it fails to ask 'why?'

In a very real sense, and regardless of whatever else it may be, the con-flict between the West and Islam is a battle of ideas and ideals, fought on several fronts, both at home and abroad. In this context, it is relevant to note that within the intellectual climate of Europe and the United States, secular and faith-based self-understandings of what it means to be Western are engaged in a direct and highly visible struggle over the ability to define a cultural meta-narrative. As Olivier Roy (2007: xiii–ix) has noted, "when one opposes the West and Islam, it is by putting forward the Christian origins of Western culture or, on the contrary, by emphasizing its secular-ism. In other words, when we question Islam's capacity to become 'Westernized,' we are referring to two different forms of Westernization: Christianization and secularization." As this contest is being fought on ontological, epistemological, and practical every-day political grounds, Islam and Islamism are employed in both faith-based and secularist narra-tives as a warning sign; an emblematic bogeyman that threatens their particular imagining of the West unless their own specific prescriptions are adopted. Proponents of a faith-based narrative point, among other things, to the threat of alien religions to their understanding of 'traditional Western values,' while their secularist protagonists argue more generally that the phenomenon of religious fundamentalism, or even religiosity, has laid siege to reason and threatens the natural progression of mankind, expressed most fully in Enlightenment secularism – which equates to 'con-temporary Western values.' The common denominator is a conviction that the West, its imagined values and practices are superior and require safeguarding. It is important to note that both the religious and secularist sides contain considered ontological and epistemological arguments along-side opportunistic and instrumental (and often flippant and hysterical) appropriations of the core concepts involved. But whether the argument is scholarly or opportunistic, the West is almost always defined in terms of its most agreeable principles – Enlightenment rationalism, individualism, tolerance – while reference to horrors such as pogroms, the Holocaust, or Stalinism are conspicuously absent. The non-West, on the other hand, is depicted as emotional, communitarian, despotic, violent, and traditionalist (Huntington 1993a; 1993b). Such caricatures obscure the sociopolitical diversity involved in any and all cross-cultural analysis.

While the intellectual tradition of Europe, or the West, has been unique in terms of its particular development and trajectory, this uniqueness has lent itself to an exceptionalism that in turn creates the illusion of a universally self-evident superiority. This is by no means a recent development. Hegel, one of Europe's most influential Enlightenment philosophers, viewed philosophy, not as "a timeless *a priori* reflection upon eternal forms," but "the self-consciousness of a specific culture, the articulation, defense, and criticism of its essential values and beliefs" (Beiser 1993: 252). This idea is perhaps most succinctly encapsulated in his famous statement, "Philosophy is its own age comprehended in thought" (Hegel 1967: preface). This historicism was coupled with an understanding of the movement of history as the realization of the thought of God; a movement that inexorably pointed to Enlightenment Europe as its universal apex and destination. The Hegelian understanding of Enlightenment Europe was thus a vision of a culture that was spiritually, intellectually, and culturally superior by necessity. Today, the original version of Hegelianism finds few proponents, but its reverberations within European politics and philosophy were immediate, profound, and lasting. Even some of Hegel's most vehement critics have adopted key elements of his philosophical schema. Among those who are thus intellectually indebted to Hegel are thinkers as varied as Karl Marx, Benedetto Croce, Oswald Spengler, Shlomo Avinieri, and Francis Fukuyama – whose primary common denominator is some form of Western exceptionalism; what today is referred to as ethnocentrism. Karl Marx and his associate Friedrich Engels, for instance, rejected the notion that a true revolution could take place outside Europe because "the revolution which modern socialism strives to achieve is . . . the destruction of class distinctions . . . Among savages and semi-savages there [. . .] often exist no class distinctions, and every people has passed through such a state" (Marx and Engels 1962: 49). Non-Europeans, they believed, were trapped in a false consciousness. A similarly linear conception of history is evident in the earlier works of one of the most strident advocates of liberal democracy in the post-Cold War era, Francis Fukuyama. In his seminally important work, *The End of History and the Last Man*, he follows an extended quote from Hegel by explaining how the "twin crises of authoritarianism and socialist central planning have left only one competitor in the ring as an ideology of potentially universal validity: liberal democracy, the doctrine of individual freedom and popular sovereignty." He goes on to suggest that "the liberal idea" is emerging victorious and "for a very large part of the world, there is now no ideology with pretensions to universality that is in a position to challenge liberal democracy" (Fukuyama 1992: 42, 25). This argument is exactly analogous to Hegel's view of his surroundings as the apex of history, and to Marx and Engels' understanding of their society as unique in harboring the conditions necessary for universal emancipation.

It is within the legacy of this linear, essentialist, and self-sufficient historiography that we find Paul Berman and other neo-Orientalists, as they trumpet the embattled superiority of 'Western values' over Islamic modes of governance; a synthesis of post-Hegelian historiography and a view of intercultural relations derived from Huntington's clash of civilizations hypothesis. The latter, it has been noted, builds on imaginings of Islam produced by dedicated, yet culturally ignorant Christian missionaries in the early twentieth century (Bulliet 2004: 47–94). As Ali Mirsepassi (2002: 53) notes in a critique of Huntingtonian understandings of macro-cultural dichotomies, "Everything fits in advance to a preconceived model, and in this unconscious imposition there is a blindness to specificity, detail, ultimately to actuality, and hence the possibility of dialogue and understanding is foreclosed." In an important sense, the narratives that frame our understanding of Islamism appear to be moving ever-further from the realities of actual Islamists. If the Christian missionaries' understanding of conflicting civilizations was removed from an understanding of Islamic hermeneutics and Huntington's development went on to remove understanding of the local and particular within Islam, Paul Berman has continued the movement by also de-territorializing the clashing civilizations. On Berman's view, Islamists' supposed rejection of liberal values of tolerance, dialogue, democracy and secularism are an expression of a universal ideological tendency that crosses continents and centuries; its intellectual kin include German Romanticism, Slavophilism, Stalinism, Fascism and, not least, Nazism. Islamism is defined as a religious yearning that hinges on revulsion with Western civilization and an adamant rejection of the consequences of the Enlightenment, which are embodied in the worldviews of liberalism. According to Berman, the war on terror should not be understood as, a clash of civilizations, or a conflict between a global ruling class and its subordinates. Rather, it is humanity's clash with itself: a war of ideas and incompatible worldviews; the free world's encounter with a timeless totalitarian fiend. The human soul, Berman contends, whatever the country or culture, has always seemed to have an infatuation with violence, mayhem and cults of death. Thus, the struggle against Islamism and terrorism – intertwined in the US-led war on terror – is part and parcel of an existential battle that has previously led to freedom's fight against a variety of other totalitarian fiends before coming up against zealous Islamic radicals "who looked on every new event in the world as a stage in Judaism's cosmic struggle against Islam." The war against terror is, Berman notes, a "war of ideas" (Berman 2004: 182).

Buruma and Margalit refer to the ideas of the enemy in this war as Occidentalism. The term refers to a perspective, embraced by communitarian extremists across geographic and cultural divides, that the West is soulless and rationalistic; that liberal Western societies not only lack absolute values, but are arrogant, feeble, greedy and decadent. Against this, occidentalists set their own willingness to "self-sacrifice for a higher cause, for an ideal world, cleansed of human greed and injustice . . . Choosing to die a violent death becomes a heroic act of human will" (Buruma and Margalit 2004: 72). This formula, they argue, is the same under the leadership of "the Fuhrer, the Emperor, God, or Allah" (Buruma and Margalit 2002). Occidentalism is, in a sense, a mirror image of Edward Said's Orientalism, the construction of negative stereotypes of the cultural outgroup in order to maintain the cohesion, solidarity, and superiority of the ingroup. As an observation limited to the generalizing tendencies of Oriental as well as Occidental thinkers who are dedicated to a cause, Margalit and Buruma are surely correct. However, like Berman, they deny the existence of clashing civilizations, not because it fails to describe geopolitical realities, but because it is not general enough. Islamism is merely a manifestation of a general human tendency towards destruction and wickedness; a virus that has traveled from host to host throughout history. Most religions, but especially the monotheistic ones, "have the capacity to harbor the anti-Western poison," they argue, "and varieties of secular fascism can occur in all cultures." Thus, the current conflict is a battle, "not between East and West, Anglo-America and the rest, or Judeo-Christianity and Islam. The death cult is a deadly virus which now thrives, for all manner of historical and political reasons, in extreme forms of Islam" (Buruma and Margalit 2002). In their account, what is distinctive about the Islamic version of Occidentalism is the particular manner in which it glorifies death, rejects liberalism, and seeks a divinely ordained alternative structure. Its core content, however, is as old as human intolerance itself.

The consequence of this tendency towards ever-increasing abstraction is a movement further away from the realities of Islamist struggles, not only their local experiences and projects, but even their self-understanding of overarching commonalities. Out of a multitude of particularities, Berman and his cohorts are able to construct a single meta-narrative defined by a rejection of Western values as they are understood by Berman and his cohorts. The analytical value of such models is virtually zero, because every differentiating factor disappears from view and with them our ability to understand the diversity, complexity, and actual choices made by actual individuals, groups, and movements. Within Berman's schema, he is able to see a direct link between al-Qa'ida's suicide pilots on 9/11 and Hamas' ranks of suicide-bombers, serving as proof that radical Islamism as a whole is detached from rationality and reason. Hamas' rejection of the negotiations at Camp David in 2000 and the subsequent outburst of violence in the Occupied Territories – with the Islamist groups taking the initiative, especially as they resorted to suicide attacks against Israeli civilians in June 2001 – display, according to Berman, that Hamas has no interest in peace, that it loathes the two-state solution and that, beyond the idealistic goal of abolishing Israel and "establish[ing] the reign of the *shari'ah* in every corner of the land," death and martyrdom have become goals in and of themselves (Berman 2004: 134–5). From his theoretical vantage point, he is entirely unable to see anything but a continuation of the nihilism that characterized the totalitarian ideologies of twentieth-century Europe. The social and political affairs of Palestine and the policies of Israel become incidental, or epiphenomenal.

Neil Curtis has argued that Berman's narrative takes an "idealistic route" that ignores the materialist structures of imperialism; that his approach conceals a "dangerous weakness" that permits him to "perpetuate the myth of an external threat" based on ideas alone, and therefore "serves to hide a much more endemic and structural threat" (Curtis 2004: 141). The political utility of this is self-evident. As Ralph M. Coury remarked about Berman's tendency to negatively stereotype all Arab political expressions, "If the dog is to be put down, it must first be declared mad" (Coury 2005: 15). "The rhetoric of evil," Curtis notes, "automatically establishes sufficient cause by imputing some essential character to the perpetrators." Something that is merely 'wrong' does not carry its own sufficient cause but remains open to further analysis, judgment, and discussion. To condemn something as evil, however, is to point to both cause and effect. "Evil people do evil things" (Curtis 2004: 141). Thus, Berman, Buruma, and Margalit are able to define as Western all that is good and benevolent, while all malevolence and irrationality – including its specifically European post-Enlightenment manifestations – are defined as 'not us.' In this way, the European civilization that enabled and perpetuated the Holocaust is absolved of its crime, while Islamists – who had nothing to do with the event – are pronounced guilty by association.

What Islamists have promoted in various places and at various points in time may be understood, not as one-dimensional incarnations of evil, but as socioculturally and religiously grounded doctrines and schools of thought that absorb and channel discontent into messages and strategies for resistance. Indeed, such a project can easily appear extremist and fanatic – and the further removed the observer and his frames of reference, the more incomprehensible the local reality. What is missing in the range of accounts described above, from Lewis and Ajami, to Huntington, Berman, and Buruma and Margalit, are the often turbulent, brutal and humiliating conditions in which Islamist struggles and agendas gain their *raison d'être* and are able to resonate. Perhaps it needs to be recognized that the perception of 'liberal values' among Western political and intellectual elites is not shared by those who are at the receiving end of neo-colonial domination. This will be discussed fully in chapter 3. Suffice it for the moment to note, with Graham Fuller, that "political Islam cannot properly be viewed as an alternative to other ideologies such as democracy, fascism, socialism, liberalism, and communism" because it cannot be placed anywhere on an ideological spectrum. It is more useful, he argues, to see it as "a cultural variant, an alternative vocabulary in which to dress any one of these ideological trends." While certain predispositions can be identified – conservative social agendas, calls for political change, defensive cultural/nationalist postures, and rhetorical calls for implementation of Islamic law – it is difficult to show that Islamism is a distinct political program in itself. Instead, Fuller contends, Islamism is a political movement that makes Islam the linchpin of its own political culture, but thereby provides a basic theme that allows for significant variations. "Islamism is therefore not an ideology, but a religious–cultural–political framework for engagement on issues that most concern politically engaged Muslims" (Fuller 2003: 193).

With the discussion of Berman's contribution to the field, we have already passed onto the Islamist-terrorist nexus. The study of Islamism is deeply importuned by its own standard terminology, and the prevalence of the concepts 'terrorism' and 'fundamentalism' has hampered efforts at understanding. Edward Said has pointed out that such concepts derive "entirely from concerns and intellectual factories in metropolitan centres

like Washington and London" and pose "fearful images that lack discriminate contents and definition, signifying moral power and approval for
whoever uses them, moral defensiveness and criminalization for whomever
they designate" (Said 1993: 288). These are mechanisms of intellectual self-
preservation, ensuring that those to stand to gain from the prevailing order
are never challenged by the arguments brought by those marginalized or
repressed by it. Instead, terms like 'fundamentalism' and 'terrorism'
ensure that groups and movements thus labeled do not get a hearing; that
they remain trapped in an effort to justify their existence, which has been
predetermined by the terminology as evil and immoral. Robert Fisk has
noted how the Israelis, after the Israeli invasion of Lebanon in 1982, applied
the label 'terrorist' on the Palestinians as a deliberate discursive means; a
tool to deprive them of a cause rooted in real conditions of destitution and
expulsion. "By labeling the Palestinians as terrorists," he notes, "the Israelis
were describing their enemies as evil rather than hostile. If the Palestinians
could be portrayed as mindless barbarians, surely no sane individual would
dare regard their political claims as serious" (Fisk 2002: 388).

While this may make tactical sense from an information management
perspective, the rigorous scholarly study of terrorism ought to be in the
interest even of those who simply want to understand an enemy in order
to combat it. Nevertheless, the persistent conflation of Islamism with terrorism has made it difficult to understand and explain it as a social phenomenon. "Words and names," Julie Peteet suggests, "form the substance
of representations and as such they form a field of intense meaning and
activity" (Peteet 2005: 157). Michael Bahtia has similarly argued that a name
has power to the extent that the way in which the name is selected, adopted
and deployed disappears from view, while a range of "normative associations, motives and characteristics are attached to the named subject.
By naming, this subject becomes known in a manner which may permit
certain forms of inquiry and engagement, while forbidding and excluding
others" (Bahtia 2005: 8). Peteet argues that these narratives are instruments
of power that regiment a "hierarchy of credibility" in which the narratives
of the dominant group are accepted as "objective and legitimate" while
those of the subaltern group "are derided as crudely fashioned propaganda
and thus met with contempt" (Peteet 2005: 155). That the term 'terrorism'
is essentially a place holder for whatever content one wishes to represent
as evil and immoral is illustrated by the fact that it is deployed by conflicting sides with equal vehemence. For instance, Ayatollah Taskhiri, an Iranian
religious scholar, has defined terrorism as an "act carried out to achieve an
inhuman and corrupt objective and involving threat to security of any

kind, and in violation of the rights acknowledged by religion and mankind" (Tashkiri 1987). Not surprisingly, Taskhiri accuses the United States of being the "mother of international terrorism" by oppressing peoples, strengthening dictatorships, and supporting the occupation of territories and savage attacks on civilian areas (Tashkiri 1987).

As one author notes: "Terrorists are, or have become, a Platonic essence: they never change, they have no history, they simply terrorize" (Marrouchi 2003: 13). Local realities and aspirations remain concealed by a single concept – terrorism – which tell us nothing about the research subject, but generally speaks volumes about those who wield it. Mustapha Marrouchi argues that terrorism, "more even than Communism and Islamism together, has come to dominate and embody everything 'we' do not like, from the poisoning of one Tylenol container to the October 1983 destruction of the Marine Barracks in Beirut, to the Sandinistas, the Soviets, Libya, Iran, Syria, the PLO, Noriega, Aideed, Milosovic, and of course, Osama bin Laden, who stands as the apex of world terrorism" (Marrouchi 2003: 8). Dag Tuastad has described this tendency of knowledge production as 'symbolic power,' which he argues is the "power to construct a hegemonic version of reality" (Tuastad 2003: 591). As regards the specifically Western terrorism narrative, Tuastad advances the so-called new barbarism thesis, which he describes as akin to Orientalism in that it creates "presentations of political violence that omit political and economic interests and contexts when describing that violence" and instead reduces political violence to the "resurgence of tribalism" and "cultural backwardness among peripheral, non-civilized groups." *Ipso facto*, the violence of the Other is "irrational and cannot be stopped by means of diplomacy or conciliation" (Tuastad 2003: 591). Inevitably, in both media and scholarship, the realities and narratives of the supposed barbarians are reduced to mere militant sound bites. Where the Orientalist and neo-Orientalist narratives on Islam and Islamism conceal diversity by its insistence on cultural cohesion, the terrorism discourse, as one scholar has remarked, is simply "thought-deadening...If someone commits 'politically motivated mass murder,' people might be curious to the cause of grievances which inspired such a crime, but no cause or grievance can justify or even explain 'terrorism,' which all right-thinking people must agree is the ultimate evil" (Whitbeck 2002: 28).

The continuing prevalence of the concept of 'Muslim fundamentalism' presents similar, but more subtle difficulties, and derives from the inability, or perhaps unwillingness of post-Enlightenment Western scholarship to take seriously groups and movements located at the intersection of religion and politics. As Robin Wright has noted, 'fundamentalism' as a concept is loaded with assumptions of inflexibility and backwardness; like 'terrorism' it predisposes the audience to a particular view of anyone thus described and is therefore inherently unable to encompass the "forward-looking, interpretive and often even innovative attempts" by Islamists to restructure their social and political environment (Wright 1992: 131). Similarly, Najib Ghadbian argues that fundamentalism, "with its judgemental tone and its implications of literalism, antimodernism, and fanaticism, is a term for those who have already made up their minds about all Islamists and is therefore inappropriate for scholarly research" (Ghadbian 1997: 7). Indeed, it is a word, like 'terrorism,' that has become a buzzword laden with emotion, assumptions and presuppositions.

A common objection to the use of the term 'fundamentalism' in the Islamic context is that it is utterly rooted in a specifically US Protestant experience, whereby the Bible came to be understood, not only as the word of God, but as literal, accurate historical documentation. In a series of paperbacks published between 1910 and 1915 entitled *The Fundamentals*, the American Protestant evangelist Reuben A. Torrey articulated a Christian response to modernist ideas. The idea was that Christians should overcome denominational division, caused by differing responses to the challenge posed by modern science, by gathering around a set of 'fundamentals.' This idea guided Torrey's subsequent establishment of the World Christian Fundamentals Association. This Protestant response to liberal theology had very little in common with most varieties of Muslim experience, theologically as well as sociologically. Beinin and Stork argue that the term is meaningless in the context of Islam because all believing Muslims view the Quran as "the literal (hence absolutely true) word of God as revealed to his Prophet Muhammad through the intermediary of the angel Gabriel" (Beinin and Stork 1997: 3). Rather, they suggest, the truly important conversation within Islam, and among Islamists, focuses on how the Quran is to be understood and applied. This conversation includes a wide range of open-ended ideas, points, counterpoints and strategies which the term 'fundamentalism' is simply unable to encompass. Similarly, on a sociological level, Torrey's attempt to unite fragmented US Protestantism in the face of liberal theology and scientific progress is only a relevant parallel if one imagines away the range of different structural realities – cultural, political and economic – within which Islamists emerge, and instead simply assumes that reactive theology is the single most important factor.

Roxanne Euben accepts the term 'fundamentalism,' which she describes as referring to "contemporary religio-political movements that attempt to return to the scriptural foundations of the community, excavating and reinterpreting these foundations for application to the contemporary social and political world" (Euben 1999: 17). That is, these movements tap into – and are expressions of – a widening critique of secular modernity that is perceived to have lost direction and meaning; a counter against a modern condition whereby secular science and ideologies have undermined, yet been unable to replace, faith-based ethics and morals. Yet, as noted above, profound problems attach to the notion that Islamists are driven by a simple urge to combat modernity and secularization, and while some groups and movements may indeed be interested in the recreation of a 'golden age,' others are not. As Sayyed Muhammad Husayn Fadhlallah – a leading Shi'a *marj'a al-taqlid* (an authoritative interpreter of Islamic law and tradition) – noted,

> We are not fundamentalists the way Westerners see us. We refuse to be called fundamentalists. We are Islamic activists. As for the etymological sense of *'usuliyya* ('fundamentalism'), meaning returning to one's roots and origins (*'usul*), our roots are the Qu'ran and the true Sunnah or way of the Prophet, not the historical period in which the Prophet lived or the periods that followed – we are not fundamentalists (*'usuliyin*) in the sense of wanting to live like people at the time of the Prophet or the first Caliphs or the time of the Umayyads ... (Fadhlallah 1995: 62)

The Fundamentalism Project, an interdisciplinary effort engaging a multitude of scholars over a number of years, sought to explain the rise, appeal, and dynamics of fundamentalist groups within all the major world religions. The project resulted in a series of five book volumes (Marty and Appleby 1991–5), and many of the individual case studies within these volumes were instances of truly groundbreaking scholarship. However, the subsequent attempt by key collaborators to extrapolate a unifying explanation of fundamentalism, referred to as strong religion, resulted primarily in a number of abstractions and generalizations (Almond, Appleby, and Sivan 2003). In fact, the problems of strong religion may be fruitfully understood as an indicator of Western post-Enlightenment academia's inherent inability to constructively grapple with the interface between religion and politics. It would seem fairly obvious that an attempt to construct grand unifying explanation for a supposedly global phenomenon said to include the Society of St Pius X, Bob Jones University, al-Qa'ida, Neturei Karta, the Iranian government, and Hindutva necessarily results in either extreme vagueness or intense essentialism. Strong religion, as a concept, results in both. As the authors search for the lowest common denominator, much of the language, structures of belief, and patterns of behavior ascribed to fundamentalists are in fact those of sincere, ordinary believers. For instance, it is argued that fundamentalists are set apart by believing that theological study, in order to have value, must be affirmed through concrete commitment, and by holding that one ought not only to believe the Bible but to live in accordance with its precepts (Almond, Appleby, and Sivan 2003: 46). Perhaps a particularly instructive train of thought is the notion that fundamentalist leaders take it upon themselves to cherry pick pieces of text and tradition that suit their agendas. From this notion, the authors go on to suggest that the fundamentalist effort hinges on "the need to bolster the authority of the contemporary guardians of the faith" because the enemies of the faith are powerful and the struggle is a potentially existential one (Almond, Appleby, and Sivan 2003: 18). In reality, the process of redefining understandings of authoritative text, rethinking and perhaps even discarding earlier applications is part of a dialectic relationship within and between religious groupings; it is conducted by fundamentalists and modernists alike. The practice and purpose of picking and choosing within text and tradition could as easily be applied to the modernist leadership of the Episcopal Church in the United States as to the *shura* council of Hezbollah. However, by making hermeneutic manipulation and assertion of leadership a part of the extended definition of fundamentalism, the authors imply that those practices are not engaged in by non-fundamentalists. More importantly, the authors imply that these practices, as they inhere in fundamentalism, aim at supporting a new-fangled and radical departure from the historic mainstream. We have thus yet again come up against scholarly pronouncements on what is and is not the real tradition and teaching of a given religious tradition; the linear progress from which fundamentalists supposedly deviate. Thus, rather than understanding competing interpretations and applications as parts of the totality of a tradition, strong religion is in fact defined as a betrayal of real religion. The Orientalist practice of defining the essence of Islam has here been augmented to include the essence of all religious belief systems.

Perhaps the most serious problem is that this term 'fundamentalism' assumes, and then widens, a rift between religious–political movements and those of a secular nature. The authors of *Strong Religion* suggest that what they call 'fundamentalism' encompasses the most prominent characteristics and traits that determine actors' strategies and objectives. This elevation of religiosity to *locus definiens* thus distorts real on the ground commonalities in order to create new commonalities that are, at best, abstract misrepresentations. On this view, Hamas, for instance, is understood to have more in common with the Zionist settlers on the West Bank than with its fellow Palestinian strugglers in secular groups such as PFLP and PFLP-GC. Gone are the structures of the real world, replaced with a nominal commonality of deviant spirituality. What, exactly, is thus explained? How does the notion of 'fundamentalism' in any way simultaneously elucidate the activities of Hamas in Palestine, *al-Muhajiroun* in Europe, *Jemaah Islamiyya* in Indonesia, and *Lashkar e-Tayyiba* in Kashmir? As Mark Juergensmeyer has noted, fundamentalism is not only more accusatory than descriptive, as well as an imprecise category for cross-cultural comparison, but describes attributes motivated solely by religious belief and therefore does not admit of broader social and political concerns (Juergensmeyer 1993: 4–6). Somewhat astonishingly, the authors of *Strong Religion* seem to agree, actually conceding that fundamentalism is a typology that does not exist in the real world. They recognize that not only do these defenders of tradition against modernity adopt and adapt to the modernity within which they exist, but also that political involvement fosters compromise and accommodation. When fundamentalists "played politics" the result was that the "exclusivist, dogmatic, confrontational mode" – by which the project itself had defined its research subjects – was modified "to such a degree that the word fundamentalism or its cognates is no longer appropriate" (Almond, Appleby, and Sivan 2003: 12). At least for the purposes of describing Islamism, when the abstraction of 'fundamentalism' was brought into the real world, it no longer described anything.

As noted above, Euben approves of the term, but ends up filling it with a very different content. To her, 'fundamentalism' entails a discursive critique against the conditions of the modern world and its foundational assumptions, providing a perspective that is "profoundly critical of as well as constituted by assumptions regarding the requirements of modernity and modern politics" (Euben 1999: 18). Voll noted in 1979 that a constant theme in the history of Islam has been the nature of the relationship between "the community of revelation and the cultures with which it came into contact." As remnants of local popular cults and the "great traditions" of other civilizations have contended for a role in the expression of Islamic tradition, "the basic line of conflict was in defining how literally Muslims should interpret their authentic tradition and how free they were to utilize elements of other cultures which were not explicitly sanctioned within the early revelation" (Voll 1979: 150). What Islamists could be said to share is a reappropriation of Islam to serve as the fundamental and authoritative guide for their diverse social and political projects. That does not seem enough to justify the use of the term fundamentalist, however, largely because what is thus accurately described is minimal in comparison to what is obscured and distorted by the term's generalities and inaccurate connotations. More importantly, the term suggests and reinforces the notion that it is religion that is at the heart of the matter – whatever the matter is – rather than the variety of encounters of Muslim populations with the world around them; that religiosity, rather than its context, is the seedling of activism and militancy.

To reiterate, while the quest to establish an Islamic state is often portrayed by commentators as the ultimate ideal for Islamists, one must be cognizant of the basis on which this state is to be founded; that is, the imperative for society to be ruled by Islamic law. The many and profound differences among Islamists notwithstanding, what they do hold in common is a rejection of one of the key assumptions of the post-Enlightenment ethos of Western modernity: the idea that human reason *alone* is capable of serving as the foundation for a just society. In Islamist thought, such an assumption is naïve at best, disastrous at worst, given that the human being is by nature arrogant, selfish, and greedy, and thus prone to corruption and injustice. Human reason cannot keep in check these destructive tendencies, and humans are therefore in need of guidance through a moral code. For instance, according to Rajaee (1983: 42), Khomeini understood man as "a creature with various dimensions but governed by two conflicting drives: passion and desire versus the need to perfect himself spiritually." However, as long as humans are convinced of their capacity to become superior, they are also capable of degeneration. Khomeini suggests that

> if a person acquires a house, he will begin to desire another house. If a person conquers a country, he will begin plotting to conquer another country. And if a person were to conquer the entire globe, he would begin planning the conquests of the moon or Mars... If this animal that has broken its bridle is allowed to roam freely outside all recognizable bounds, it is left to itself and no attempt is made to train it, it will desire everything for itself and be prepared to sacrifice everyone to its desires. (Algar 1981: 331)

Religious decrees serve to stem these tendencies. "The prophets," Khomeini asserts, "came to tame this unbridled beast and to make it subject to certain restraints" (Algar 1981: 330) That is, Islamic law, *shari'ah*, is understood as an effort to *discipline* and control these innate and destructive human passions in order to "protect the humans from themselves" and are thus part and parcel of the Islamist understanding of how to create an equitable polity. The rationalistic secular order thus provides a path to deviation from man's divinely ordained purpose, guided as it is by the idea that the human spirit should flourish unrestrained. On the contrary, this leads mankind into what the Tunisian Islamist thinker Rachid Ghannouchi has termed *tawahush* ('barbarism'). "Humans, by nature, have a readiness to become brute," he argues and suggests that the age of Enlightenment that liberated the human mind from religious decrees was both a blessing and a curse to the world, depending on which historically contingent dimension one looks. In the West, modernity has come to imply that political liberalism finally would be able to dominate the political order, having overcome feudalism, fascism, and communism. Ghannouchi notes that this is exemplified in the "democratic system and the recognition and defense of rights and freedoms" (Ghannouchi 2000: 117). But he adds that there is a darker side to the philosophical dimension of liberalism because it is based on the belief in the absolute ability and autonomy of the human mind to organize life; on the precedence of the individual over his community; on the exclusion of religious authority and values from public affairs; and on the rejection of man's metaphysical dimension in favor of the fulfillment of material needs. For this reason, according to Ghannouchi, Western liberal democracies grant basic rights to their own citizens, even as their underlying philosophy and *weltanschauung* fail to offer any relief for the Third World, upon the exploitation of which Western material privileges and power are founded. Thus, *tawahush* has been and remains a basic building block in the liberal democratic order. It has been nourished historically through colonialism and its processes of inequality driven by racism and materialism. This structural order persistently reproduces itself, evidenced in today's Western support for favored Arab despots at the expense of the rights of the populations, and for the Israeli state at the expense of Palestinian rights (Ghannouchi 2000: 117).

While Westerners may thus benefit from democracy, tolerance, and civility in their own countries and societies, *tawahush* is continually present because these blessings are enabled by expansive social welfare programs and high material standards of living that are financed and facilitated by the colonial and neo-colonial exploitation and repression of the world's poor. The so-called civility of the Western democracies is thus rooted in material riches garnered through an essentially unjust and repressive historical trajectory. In this, Ghannouchi echoes the view of Jean-Paul Sartre, in his preface to Fanon's *The Wretched of the Earth*, that "there is nothing more consistent than a racist humanism since the European has only managed to become a man through creating slaves and monsters" (Fanon 2001: 22). In contrast, according to Ghannouchi, many Third World countries enjoy civility, not because of rationalism or materialism, but due to their abidance by norms and ethics decreed by religious convictions. Central to this religious logic is *taqwa* (the fear of God) and the belief in transcendence and the hereafter. Humans, Ghannouchi asserts, are by nature more willing to satisfy their desires than to follow their conscience. Islam recognizes this weakness and addresses it by allowing space for 'transcendent self-interest.'; "Benefit is not restricted to this life... Individuals are trained to sacrifice their own personal interests to serve the public interests; they do so because they are promised a great reward if they forfeit what is immediate and temporary in exchange for that which is delayed but everlasting" (Ghannouchi 2000: 119). While on a basic level, belief in transcendence and reckoning in the after-life are generic features of religious conviction, among Islamists they are deeply politicized. Ghannouchi suggests that *iman* (belief) "plays an essential role in sustaining the determination of individuals and communities to rise up against injustice," and that such religious belief neutralizes "the pragmatists, who like to use the pretext of an unfavorable imbalance power to justify inaction." From this perspective, losing one's life in the effort to attain social justice, to become a martyr, "is not wasted and the sacrifice not in vain... It is understandable that a Muslim may lose his life struggling against oppression, and for this faith promises a great reward in the life after death... Martyrdom in the Islamic standard is not failure, and a martyred is an aspirant who offers his life for what is much more valuable, and at the same time, eternal" (Ghannouchi 2000: 115).

Islamist thought thus entails a rebellious thrust that politicizes religious precepts by stressing how political action in the here and now will be rewarded in the hereafter. To some Islamists, like Hezbollah, *taqwa* does not only encourage believers to chart a political course of action, but it *obliges* them to do so. On this view, political indifference equals impiety. To Khomeini, this transcendence makes Islam a superior instrument for socio-economic betterment. He urged the Muslims to not look elsewhere for remedies to their countries' maladies since they already possessed the tools of Islam, which far surpass the efficacy of the materialism and rationalism advanced by the West.

> For the solution of social problems and the relief of human
> misery require foundations in faith and morals; merely acquir-
> ing material power and wealth, conquering nature and space,
> have no effect in this regard. They must be supplemented by,
> and balanced with, the faith, the conviction, and the morality
> of Islam in order to truly serve humanity instead of endanger-
> ing it. This conviction, this morality, these laws that are needed,
> we already possess. So as soon as someone goes somewhere
> or invents something, we should not hurry to abandon our
> religion and its laws, which regulate the life of man and *provide
> for his well-being in this world and the hereafter.* (Euben 1999:
> 119 20)

In this context, it is instructive to consider Khomeini's open letter to Russian
leader Michail Gorbachev in 1989, when the Soviet Union was crumbling
and looking to the capitalist West for solutions to its predicament:

> Reality must be faced. The main problem confronting your
> country is not one of private ownership, freedom and economy;
> your problem is the absence of true faith in God, the very
> problem that has dragged, or will drag, the West to vulgarism
> and an impasse. Your main problem is the prolonged and
> futile war you have waged against God, the source of existence
> and creation...It is clear to everybody that from now on
> Communism will only have to be found in the museums of
> world political history, for Marxism cannot meet any of the
> real needs of mankind. Marxism is a materialistic ideology
> and materialism cannot bring humanity out of the crises caused
> by a lack of belief in spirituality [which is] the prime affliction
> of the human society in the East and West alike. (Khomeini
> 1989)

Khomeini's vision of world politics was shaped by the Cold War stand-
off, and he believed that the political ideas of both sides were aimed
solely at material gain, regardless of the long-term consequences for
both their own, as well as other people. "The threat to the world today
stems from the two superpowers," he asserted. "They have manipulated
the world under their own control and use it for their own interests"
(Rajaee 1983: 74). Thus he believed that the logic of this world order is
firmly focused on the acquisition and maintenance of power. "It is lust
for power," Khomeini remarked, "which motivates America to commit

crimes unknown to history," which is the natural outcome of a world governed by the chimera of human reason (Rajaee 1983: 75). Regardless of whether it is accurate or inaccurate, variations on this analysis are part and parcel of the multitude of Islamist narratives and agendas that have been concealed by the fictitious monolith – static, unsophisticated, premodern – constructed by the dominant voices within Western scholarship.

3

'The Fanonian Impulse': Islamism as Identity and Ideology

The modern encounters between the Western states and Muslim nations have been framed, almost without exception, by colonialism, occupation, and domination. The medieval period had seen a protracted and fierce struggle for sociopolitical hegemony that pitted Western Christendom against Islam, Jewry and Eastern Christendom, but the geopolitical turbulence was not permanent. After the expulsion of the Moorish rulers from Spain in 1492, three centuries of quiet border consolidation followed; certainly quiet relative to the Protestant–Catholic warfare that ravaged Europe following the Reformation. Between the Islamic and European states, stable geopolitical boundaries came to be defined by religious confession with the exception of the Balkans, where Eastern Christians remained subject to the Ottoman Caliphate, as did the Christian communities of the Levant and Asia Minor. Following the Enlightenment, as Ali Rahnema points out, that all changed: "it was not until the 1800s that Europeans made an attempt once again to redraw the geographical map in their own favor, and subsequently visited Muslims living in a long geographical stretch from Morocco to Indonesia. This time they came as conquerors" (Rahnema 2008: xxvi). Nineteenth-century Europe was experiencing revolutions and political turbulence, even though, or perhaps because its peoples shared an experience of unprecedented advances in the human, social, and hard sciences. Rationalist, humanist, and utilitarian philosophies and ideologies, which drew on but also fed into this new level of human achievement flourished. Together with technological and scientific advances, these new ideologies enabled a spectacular expansion of commerce and industry, and "unleashed the energies and capacities of capitalism and finally shaped the European commercial and political penetration around the world" (Rahnema 2008: xxvi–xxvii).

The peoples within the slowly declining Ottoman Empire, however, had a very different experience of European ascendancy; the wealth of Europe was made possible in part by the exploitation of other parts of the world, including the Islamic world. Napoleon's armies invaded Egypt in 1798 and were expelled by British forces in 1801, which went on to maintain British political and economic hegemony in Egypt until the overthrow of the monarchy by the Free Officers in 1952. Egypt's integration into the world market as an exporter of cotton and importer of cloth, capital goods, and military hardware, and the loan repayments following the construction of the Suez Canal 1859–69, led to a huge national debt and eventual bankruptcy, while British and French entrepreneurs together with local elites, made huge profits. In 1830, France placed Algeria under military rule, incorporating it into mainland France in 1871; as a 'protective' measure, France also invaded Tunisia in 1881 and imposed a protectorate. To safeguard its new possession against a strong local resistance, France fought a brutal counterinsurgency, culminating in the massacre of some 1,000 men from the Oula tribe in 1847. The Algerians were 'pacified' and remained under French rule until 1962. In Iran, as early as the first decade of the nineteenth century, the increasing presence and power of Europeans throughout the Near East convinced the Qajar rulers that Westernizing reform was needed. In order to stay afloat on the colonial commodity market, local elites turned competition into corruption and monopoly. Beginning in 1865, a string of trade concessions were granted to European powers, culminating in a fifty-year tobacco monopoly granted to an Englishman in 1890, to the detriment of local merchants, traders, and workers. Elsewhere, colonial exploitation as a mode of interaction had begun earlier. On the Indian Subcontinent, the British encounter with Islam had been defined by the activities of the East India Company ever since its royal grant of trading monopoly in 1599. The Mughal Empire – a Muslim, Persian speaking imperial power that had ruled what today is India, Pakistan and Bangladesh since the early sixteenth century – was destabilized and exploited by the company until the last emperor was finally exiled in 1858 and replaced in 1877 by Queen Victoria, styled "Empress of India." Elsewhere in Asia, the Dutch East India Company, chartered in 1602, had quickly gained sovereign rights over Muslim populations in Indonesia and Malaysia. At the peak of its power, in 1669, the Dutch East India Company had forty warships, 150 merchant ships, 50,000 employees and an army of 10,000 soldiers, bringing into fine focus the symbiotic relationship between economic exploitation and political subjugation.

The imperialist footprint was vastly different in each locality, as were the specific interactions with local populations and rulers. At the same time, the identity and collective sense of Self around which local resistance was formulated in these various locations was that of Islam. Islamic leaders became the natural focal point for popular aspirations, while corrupt local elites and their European taskmasters became focal points for discontent and resentment. As Rahnema noted with regards to the Egyptian experience, "the most simple and common line of demarcation between them and the intruder was their sense of being Egyptian imbued with their religion" (Rahnema 2008: xxviii). In each place, two different approaches to resistance crystallized. One was a belief that in order to defeat the local despots and repel their masters, the 'evidently superior' laws, philosophies, and ideologies of Europe needed to be adopted and adapted to the local milieu. The other was a belief that local custom and practice – the chief organizing factor of which was Islam – contained the solution to the ongoing problems created by the encroachment of foreign laws and ideologies, and that the way forward was reification and purification of authentically local alternatives to the ways of the Europeans. These two schools of thought were by no means exclusive. Indeed, cross-fertilization and rivalry led both sides to adapt, develop, and progress. What is important to note is that, regardless of whether the flavor was modernist or anti-modernist, the first generation of the resistance against European exploitation and domination was guided by Islamic leaders; religion provided a natural organizing principle in societies where the main point of demarcation between natives and foreigners was religion. Thus, in Algeria, the first resistance effort against the French invasion in 1830 was organized by Islamic and tribal leaders (Ruedy 1992: 55). In the Sudan, Muhammad Ahmad ibn al-Sayyid Abdallah, claiming to be the Mahdi – in the Sunni tradition, a great reformer and renewer of Islam – raised an Islamic tribal army, declared war against the Egyptian authorities administering Sudan in 1881, successfully fought the British forces, and in 1885 took Khartoum and briefly asserted Sudanese independence. In Egypt, in the second half of the nineteenth century, the first to articulate an anti-colonial discourse were Islamic intellectuals, including Rashid Rida and Muhammad Abdu. During the first half of the twentieth century, in Palestine, it was the preacher Izz al-Din al-Qassam and the Grand Mufti of Jerusalem, Hajj Amin al-Husseini, who led the first stirrings of resistance against Zionist settlement.

Throughout the Western colonial and neo-colonial encounter with Islam, as with other native cultures and belief systems, scholarship has been harnessed to 'explain' the native in ways that justify exploitation and subjugation by reference to primitive urges, immutable belief systems, and other innate qualities. In the previous chapter we saw how these explanations remain prevalent even today, and how they fail to account for the complexity and diversity within the Islamist universe. How, then, are we to understand properly the social, ideological, and psychological mechanisms of the contemporary third generation of Islamist resistance – following as it does on the first generation's reaction shaped by Islam and the second generation's effort shaped by nationalism and leftist third worldism? Why does it seem so often to result in violent behavior? One of the most reviled characters in Western literature, Shylock the Jew in Shakespeare's *The Merchant of Venice* – perhaps the paradigm of the essentialized and dehumanized Other – can shed some initial light on the matter. In the opening scene of the third act, Shylock explains why he has demanded a pound of his Christian tormentor Antonio's flesh in the eventuality that the latter forfeits on a loan. Antonio's friend Salerio asks, "Why, I am sure, if he forfeit, thou wilt not take his flesh: what's that good for?" to which Shylock responds:

> To bait fish withal: if it will feed nothing else, it will feed my revenge. He hath disgraced me, and hindered me half a million; laughed at my losses, mocked at my gains, scorned my nation, thwarted my bargains, cooled my friends, heated mine enemies; and what's his reason? I am a Jew. Hath not a Jew eyes? hath not a Jew hands, organs, dimensions, senses, affections, passions? fed with the same food, hurt with the same weapons, subject to the same diseases, healed by the same means, warmed and cooled by the same winter and summer, as a Christian is? If you prick us, do we not bleed? if you tickle us, do we not laugh? if you poison us, do we not die? and if you wrong us, shall we not revenge? If we are like you in the rest, we will resemble you in that. If a Jew wrong a Christian, what is his humility? Revenge. If a Christian wrong a Jew, what should his sufferance be by Christian example? Why, revenge. The villainy you teach me, I will execute, and it shall go hard but I will better the instruction.

Powerfully and head-on, Shylock confronts the hypocritical Christian self-image of generosity and righteousness. A man at the breaking point, he feels that he can take no more of the disrespect and suffering that has been his lot, and that of his people. Shylock delivers a statement that contains a plea as well as a reflection on the causes of his despicable decision; a plea to be heard and seen as a fellow human being, through action that mirrors that of his tormentors. It is through scorn and cruelty at the hands of the Christian elite that he has come to know them, regardless of their oblivious self-righteousness, and it is by repaying in kind, he believes, that he can best strike back while at the same time regaining his own humanity. To Shylock, the Christian ideals of humility, love, and justice are simply not real because these values have not been part of his experience of Christian conduct. We cannot comprehend Shylock by merely examining his actions – his dedicated focus on cutting a pound of flesh from the side of Antonio – which in isolation seem only bizarre and irrational. Nor can we comprehend him by ascribing to him some immutable essence; indeed, the notion of the 'eternal Jew' is a racist fantasy that has inflicted untold damage on Jewry since its invention in the Middle Ages. Rather, we may understand Shylock only when we listen to his words and take them seriously. Hannah Arendt noted that, "In acting and speaking, men show who they are, reveal actively their unique personal identities and thus make their appearance in the human world.., This disclosure of 'who' in contradistinction to 'what' somebody is – his qualities, gifts, talents, and shortcomings   is implicit in everything somebody says and does" (Arendt 1958: 179).

Antonio is the cause of and inspiration for Shylock's will to violent and bizarre action, yet he and his fellow Christians are oblivious of the relationship. While audiences throughout the centuries may have focused on the colorful and enigmatic Shylock, it is important to note that as we learn about his turpitude, cruelty, and wickedness, we are in fact learning about what has been done to him; every indictment of Shylock the Jew is also an indictment of Antonio the Christian. Yet there is a further level, as meta-narrative, at which the example of Shylock is instructive. Even as the writer of the play gives voice to sincere and basic human grievances, and as the audience comes face to face with the inescapable logic of an unpalatable argument – Shylock himself remains a caricature. The character that Shakespeare presents is a distorted representation of a threatening Other; a repulsive, greedy incarnation of anti-Semitic fantasies. That representation in and of itself guarantees that whatever Shylock says or does, he will not be given a fair hearing by the play's audience. The discursive framework is such that his voice will remain that of the threatening Other – even as we hear him argue logically on the basis of shared humanity. The modern study of Islam and Islamism has gone even further and sought to erase entirely the Antonio by whom we can make sense of Shylock. Lewis, Ajami, and Berman, as well as a multitude of terrorism experts have contributed to this effort. It can be argued that the primary purpose of the hegemonic discourse of the West is to create a Shylock without having to acknowledge the existence of an Antonio. Indeed, the closest living relative of 'the eternal Jew' may well be the 'eternal Islamist'; someone who incarnates all our fears and fantasies, a self-contained evil whose villainy transcends time and space, whose words we cannot hear even as they are being spoken.

The literature on what makes Islamic activism and Islamism different is bountiful, but analyses of how or whether it may conform to more universal norms of political conduct – as socioculturally contingent expressions of human agency and cogency – are comparatively scarce, although not entirely absent (Ayoob 2008; Moghaddam 2008a). Yet the eternal and essential qualities ascribed to Islamists bar them from ever entering the human world. In the twentieth century, the sort of relationship between oppressor and oppressed into which Shakespeare's play gives a brief but finely focused insight, has been recognized as key element in Third World liberation struggles across the global south. Following the 1847 massacre of the Oula tribe in Algeria, a French investigative commission noted that, "we have surpassed in barbarism the barbarians we came to civilize" (Stora 2001: 5). Indeed, actions have consequences, and Sartre noted that the Algerian revolutionaries had been taught violence by the structures by which they had been oppressed. "In the savagery of these oppressed peasants," Sartre asks; "does [the European] not find his own settler's savagery, which they have absorbed through every pore and for which there is no cure?" (Fanon 2001: 14). He continues:

> You said they understand nothing but violence? Of course; first, the only violence is the settler's; but soon they will make it their own; that is to say, the same violence is thrown back upon us as when our reflection comes forward to meet us when we go towards a mirror... The native cures himself of colonial neurosis by thrusting out the settler through force of arms. When the rage boils over, he rediscovers his lost innocence and he comes to know himself in that he himself creates his self. (Fanon 2001: 15, 18)

Fanon, who emerged as one of the great theoreticians of revolutionary psychology, argued that this relationship, whereby the native is first dehumanized by means of generalities and stereotypes, creates a Manichean world that defines the native's violent rebellion. Paralleled by Shakespeare's Shylock, it is not the lofty abstract ideals of European civilization that anger the subaltern revolutionary, but the utter absence of those ideals in relation to the colonized subjects. Fanon describes a colonial situation in which "The violence with which the supremacy of white values is affirmed and the aggressiveness which has permeated the victory of these values over the ways of life and of thought of the native mean that, in revenge, the native laughs in mockery when Western values are mentioned in front of him" (Fanon 2001: 33). To Fanon, the salient protagonists were white colonizers and dark natives. Elsewhere, the same dynamics have applied to different actors. In Palestine, for instance, Fatah announced its liberation struggle in similarly existential terms:

> With revolution we announce our will [and existence], and with revolution we end this bitter surrender, this horrifying reality that the children of the Catastrophe experience everywhere ... With revolution we will restore our people's self-confidence and capabilities, and restore the world's confidence in us, and respect for us. (Sayigh 1999: 88)

The existential angst that the struggle gave voice to – and which enabled the struggle in the first place – continued as part of the dynamics of the Palestinian movement and fed straight into the emergence of the Palestinian Islamist trend some three decades later. A seemingly endless cycle of violence and counter-violence taught the mainstream of the Palestinian movement that in order to actualize their humanity – to become fully equal to their oppressors – violent action, not subservient negotiation, was required of them. The puzzlement and moral revulsion of Western observers against Islamism was perhaps never so great as when Hamas initiated its use of suicide operations. Evidencing a remarkably short historical memory span, the American commentator Charles Krauthammer, in a lament over the savagery of Hamas, argued that the advent of suicide bombings "coincides precisely with the era of Israeli conciliation and attempts at peacemaking. It is precisely in the context of the most accommodating, most conciliatory, most dovish Israeli policy in history that the suicide bombings took hold" (Krauthammer 2002). What Krauthammer ignores is that these Israeli moves of reconciliation were utterly irrelevant to the actual life-experiences of the people still living under occupation. Instead, what was relevant to Hamas and its constituents was the continuing steady stream of Palestinian civilian casualties. The lofty pledges of Yitzhak Rabin obscured this reality from the international community's view, but to those engaged in the struggle, on the ground, the principled self-righteousness of the West and Israel was neither here nor there. On February 25, 1994, Baruch Goldstein, a US-born resident of the Kiryat Arba settlement in Hebron opened fire with an assault rifle on worshippers at the Ibrahimi Mosque in Hebron, killing twenty-nine and wounding 125 before being overpowered and killed by an outraged crowd. It was this event, which a Hamas cadre later described as "the first suicide attack in the history of the Palestinian–Zionist conflict," that brought a turning point in Hamas' tactics (Hamas cadre to author, April 2004). Like the other factions, Hamas had previously engaged primarily in drive-by shootings, stabbings, and car bombings in the Occupied Territories, distinguishing itself only by the frequency of its attacks. In response to the Hebron massacre, however, Hamas introduced the tactic of suicide operations inside Israel, irrevocably changing the face of the conflict.

> Hamas declared itself in 1987 and it stated clearly that its mili-
> tary action was directed against the military forces of the Zionist
> entity, not at civilian people either inside or outside Palestine.
> But every day the Zionists were killing our women and children,
> destroying our houses and cutting down our trees. After the
> attack against the Ibrahimi Mosque...Hamas decided that it
> had no choice but to repay the Zionists in kind. (Strindberg
> 2001: 64)

Hamas' first attack on civilians inside Israel took place in Afula on April 6,1994, killing eight, and its first suicide operation struck Hadera one week later, April 13, killing five. In a statement circulated following the attacks, Hamas proclaimed that "the outrageous criminal actions of the Zionists against the Palestinians...in which Zionist soldiers did not discriminate between civilians, forced the al-Qassam Brigades to treat the Zionists in the like manner. Treating like with like is a universal principle" (Hamas 1994). Yahya Ayyash, the engineer responsible for development of Hamas' bomb making expertise until his assassination by Israel in 1996, was quoted as saying that the use of "human bombs" was a way to "make the occupation that much more expensive in human lives, that much more unbearable" (Kafala 2004). Hamas' own explanation for its decision to target Israeli civilians thus accorded with Fanon's assertion that

> He of whom *they* have never stopped saying that the only
> language he understands is that of force, decides to give utter-
> ance by force. In fact, as always, the settler has shown him
> the way he should take if he is to become free. The argument
> that the native chooses has been furnished by the settlers, and
> by an ironic turning of the tables it is the native who now
> affirms that the colonialist understands nothing but force.
> (Fanon 2001: 66)

That Hamas wanted to sabotage the 'peace process' is evident, but the reason was not some principled dislike of peace – it was a principled hatred for the implications of a peace built on the subservience of the Palestinians; on the inability to confront the enemy with the humanity of the native. In this context, local decision makers who adopt the enemy's narrative are seen as part of the problem. Not merely dishonorable, but downright dangerous to the ability of the people to raise itself from its imposed subhumanity.

The Manichean world created by the legacy of imperialism and colonialism has had profound repercussions for all major Islamist movements, which have emerged as responses to the failed liberation struggles of the leftists and nationalists. As third-generation resistance fighters, they had to appropriate and redefine the struggle, drawing on the first generation of Islamists in the nineteenth century, as well as the second generation of increasingly fatigued leftists and nationalists. Contemporary Islamist agendas are certainly not beamed straight from the orthopraxis of an imagined Muslim community at Medina in the seventh century, but have emerged within their own communities, nations and struggles. Meanwhile, Bernard Lewis is able to claim that

> We are facing a mood and a movement far transcending the level of issues and policies and the governments that pursue them...This is no less than a clash of civilizations, the perhaps irrational but surely historic reaction of an ancient rival against our Judaeo-Christian heritage, our secular present, and the worldwide expansion of both. (Lewis 2004: 330)

As our case studies illustrate, Lewis gets it exactly backwards: the emergence and formation of each Islamist group is a product of local exigencies and developments, not transcendent narratives of clashing civilizations. Even al-Qa'ida and its affiliates – arguably the most transcendent and global of Islamists – are products of local interactions and contexts. That these local conditions are situated within, and products of a global system does not mean that the correct level of analysis is the latter rather than the former; if so, then any and all domestic political events should be analyzed within a world systems context, lacking the specificity capable of distinguishing one movement from another. Also, the fact that Western governments and interests are more often than not party to the sociopolitical impositions against which the Islamists revolt does not translate into a war against Western values. Cognizant of the plight of Shylock, and following Fanon, one must ask: how can one assume that they are battling Western values when the West does not expose them to its values, but merely to the means with which it enforces its hegemony?

In 1967, the Carmelite monk and philosopher Thomas Merton recognized in the Vietnam war, and in the structural injustices that maintained racial and economic segregation in the United States, a parallel to the treatment of Shylock. "Instead of preaching a theology of the Cross for others and advising them to suffer patiently the violence which we sweetly impose, with the aid of armies and police, we might conceivably recognize the right of the less fortunate to use force, and study more seriously the practice of non-violence and humane methods on our own part when, as it happens, we possess the most stupendous arsenal of power the world has ever seen" (Merton 1967: 10). Without ideological sympathy for the leftist movements of the Third World, Merton was nevertheless able to see the relationship between oppressive structures and revolutionary violence. Importantly, in his attempt to develop a Christian theology dealing cogently with the cycles of oppression and violence, Merton recognized that it was far from always situated in the relatively visible context of direct colonial domination. Instead, he noted:

> Violence today is white-collar violence, the systematically organized bureaucratic and technological destruction of man... It is this polite, massively organized white-collar murder machine that threatens the world with destruction, not the violence of a few desperate teenagers in a slum. But our antiquated theology myopically focused on individual violence alone fails to see this. It shudders at the phantasm of muggings on our own doorstep, but blesses and canonizes the antiseptic violence of corporately organized murder because it is respectable, efficient, clean, and above all profitable. (Merton 1967: 6, 7)

Merton's observations on Western theology are applicable also to its ideological assumptions. The Western scholarly tradition of regarding liberalism in the abstract, as an ideal and idealized model of the world, fails to account for the realities that attend the enforcement of Western hegemony. For this reason it is unable to shed light on the resistance of the subaltern. Fanon's 'methodological individualism' circumvents this blind spot by juxtaposing individual action and societal context, focusing on the opportunities and constraints imposed by social structures and institutions on subaltern attempts to realize individual or collective interests (Jindau 1986: 126). The resistance of individuals and groups is linked to the institutions and complex social networks they encounter and revolutionary ideologies often stem from everyday experiences; social roles, norms, and cues are both operationalized and transformed through acts of resistance. In his own studies, Fanon used sociopolitical snapshots to give "a comprehensive perspective and analysis of a country and a people in revolution" and demonstrated the value of descriptive data in the linking macro and micro analysis (White 1996: 101). That linkage remains crucial for an understanding of Islamist militancy and activism.

Cultural symbols and norms have social significance because they are identified with 'authentic existence' and as such are likely to eventually become reified as tools of resistance. Thus, for instance, Palestinian nationalism in the Occupied Territories during the second intifada in Palestine 2000–4, took on an increasingly Islamist tenor while remaining essentially nationalist in focus. The Islamists remained dedicated to the national cause, while many nationalist movements 'Islamized' their discourse, symbolism and actions because, as Ahmad Jibril, a senior Palestinian nationalist leader had presciently remarked during the first intifada, "the touchstone of Islam today is jihad for the liberation of Palestine" (Jibril 1989: 6). This testifies to the importance of Fanon's observation that, at some point in every struggle for national liberation, "the customs, traditions, beliefs, formerly denied and passed over in silence are violently valorized and affirmed," and that, in revolutionary praxis, "the plunge into the chasm of the past is the condition and the source of freedom" (Fanon 1988: 43).

Islam is not uniformly, and far from always easily mobilized as a framework for national resistance. Vedi R. Hadiz uses the term "neo-third worldism" to signify Islamist groups and movements that define non-Islamist counterparts as enemies to be confronted regardless of commonalities within a national dimension. As such, it is an extension of the thought among some first-generation Islamists, mentioned above and returned to in subsequent chapters, that reification and purification of indigenous praxis and customs is the superior way to wage a resistance struggle. It emphasizes an inward-looking focus on a supposedly 'pure' Islamic identity – the golden age myth of the Salafi trend – but does so as a result of social factors; this is neither novel, nor can it be understood in isolation from the colonial and neo-colonial experience. Social symbols represent ideology and control over those symbols implies control of the ideological foundations of society. In the words of George Orwell, "he who controls the present, controls the past. He who controls the past, controls the future" (Orwell 1949).

Islamist modernism and nativism have, since the very beginning of the modern Islamist movement, been engaged in the struggle to acquire control over Islamic symbols, a struggle that currently lies at the heart of the Islamist project. Neo-third worldism is an extreme form of nativism, "the doctrine that calls for the resurgence, reinstatement or continuance of native or indigenous cultural customs, beliefs, and values" (Boroujerdi 1996: 14). Writing about Indonesia, Hadiz points out that this Islamist neo-third worldism is not a polar opposite to third worldism but "a more inward-looking version" of it, "characterized by indigenism, reactionary populism and strong inclination towards cultural insularism... nostalgia for a romanticized, indigenous, pre-capitalist past." Hadiz argues that, in the Indonesian context, this nativism emerged with the decline of third worldism in the post-Cold War era as a "sorry riposte to the triumphalism of unbridled US power" (Hadiz 2004: 56). Ali Fayyad, a Hezbollah parliamentarian and one of the movement's leading intellectuals, sees this fault line as crucial to contemporary Islamism, and explicitly situates his own party's theological and philosophical foundation within a third-worldist school of thought, contrasting it with the neo-third worldist insularity of al-Qa'ida:

> We practice the idea of *umma* ['nation'], taken from the root *amma*, which means 'to go,' 'to move forward,' 'to have some place as your destination.' The idea is that a group has a common objective, a common goal to struggle for. This means that the *umma* must be flexible and not rigidly conceived... There may be many roads towards reaching this goal, not just one. This differs from the conception of the *umma* as a group, which is held by the Wahhabis. Their conception of the *umma* does not imply plurality, they believe in one solid entity. Our conception involves plurality. Taking this from the theoretical to the practical level, it enables us to say that the *umma* includes a variety of parties, currents and sects. All these are Muslims, those concerned with the faith and those who are not. Even secular Muslims are a part of this *umma*. This is completely different from the thought of the Wahhabi movements... By extension, this implies that the conception of the *umma* may also include non-Muslims, Christians and Jews... If we apply this notion of the *umma*, we can never endorse the notion of *takfir* [declaring Muslims to be apostates]. (Fayyad to authors, March 2004)

Indeed, Fanon warned of nativism and attempts to recreate 'authentic existence,' something he believed was most likely when progressive alternatives appeared exhausted. One way of understanding these differences in the use of Islam as an instrument of resistance has been suggested by the Iranian philosopher Abdolkarim Soroush. He has argued that "one of the greatest theoretical plagues in the Islamic world" is that some Muslims are "gradually coming to understand Islam as an identity rather than truth" (Soroush 2000: 34). Describing the neo-third worldist trend, although in other terms, Soroush deplores the tendency of growing numbers of Muslims to commit themselves to Islam as a means of resisting the centrifugal powers of globalization, rather than as divinely revealed truth. To him, the commitment to Islam as identity is "by its very nature, belligerent and bellicose," while a commitment to Islam as truth – in the sense of a divinely revealed foundation of knowledge and action – "can coexist with other truths. . . . I don't argue that Muslims have no identity but that Islam should not be chosen for the sake of identity" (Soroush 2000: 34).

Whether we like it or not, and regardless of whether specific courses of action make sense to us, Islamist struggles of both the third worldist and nativist kinds are at root anti-colonial liberation struggles. Within such struggles, as Robert Malley (1996) has noted, the quest for dignity is a common denominator. According to John Holloway, 'dignity' as a political category is invariably subversive because "the consistent pursuit of dignity in a society based on the denial of dignity is in itself revolutionary" (Holloway 1998). That is, it breaks down the social rules and norms that obscures, consolidates and reproduces marginalization and oppression. Writing about the Zapatista struggle in Mexico, Holloway argues that, "if dignity were simply the assertion of something that already is, then it would be an absolutely flabby concept, an empty complacency" (Holloway 1998). To simply assert human dignity as a principle, he argues, would be either a meaningless generality or even serve to "obscure the fact that existing society is based on the negation of dignity. Similarly, if dignity were simply the assertion of something that is not, then it would be an empty daydream or a religious wish. The concept of dignity only gains force if it is understood in its double dimension, as the struggle against its own denial."

Colonialism and neo-colonialism are enabled by the 'colonized mind,' which, by their very structures, they seek to foster. Islamism, as one of a number of liberation ideologies, seeks to break loose from this mental mould and in the process turns against the structures that underpin it and the hegemon that enforces it. Third World liberation strategists through-out the modern era have argued that the weakness of the subaltern stems from a perception of inferiority, from fear of the neo-colonial powers and their local enforcers, or the belief that the superiority of the colonizer is natural; that Western ways really are better. As Paul Nursery-Bray suggests, the ideology of racism "imprisons the natives within a value system that construes their identity in the negative terms of inadequacy and impotence" (Nursery-Bray 1980: 137). Indeed, the colonial and neo-colonial order is inherently racist, and its underlying logic of stratification and hierarchy must be consumed and accepted by the subalterns in order to be consolidated and reproduced. Only racism (explicit or implicit) could justify the exploitation of resources, the imposition of borders and exploit-ative financial regimes, the creation and maintenance of corrupt but pliant local despots, all the while marketing the values that sustain this order as morally superior. "It is not possible to enslave men without logically making them inferior through and through," Fanon contended, "And racism is only the emotional, affective, sometimes intellectual explanation of this inferiorization" (Fanon 1988: 40). The epistemology of colonial and neo-colonial domination is racism and its ontology is violence; these are the twin pillars upon which the *status quo* rests. To Fanon, neither reasoning nor supplication would change reality; the liberation of native peoples had to be seized. The political order would not yield but to counter-violence and a reification of the native self and only armed resistance could break down the political and economic, as well as intellectual and mental struc-tures that kept the system together. The native "knows that he is not an animal; and it is precisely at the moment he realizes his humanity that he begins to sharpen the weapons with which he will secure his victory" (Fanon 2001: 43).

One of Fanon's main ambitions was to understand and remedy these conditions of inferiorization and submission. While he was neither unique, nor entirely original in his theoretical elaboration – accounts of peoples resisting domination and oppression are surely as old as historiography itself – he identified and articulated a dynamic that, to coin an expression, may be referred to the *Fanonian impulse*. By this is meant *the psychological impact of insurgence and resistance on the native Self, and the translation of that impact into political currency, tactics, and strategy*. As the case studies intend to demonstrate, Fanon's delineation of the epistemological and ontological structures of oppression in the colonial system, as well as his doctrine on how to confront and over-come it, have been prevalent among a wide range of anti-colonial and postcolonial thinkers and ideologues, not the least among many of today's Islamist movements.

In one of Fanon's more controversial and most heavily criticized claims, which is acutely relevant to today's debate on terrorism and political violence, he suggested that violence on part of the colonized is 'therapeutic'; that the act of taking up arms in and of itself serves to restore the native's self-respect and hence 'de colonize the mind.' Political controversy notwithstanding, this is not an unfamiliar line of thought within Western post-Enlightenment scholarship, but in fact closely akin to the Hegelian dialectic process whereby we come to know who we are in relation to what we are not. In his *Phenomenology of the Spirit*, Hegel wrote that,

> Self-consciousness exists in and for itself when, and by the fact that, it so exists for another; that is, it exists only in being acknowledged...Self-consciousness is faced by another self-consciousness; it has *come out of itself*. This has a twofold significance: first, it has lost itself, for it finds itself as an *other* being; secondly, in doing so it has superseded the other, for it does not see the other as an essential being, but in the other sees its own self. (Hegel 1977: 111)

With characteristic bluntness, Sartre correctly identified the relationship when he noted that, "to shoot down a European is to kill two birds with one stone, to destroy an oppressor and the man he oppresses at the same time: there remain a dead man, and a free man; the survivor, for the first time, feels national soil under his foot" (Fanon 2001: 119). To Fanon, the violent structures within which the native self-consciousness emerges as a quest for dignity makes violent rebellion an ontological necessity.

The notion of violence as therapeutic does not amount to a glorification of the same, but a lamentable recognition of the wretched condition of the native. In fact, describing it as an illness, or ailment, in search of a remedy makes it very clear that it is not a desirable, good or natural state for a human being to find himself in. The structural violence of the colonial and neo-colonial system makes armed resistance an expression of equality and, following Hegel's logic, an expression of Self over and above the Other. This, then, is the broader socio-psychological dynamic behind the claim by Abu Imad al-Rifa'i, Palestinian Islamic Jihad's chief representative in Lebanon, that

> Wherever people feel that their dignity is trampled upon, people will rise and resist. Look at the killings [in Palestine], the

> destruction of homes, the checkpoints, the unethical practice
> by Israeli soldiers against women and children. Palestinians
> cannot sit idle while they see these violations of their dignity.... A
> human being without dignity has no life. I don't think that a
> human being can live without dignity, and if he does, then he
> ceases to be a human being. (Al-Rifa'i to authors, March 2004)

Thus, armed resistance not only carries with it the promise of political
liberation but constitutes in and of itself the means of psychological emancipation. By the act of taking up arms, an objective has already been met;
on this psychological level it matters less whether the struggle is ultimately
successful. This is not to deny that Islamist violence also fills a more traditional instrumental function, aimed at inflicting damage on the enemy,
thereby achieving tactical and strategic objectives. Nevertheless, as Robert
C. Young, a leading theorist of postcolonialism, has suggested, the violence
of anticolonial resistance movements fills a psychological function by
offering "a primary form of agency through which the subject moves from
non-being to being, from being an object to a subject" (Young 2001: 295).
This psychological and emotional aspect of emancipation – regardless of
whether one agrees with it – underlies the activities of all the groups
treated in the case studies, including al-Qa'ida. Following the 9/11 attacks,
bin Laden suggested that

> just as they're killing us, we have to kill them so that there will
> be a balance of terror. This is the first time the balance of terror
> has been close between the two parties, between Muslims and
> Americans, in the modern age. American politicians used to do
> whatever they wanted with us. The victim was forbidden to
> scream or to moan... ("Transcript" 2002)

Often the instrumental tactical and strategic choices can only be made
sense of if one first understands the underlying Fanonian impulse. The
hopelessly asymmetrical nature of most conflicts in which Islamists are
currently engaged across the globe means that their chances of political
success often seem infinitesimal – yet they struggle. Not because of some
essential and immutable violent quality that inheres in Islam, but because
the ability to inflict damage on the enemy reifies a sense of Self, which in
turn translates into political capital in the ongoing struggle to define the
nature and trajectory of Islam.

   If the Fanonian impulse constitutes an overarching commonality among
Islamist movements, how are we to understand local specificity and the

divergent, often conflicting Islamist tactics, strategies, and agendas? There is widespread scholarly acceptance throughout the social science disciplines that research on social and political phenomena must somehow be done in context, that is, analyzed with reference to internal or external features that can 'give sense' to them. On a global level the language and symbols of Islam – including their appropriation and reification through the Fanonian impulse – constitute a macro-context capable of framing a common discourse. On a local level, the very same features also constitute the building blocks of micro-contexts, but on this level imbued with specific local meanings and implications. On the macro-level, the language and symbols of Islam are necessarily abstract; on the local micro-level, they are practiced and practical, lived and applied; globally we deal with principles and theories, while within the local context we deal those principles and theories acted out as culture.

Both context and culture are notoriously difficult concepts. Anthropologist Roy Dilley argues that the process of contextualization has largely been seen as unproblematic. Conventional wisdom suggests that we should appeal to features and characteristics surrounding a phenomenon in order to illuminate it and to understand or give sense to it. Anthropologists interpret social and cultural phenomena with reference to something called 'context,' but "this apparently simple notion that it is context that gives form to our interpretations raises important questions about what a context is, how it is defined and selected, and by whom" (Dilley 1999: 1). Without taking seriously the simultaneously local and global dimensions of Islamism, present contexts for studying Islamism, as indicated above, tend to range from ill fitting to phony. They moreover tend to share the characteristic of being entirely constructed and imposed by the Etic, the social scientific researcher, with little or no reference to the way in which the Emic, the research subject, perceives his or her milieu, speech, and action. The contributions that have been allowed to define the scholarly discourse of the West have failed to make sense of Islamism precisely because they have refrained from addressing its local, dynamic human and sociocultural dimensions. Yet political speech and action can be 'given sense' only when located on a 'cultural map,' which – although fluid and transient – allows us to find our way through the norms, cues, and idiosyncrasies of a given place at a given time. Over-reliance by scholars on their own sociocultural frames of reference have proven time and again to be inadequate. Riding roughshod over the Islamists' own narratives, scholars have misinterpreted Islamist speech and behavior, and as a consequence misrepresented their agendas and objectives. The activities of groups and movements have been examined within contextual frameworks that have been either ill fitting, such as those centering on clashing civilizations and regional security concerns, or specious, such as frameworks for studying terrorism, or ideas of Islamic immutability and essences.

Because Islamism is generally conceived of as *a political threat or problem*, much of the extant literature comes from the field of political science. This particular discipline has not spent much time problematizing the issues of context and contextualization, and is particularly insensitive to cultural difference. Its forte is rather to formulate and apply macro-level models and paradigms capable of explaining political behavior and processes across social and cultural boundaries, alternatively to construct universally applicable models of political behavior and apply these to (or extrapolate from) specific countries or regions. The focus is thus set at a high level of abstraction, and micro-level idiosyncrasies are important primarily because of what they tell us about the whole, through their ability to validate or correct paradigmatic models. Political science would thus be capable of making sense of Islamism as a macro-level phenomenon, were it not hampered by the range of assumptions and presuppositions examined in the previous chapter. Instead, studies of Islamism within political science have tended to be analogous to Lévi-Strauss' anthropological work on myth (1963; 1966), which removed the processes of oral accounts from their performative contexts in order to establish pan-cultural features of the "savage mind." Dilley's description of Lévi-Strauss' efforts could easily be transposed onto terrorism studies: "The specificity of local cultural contexts becomes the object of his generalizing project that seeks certain kinds of symbolic phenomena in particular localities, seen simply as moulds which give shape to fundamental principles" (Dilley 1999: 21).

The alternative is sociological and anthropological studies, in which local context is a core concern. While contributions from these disciplines are far less prone to exoticism, they generally fail to take into account the macro-level commonalities, if for no other reason than the fact that they have little or no interest in that level of abstraction. Due to the compartmentalization of academia, the two approaches almost never combine, serving instead as the Scylla and Charybdis of research on Islamism; those who avoid the pitfalls of one generally fall into the traps of the other, giving accounts of specific issues or groups that may be accurate and insightful, but nevertheless truncated views of 'the Islamist story.'

The act of interpreting the significance and meaning of social phenomena may be thought of as establishing how they are connected. Dilley has suggested that, "A phenomenon is connected to its surroundings;

contexts are sets of connections construed as relevant to someone, to something or to a particular problem, and this process yields an explanation, a sense, an interpretation for the object so connected" (Dilley 1999: 2). Yet this process is by no means unproblematic. Relevance is difficult to delineate to the point that 'relevant context' may be practically unbounded, which in turn means that any attempt to be thorough in understanding context "leads to total contextualization, in which everything becomes the context of everything else" (Scharfstein 1989: xii–xiii). An additional matter is the problem of 'contextual direction,' as scholars working within philosophy of language have identified three distinct spheres of context. First, the external context, which is created by making a connection between one domain of phenomena (say, Islamist language) and another (the world). On this view, language can be ascribed meaning insofar as it relates to or describes 'objective reality.' Second, the internal context, which is created by making a connection not with things outside the object of inquiry, but internal to it. Here, meaning involves connections and significant relations within language itself. Third, the mental or psychological context, which is created by focusing attention on the minds of the individual agents whose particular use of language we study, their intentions and inner states. "The mind, it could be suggested, becomes a particular kind of context that environs the object of study ..." (Dilley 1999: 13).

These originally philosophical distinctions contain important insight for the relationship between the Fanonian impulse, the local structural context within which that impulse is stimulated, and the global macro-context of a shared Islamic language and symbolism. In anthropology, these three levels of context are roughly the content of universalism, contextualism, and psychologism, distinct and conflicting models for interpreting and understanding behavior and custom. In order to understand Islamism, however, we are required to see the models as complementary. While these contextual spheres will be elaborated and illustrated in the case studies, we may note that they could be considered analogous to interpreting Islamist speech and action with reference to its significant local and global context; with reference to the hermeneutical process of Islamic scholarship capable of creating both local and general meaning; and with reference to the psychology of resistance, the Fanonian impulse.

Anthropologist Bronislaw Malinowski coined the phrase "context of situation" in order to address the pragmatic circumstances in which "the context of words," language, as a mode of action, was used and articulated. He argued that "the meaning of a word must always be gathered ... from an analysis of its functions, with reference to the given culture" (Malinowski

1993: 6). In his later writings Malinowski restated the "context of situation" as "the context of culture," arguing that translation and interpretation must take place against the "cultural background of society" (Malinowski 1935: 17–18). Culture may be thought of as a socially negotiated network of polyvalent practices, narratives, and images that generate meaning and inform speech and action. In every human culture, there are sets of behaviors, some of which are (more or less) predictable and regular and thus capable of being accounted for in generalized and, admittedly, stereotypical patterns. These are social norms or cues that help members of a culture to know how to interact with one another and with strangers, but they do not imply that human beings are in some way "cultural dopes who act unconsciously in accordance to underlying structures of shared symbolic meaning" (Goodwin and Duranti 1992: 96). Social and cultural norms do not acquire the status of social law (Esler 1987: 6). Rather, to talk of sociocultural norms and cues entails only the observation that whenever we speak and act in life, we do so from within a context of cultural conditioning, from a socially constructed and inculturated sense of how and why we function as human beings and relate to one another, the roles we adopt and the values by which we are motivated. Ingold has correctly pointed out that when a fieldworker investigates cultural parameters, "what we do not find are neatly bounded and mutually exclusive bodies of thought and custom, perfectly shared by all who subscribe to them, and in which their lives and worlds are fully encapsulated" (Ingold 1994: 330).

Context, then, includes both the general setting and the immediate situation in which a word is used, and in which, for our purposes, action takes place. Understanding context as setting is a fruitful way of shifting the focus from analysis of words and sentences to conceive of language as a mode of action, examining how people deploy language in order to accomplish action (Goodwin and Duranti 1992: 17). Setting, a set of recognized conventions, gives certain words and sentences particular meaning and is reminiscent of Habermas' concept of 'lifeworld,' the immediate environment in which individuals ideally can find recognition for the validity of their communication (Dilley 1999: 18–20).

Again, the setting for Islamist speech and action is simultaneously local and global, a fact that lies at the heart of the intra-Islamist struggle for the future of the community. Concepts such as jihad, *shari'ah, ummah* and *fitna* are common to, and recognized by all Islamists everywhere. But the fact that these and other concepts are subject to a range of different local exegeses and applications means that the common setting in itself generates conflict. On the local level, by contrast, the setting consists of the common background expectancies whereby speech and action can be understood. Within what Dell Hymes (1972) terms the "speech-community," there are shared rules concerning the conduct and interpretation of speech, and for the Islamists, such speech-communities, then, exist on both the local and global level.

In this context it is instructive to note that Robert Paine distinguishes rhetoric as a particular kind of discourse, arguing that while most speech acts are "speech about something" the kernel of rhetoric is that "saying is doing" (Paine 1981: 9). The effect of the successful use of rhetoric may be to cause an audience to achieve a state of identification with a speaker, "whereby aspects of the social identity or being of the people involved in the rhetorical encounter come more closely to approximate one another" (Rapport and Overing 2000: 119). While the persuasion of an audience by a speaker is the most apparent direction of rhetoric, a speaker may also be persuaded by his or her own words. In either case, "rhetoric can be seen as an instrument by which a speaker gains or increases control over a political environment. And once this control becomes routinized, institutionalized, then control over language, over the right to speak, may be defined as an essential base of power and authority" (Rapport and Overing 2000: 119).

There is no way of understanding Hamas and its ability to resonate with its constituents apart from the local conflict with Israel *and simultaneously* the global Islamist movement that enables Hamas' existence to transcend parochialism. There is no way of understanding the Taliban apart from the local war against the Soviet Union and subsequent inter-tribal warfare, *and simultaneously* the global Islamist resurgence that was, to a significant extent, born out of the Afghan anti-Soviet struggle. Local settings supply meaning to concepts and ideas that are otherwise abstract and practically meaningless, but the transcendence and universality of those abstract principles are nevertheless crucial to the creation of common local identities. The language of Islam does not descend into localities to give sense to people's lives; the local setting creates meanings, appropriates words and symbols, that ascend to the macro-level as claims on the overarching identity of Islam. On both levels, context is both constitutive of social action and itself the product of social action; "it is both a generative principle and a resulting outcome" (Dilley 1999: 19). Moreover, "individual participants can actively attempt to shape context in ways that further their own interests" and context can thus be understood as "an interactively constituted mode of practice" (Goodwin and Duranti 1992: 6, 22). Taken together, we may understand Islamists, like other social agents, as actively interested in the use of context to create effects and outcomes.

It follows that while Islamism is based on ideological and theological principles and propelled by intergroup competition, the ways in which these are expressed and played out must be understood as informed by the social and cultural norms and cues of their local societies, as well as the norms and cues derived from their overarching Islamic identity. That is not to say that they should be considered as locked into a cultural matrix, which would reduce the argument to one based on essentialism. Culture is important, but not static. It is constantly negotiated through the creative agency of its members. It is therefore not only possible, but expected that individuals and groups within the same cultural context form different understandings of the meanings and implications of cultural practices, narratives, and images, especially if they occupy different positions within a power structure. It is also expected that competing social groups may consciously choose to emphasize and advance different interpretations of common sociocultural images and narratives in order to enhance their social position and status. It is probably evident at this point that the present study does not seek to construct a model for understanding the Islamist mind, nor is it making a claim about social norms followed by any and all members of some given cultural sphere. Instead, through the case studies, this volume is holding up a particular social phenomenon to scrutiny against the background of a range of fluid and dynamic sets of social cues provided by the cultures of Islam.

In examining Islamism as socioculturally grounded expressions of the Fanonian impulse, this study draws on social identity theory, a heuristic model of the way human identity develops in and between groups through interaction and communication. As a non-reductionist theory of group behavior, social identity theory emphasizes the significance of the subject's hermeneutic situation and group members' internally constructed social identity. Importantly, social identity theory is sufficiently elastic to allow space for different cultural contexts in which cohesive group conscious-nesses are installed in the minds and hearts of its members. It is unnecessary for present purposes to attempt a rigorous definition of a group: the simplest, and perhaps the ultimate, statement that can be made about a group is that it is a body of people who consider that they are a group. Nevertheless, in describing the experience of belonging to a group it is helpful to follow Henri Tajfel, the originator of social identity theory, in differentiating between three components. First, a cognitive component (i.e. knowledge that one belongs to a group); second, an evaluative component (in the sense that the group and/or one's membership of it may have a positive or negative connotation); and third, an emotional component (i.e. the cognitive and evaluative aspects of group membership generate emotions – such as love, pride, anxiety, loathing etc. – directed towards one's own group, as well as towards other individuals and groups that stand in certain relationships to it) (Tajfel 1978: 28).

Tajfel defines "social identity" as that part of an individual's self-concept "deriving from his or her knowledge of membership of a social group (or groups) together with the value and emotional significance attached to that membership" (Tajfel 1972: 31). The extent to which group membership contributes to a sense of self varies depending upon the level of group orientation present in the ambient culture. Markedly individualistic cultures are atypical in the world – limited, in fact, to Western Europe and North America – with collectivist attitudes being far more common (Taylor 1992). It is perhaps worth noting that, in this respect, there is a clearly discernible difference between the highly communitarian cultural spheres within which most Islamist have emerged, and the atomistic environments in which Western scholarship on Islamism has been devised.

Social identity theory adopts a distinctive position in relation to the continuing problem of the relationship between the individual and the group. Its central idea is that being categorized as members of certain groups provides an important part of the self-concept of individuals. In important ways, we learn who we are from the groups to which we belong, and in becoming members of a group we redefine who we are. Moreover, since we internalize our group memberships as part of our self-understanding, it follows that any value associated with those groups will have implications for our feelings of self-worth (Brown 1988: 20–2). From this perspective the critical question is: how, that is, through which psychological processes, are societal and group-specific norms and cues – such as those attending the Fanonian impulse – able to install themselves in the minds and hearts of individuals, affecting their speech and behavior? The answer will depend on the cultural and social context of any given group, as each environment activates different individual and collective responses and gives rise to distinct and distinctly local manifestations of Islamist thought and action.

What makes social identity theory particularly pertinent to the present study is its attendant models for understanding intergroup relations and conflict. Group dynamics are strongly affected by whether a comparative or non-comparative ethos or ideology permeates the group. What holds true for all groups by definition, however, is that they need to provide their members with a positive social identity – establish a positively valued distinctiveness from other groups – in order to maintain their existence. This group consciousness can operate on a number of levels (e.g. Muslim, Salafi, Algerian, FIS member, military cadre, etc.). Within these groups, normative evaluations define acceptable and unacceptable attitudes and behavior for group members, thus maintaining and enhancing group identity (Brown 1988: 42–8). These norms, and the politicization of these norms, are supplied by group elites. When a group finds itself in a position where it has a lower social status than another group with which it interacts, its ability to contribute positively to its members' social identities is impaired. In such situations, two types of response are open to group members who are discontent with their negatively charged social identities. One response is social mobility, which occurs when individuals leave their group to join another. The feasibility of this option depends on the permeability of intergroup boundaries, external constraints (e.g. negative evaluations of one's religious affiliation or ethnic background in the group to which access is sought), and internal constraints (e.g. disapproval of dissent) (Hogg and Abrams 1988: 54).

The second response is social change, an attempt at a positive revaluation of the ingroup in relation to the dominant outgroup. This response assumes impermeability of intergroup boundaries and overpowering internal and external constraints – such as the conditions that permeate the structures of societies subject to colonial and neo-colonial subjugation. Change, then, can be brought about through social creativity or social competition, or a combination of both (Esler 1998: 52). It is here that the Fanonian impulse becomes operative, as it uses the act of resistance to change the native's self-understanding as well as his or her actual situation vis-à-vis the hegemonic power.

Social creativity entails redefining and altering the premises of the comparative or competitive situation, and seems to be an appropriate response when the negative balance cannot be redressed. This may involve the redefinition of the value of some existing comparison, turning a weakness into strength (e.g. "the smallness of our group indicates its elite nature"). It may furthermore entail the proposition that true positive values are per definition the antithesis of those espoused by the outgroup. This, as will be demonstrated in the following chapters, is exemplified by the absolutist rejection of all 'non-Islamic' norms and values by the nativist trend. Finally, an ingroup may fix its gaze on some outgroup other than the dominant one, seeking to bring about a more favorable comparative situation. Again, the internecine struggles that bedevil the global Islamist movement – brought about by the multiplicity of local interpretations of common language and symbols – provide examples of this approach. For instance, the long-standing and public confrontation between Hamas and al-Qa'ida over the ability to define the Palestinian struggle and its wider implications is based in part on different interpretations of Islamic codes of conduct, pointing to many of the same texts – but texts that have been read in very different contexts. For the same reason, it is easier for al-Qa'ida in Iraq to turn its weapons on the 'apostate' Shi'a, than the US occupation forces, and attacks on both these outgroups serve to legitimize and enhance the al-Qa'ida ingroup's claim to Islamic authenticity.

Social competition refers to the efforts by the subordinate group to improve its actual social status vis-à-vis the dominant group. Esler has suggested that direct competition of this sort presupposes that an alternative arrangement is possible and that the comparative relationship is thus unstable (Esler 1998: 54). It seems, however, that all that is needed is a perception of that possibility in the subordinate group, causing them to undertake the competitive venture. As Fanon put it:

> For if, in fact, my life is worth as much as the settler's, his glance no longer shrivels me up nor freezes me, and his voice no longer turns me to stone. I am no longer on tenterhooks in his presence; in fact, I don't give a damn for him. Not only does his presence no longer trouble me, but I am already preparing such efficient ambushes for him that there soon will be no way out but that of flight. (Fanon 2001: 45)

Whether it is the challenge of the various Algerian Islamist groups against the national government, the Muslim Brotherhood's challenge against the Egyptian state, Hezbollah's challenge against the Lebanese status quo, or the challenge of groups within Europe's Muslim communities against the sociopolitical inferiority imposed upon them, the act of resistance is an act of social competition. In any case, "any threat to the distinctively superior position of a group implies a potential loss of positive comparisons and possible negative comparisons, which must be guarded against" (Tajfel and Turner 1979: 45). This contest lies at the heart of the fractured unity of the Islamist project.

4

Roots and Branches: From the Muslim Brotherhood to Hamas

The narrative of the Egyptian Muslim Brotherhood (MB), which overlaps with the story of the emergence of Islamism as a modern political movement, neither begins nor ends in Egypt. Rather, Egypt served as a laboratory in which a range of intellectual and political trends and tendencies from across the Muslim world came together and cross-fertilized, were refined or remolded into a new and powerful political formula. That formula was then re-exported to the Muslim world and beyond. Indeed, due to the intense interaction and interconnectedness of Islamist thinkers and their ideas in the 'Egyptian cauldron,' it is sometimes difficult to parse the lineages of the panoply of contemporary groups and movements. Hillel Fradkin, for instance, conflates a number of different terms when he writes, in a study about the MB, about the urgent necessity to understand "the worldwide Islamic phenomenon and movement variously known as Islamism, Salafism, radical Islam, militant Islam, political Islam and the like" (Fradkin 2008: 5). Yet these are not conterminous, and there is no necessary or constant connection between Islamism and militancy, nor between Salafism and political activism. Moreover, while the political philosophy of the MB shares historical roots with Salafism, as well as significant elements of its framework and objectives, the MB is not a Salafi movement. Indeed, in some places – notably Algeria and Bahrain – the MB has evolved into a primary competitor against Salafi groups.

Contemporary Islamism has its genesis in a purposive move to address an existential threat. In the mid-nineteenth century, Muslim intellectuals around the Islamic world saw their religion faced with creeping corrosion brought about by complex social and political forces. With the better part of the world's Muslims being the colonial subjects of non-Islamic Western powers, the notion of Islam's divinely appointed universal superiority had become little more than a joke. The colonial powers were enriching themselves on the basis of Muslim labor and resources, making it difficult if not impossible to direct time and treasure to local regeneration. Additionally, the colonial powers were steadily Westernizing their subservient local clients – royal families and local business elites molded entirely in the image of their Western masters – which in turn impacted the social norms and cues of society at large. As for Western scientific and technological advances, few Islamic scholars disputed that they carried the promise of social and economic improvements, but also recognized that these were primarily reserved for the purposes of the colonialists. Moreover, the ethos that accompanied this Western superiority seemed to be devoid of spiritual principles and morality; the Enlightenment had consciously separated reason and revelation, thus creating an apparent spiritual and moral void at the heart of the civilization whence it had emerged; a civilization that held the Islamic world in its clutches and therefore threatened it too with lingering political, moral, and spiritual destruction.

As a reaction to this situation, Islam was gradually forged into Islamism; Islam as a modern, action-oriented political language, in addition to its traditional theological, ethical, and philosophical content. The first generation of anti-colonial strugglers in the Islamic world were Islamic intellectuals who sought to reconcile the obviously beneficial material and intellectual advances of the West with the requirements of their own sociocultural and religious identities. It is not uncommon to hear Western pundits call for a 'Reformation in Islam,' an 'Islamic Enlightenment,' or for Islam to produce an answer to Luther or Voltaire (Rushdie 2005; Hirsi Ali 2006). The idea behind such calls seems to be that only a society that has a robust separation of church and state, and a political system based on reason rather than revelation, can adequately and justly serve its citizens. This concern with Muslim mimicry of a Western developmental matrix was expressed at least as early as 1900, when the French Foreign Minister, Gabriel Hanotaux, entered into a polemic exchange with Egyptian scholar Muhammad Abdu over the "question of Islam" (Adams 1933: 86). At the time, Hanotaux raised some of the very issues that have remained stock concerns in Western scholarship and commentary on Islam ever since: Islam's relationship with democracy and pluralism and its capacity – or lack thereof – for material progress. This exchange took place at the time, and as a consequence of the flourishing of Islamic modernism of which Muhammad Abdu was a chief proponent. According to the early twentieth-century Orientalist Charles Adams,

> Muhammadan modernism in Egypt...constitutes an attempt to free the religion of a too rigid orthodoxy, and to accomplish reforms which will render it adaptable to the complex demands of modern life. Its prevailing character is that of religious

reform; it is inspired and dominated chiefly by theological considerations. (Adams 1993: 1)

Bernard Lewis is half right when he claims that, "the struggle of the [Islamic] fundamentalists is against two enemies, secularism and modernism" (Lewis 2004: 329) Certainly, rejection of the principles of secularism is to some extent inherent in all Islamist projects. Yet Islamism, despite its religious language and seventh-century reference points, is a thoroughly modern phenomenon. Muhammad Abdu (1849–1905) and his mentor, the Persian scholar Jamal al-Din al-Afghani (1838–97) – "the first genuine modernist thinker in Islam" (Fakhry 2004: 345) – produced a body of thought that even neo-Orientalist 'terrorist experts' are forced to concede was "an anti-colonialist one. Neither was anti-Western. They rejected its political and religious domination, but not the West itself" (Migaux 2008: 273). Al-Afghani and Abdu's Islamist thought and activities are important, in part because they constitute the first modern articulations of anti-colonial sentiment in the Muslim world, in part because they feed directly into the intellectual and political activities of Hassan al-Banna (1906–49) and Said Qutb (1906–66), the founder and premier *philosòphe* of the Egyptian MB, respectively. Neither al-Banna nor Qutb copied al-Afghani and Abdu, but rather interacted with them, and developed their understandings and prescriptions in powerful and influential ways.

The context provided by the ongoing anti-colonial project, which was the chief concern of all these thinkers, allows us to make sense of the MB and the contemporary Islamism that it has spawned and inspired, as thoroughly modern. The implications are worth spelling out: if the wellspring of Islamism was a modernist anti-colonial project, then its various intellectual children and step-children cannot be adequately understood, as per the Orientalist and neo-Orientalist models, as proponents of a simple medieval faith, immutable Islamic warrior-types, eternal enemies of Western ideas and ideals, and so forth. The MB took upon itself to operationalize Islamic thought in ways that corresponded to the conditions of Muslims in the modern era, and did so in the full awareness that it was a modern movement, and that its tenets and precepts, derived from al-Afghani and Abdu, clashed with the traditional consensus on Islamic theology and jurisprudence. Subsequent generations of Islamists, and the various groups that have branched off from the MB, must by no means be thought of as determined by early MB thought, as if locked into a static intellectual matrix. Yet when Western scholars trace contemporary Islamist projects to the MB, to the scholarship on which it relied, and to the activism that it produced, these scholars – whether they recognize it or not – are clearly marking Islamism out as a modern phenomenon.

A disingenuous way to obfuscate the conclusion that Islamism represents modern, rather than medieval thought is to pronounce Islamic modernism itself as a perverter of Islam, leading to what one author has referred to as "an aberrant form...a mythicized view of original Islam" (Migaux 2008: 255). First one must ask why al-Banna or Qutb's understanding of 'original Islam' should be thought of as more mythical than a Western researchers' understanding of 'original Islam'? More significantly, the move to cast modern expressions of ancient belief systems as perversions seems to be grounded in a confusion between the terms 'traditional' and 'authentic' (O'Donovan 2007: 265–77). This in turn reflects a much broader theological conversation, cutting across religious boundaries: how do we determine if an expression of faith is 'authentic'? That is to say, by reference to what other thing can we *authenticate* it? It is beyond the scope of the present volume to get mired in that question. Suffice it for the present to note that the easy route taken by those who enshrine a particular vision of a lost golden age as authoritative for authenticity – and this is done by Orientalists and some Islamists alike – tend to equate authenticity with tradition as expressed in overt and verifiable actions: clothing, dietary habits, prayer routines, and so forth. However, understanding faith and faith communities as dynamic communities of meaning necessarily undermines such a simple equation between outward tradition and authenticity. An instructive parallel might be the movement, primarily within the Roman Catholic Church, referred to as liberation theology. Liberation theology argues that the authenticity of Christianity is determined primarily by its enacted social relevance in the lives of the poor (Gutiérrez 1988). It is certainly a modern intellectual current, impossible without the analytical categories supplied by post-Enlightenment economics, sociology, and political science, as well as the modernizing catalyst provided by the Second Vatican Council. Are we legitimately to conclude, therefore, that its proponents – Archbishops Romero and Camara, priests and theologians Leonardo Boff and Gustavo Gutiérrez, among many others – are not 'genuinely Christian'? That is exactly the leap made by Orientalists as they replicate the Salafi Islamists' simplicity, pointing to the external markers of tradition at the expense of social relevance through dynamic interaction.

John Gray, in a study of al-Qa'ida and the Salafi trend – which can be traced directly back to Abdu – has been able to claim that radical Islam is "best understood as an attempt to realize a modern European ideal" (Gray

2003: 5). He suggests that its intellectual roots may be found in the European counter-Enlightenment, which emerged in the late eighteenth and early nineteenth century. In this current, "the rational skepticism of Enlightenment thinkers such as Hume led to a rejection of reason itself" (Gray 2003: 25). A thoroughly modern movement, yet opposed to the hegemony of reason, the counter-Enlightenment included luminaries such as J. G. Hamman, who rejected reason in favor of religious revelation, J. G. Herder, who rejected of the ideal of a universal civilization in favor of cultural genius, Søren Kierkegaard, who defended religious faith as a subjective experience, as well as Fichte and Nietzsche, both elevating will over reason (Gray 2003: 25). Gray argues that it is precisely the rejection of reason that shows radical Islam to be a modern movement, and that understandings of Islamism as medievalist miss the mark because "the medieval world may have been unified by faith, but it did not scorn reason" (Gray 2003: 25).

This is certainly a valid partial view of contemporary Salafi Islamism, yet the intellectual progenitors of modernist Islam were far from anti-rationalist. The juxtaposition of reason and revelation, and of modernity and religion, as polar opposites is itself a feature of Enlightenment thought that is particularly unhelpful in trying to understand the development of Islamism as a modern political movement. By interaction, not only with the Enlightenment and counter-Enlightenment thought of the West, but also through what Elleke Boehmer (2002) has referred to in a different context as "margin-to-margin" interaction among various intellectual trends and currents in the colonized societies themselves, Islamist thought is not merely a response to, and development of *core* Western ideas and ideals of modernity, but also the product of interaction among the various actors in the *periphery*; not merely a reaction against colonial hegemony, but a unique and complex product of the range of intellectual currents throughout the Islamic world that were united by structural subservience in a global colonial system. It was this system, rather than Islam, that provided a common point of departure for modern anti-colonial intellectuals and activists from Algiers to Jakarta, some of whom emphasized Islam as the solution. Thus the trajectory of Islamist thought has been complex and versatile, but always thoroughly modern.

Al-Afghani was "a pioneer of Islamic modernism and especially of anti-imperialist activism" setting the tone for the marriage of thought and action among subsequent generations inspired by his work (Keddie 2008: 11). His intellectual output was vast and his *curriculum vitae* extensive. For our purposes it may suffice to note that his approach to religious thought, and to the absolute truths that he believed inhered in Islam, was thoroughly rationalistic. His major philosophical treatise, *Refutation of the Materialists*, took aim at that basic feature of Enlightenment thought, yet was at the same time written from a staunchly rationalist perspective. For al-Afghani, there was no contradiction between reason and religious faith; between believing in sound principles of deduction, on the one hand, and theological claims about absolute truth, on the other. Indeed, to him, the very superiority of Islam lay in its rejection of intellectual super-naturalism; in the fact that it commands its adherents to accept nothing without proof and admonishes them not to be led astray by fads and fancies. Islam, he argued, "enjoins its adepts to seek a demonstrative basis for the fundamentals of belief ... always addresses reason and bases its ordinances upon it. Its texts clearly state that human felicity is the product of reason and insight..." (Fakhry 2004: 349). As a consequence of the belief that religion and reason are fully consonant, and even though he rejected the supernaturalism of traditional cultic life, he never rejected religious belief, as some medieval rationalist had done. On the contrary, and importantly, he was fully aware that religion is a crucial element in the lives of human beings, both on the level of individual morality, and on the level of human culture. The rationality and the cultural aspects of Islam would both become dominant themes in modernist interpretations of the faith (Fakhry 2004: 350).

Al-Afghani's politics demonstrate the inadequacy of positing a simple binary choice between mimicry of the West and retreat into nativism. While his rationalist understanding of Islam was in part a product of his encounter with European intellectual trends, it was also a response to a societal need; far from mere mimicry of the hegemon, it was a formulation that was fed by, and in turn fed into local needs for societal regeneration. The achievements of the West were evident, and they were based on science and technology. Al-Afghani also understood them as beneficial – but for the corrosive nature of philosophical materialism, which appeared to have inseparably attached itself to Enlightenment thought. Thus, while intellectual elites in Europe had come to believe that rationalism and materialism must go hand-in-hand, al-Afghani believed that they could and must be separated, lest modernity become a monstrosity; an exclusively Western phenomenon that first hollows itself out, and then requires other cultures also to empty themselves of their unique spiritual contents.

The initial intellectual impetus for al-Afghani's emphasis on the need for a pan-Islamic solution to local as well as regional political predicaments was the encounter with overwhelming British military might during the so-called Indian Mutiny of 1857, at which he is believed to have been present (Rahnema 2008: xxxix). In the face of the colonial super power, localized Islamic expressions of resistance had been proven impotent. In al-Afghani's analysis, it was Islam as a supra-national school of thought, cultural matrix and spiritual motor that would provide an opportunity to stimulate the consciousnesses of intellectuals and masses, and do so far beyond the confines of any one nation. Since the problems posed by colonialism appeared to him essentially similar across the Islamic world – subservient local elites doing the repressive bidding of remote imperial masters – the pan-Islamic solution appeared to him adequate to address the colonial situation *in toto*. Pan-Islam, "an exclusion-based defensive idea" (Rahnema 2008: xxxix) able to appeal across the Islamic world was thus developed as a neutralizing response to the equally exclusion-based policies of colonialism.

This attempted antidote to subaltern status, an attempt to wrest political power and dignity back from the colonial system, was marketed relentlessly by al-Afghani, who travelled untiringly in the Islamic world (as well as Europe), teaching and agitating until his death. That "al-Afghani believed that violence was the only way to realize his purposes" (Kedourie 1992: 274) should not surprise, since the colonial order against which he sought to foment rebellion was itself maintained by violence. Fanon's analysis mentioned in the preceding chapter is directly applicable: "the argument that the native chooses has been furnished by the settlers, and by an ironic turning of the tables it is the native who now affirms that the colonialist understands nothing but force" (Fanon 2001: 66).

Muhammad Abdu studied logic, theology, astronomy, metaphysics, and philosophy under al-Afghani during the latter's time on the faculty at al-Azhar in Cairo. A reason for Abdu's interest in al-Afghani's teachings was, according to Fakhry, that the latter "not only imparted the spirit of free expression into his students, but actively spearheaded a movement of national and intellectual emancipation in Egypt" (Fakhry 2004: 351). A lack of representative institutions in Egypt had resulted in a scholarly lacuna in terms of applying the various academic disciplines to politics and public affairs. Al-Afghani had attempted to remedy this by synthesizing Islamic thought and modern politics, and Abdu carried on the endeavor. At al-Azhar, Abdu lectured on Ibn Khaldun's *Muqaddimah*, applying its analysis to contemporary Egypt, which caused him to clash with traditionalist theologians who accused him of straying from tradition. While teaching in Beirut, he taught not only traditional subjects, but also philosophy and scholastic theology (*'ilm al-kalam*), which had not previously been done in the Levant. These lectures formed the foundation of his systematic *magnum opus*, *Risalat al-Tawhid*, in which, following al-Afghani, he reaffirmed reason as the ultimate arbiter of truth and morality. Prior to the Quran, he argued, theology had drawn on the supernatural and unverifiable to establish truth. The Quran, however, revealed what

> God had permitted or prescribed the knowledge of, but did not stipulate its acceptance simply on the ground of revelation, but advanced proof and demonstration, expounded the views of disbelievers, and inveighed against them rationally . . . reason and religion marched in unison for the first time in that sacred book revealed by God to a prophet commissioned by Him. (Fakhry 2004: 352)

This unison march of reason and religion, according to Abdu, was interrupted already in the first century of Islam when political and theological differences began to fragment the community of believers. The philosophers who emerged to settle the disputes and champion orthodoxy were rationalists, but fell into error by excessive deference to the Greeks. To Abdu, the example of the 'pious forebears' – al-salaf al-salih – lay in their demonstration to mankind of a divinely appointed, perfect intellectual balance. This was the particular golden age narrative thenceforth associated with Abdu's work, and the first stirrings of Salafi Islamism. The flawed and relatively uncritical historiography of Abdu's age is less interesting than the conclusions it allowed him to draw. Fakhry explains that, to Abdu, the core of Islam is a belief in the oneness of God, which was established by reason and supported by revelation. "The blind acceptance (taqlid) of any precept or dogma is incompatible with the express teaching of the Koran, which had enjoined reflection upon the wonders of Creation and admonished believers against uncritical acceptance of the beliefs of their forebears" (Fakhry 2004: 353). Abdu's rationalism was bounded by his awareness of reason's limitations. Reason could not inquire into God, his essence, or his purposes, and here Abdu stands out, not as a rationalist but as a traditionalist. Indeed, the example of the pious forebears, which was important to him precisely because he believed they had attained the perfect balance of reason and religion, was also authoritative because they had not encumbered reason with idle and unprofitable inquiry. The pious forebears had understood and remained within the boundaries of rational inquiry and were therefore to be studied and emulated. Again it is worth noting that, to Abdu, the tension between reason and revelation was an inescapable fact of life; a tightrope to be walked, rather than a problem to be solved by discarding either one or the other. Subsequent commentators – Islamists and Western academics alike – have thus been able to find in Abdu's writings two distinct and apparently contradictory strains of thought that he himself considered inextricably intertwined.

When the French Foreign Minister Hanotaux entered into a discussion with Abdu about "the question of Islam," the concern of the former was that, despite al-Afghani and Abdu's rationalism and modernism, and despite their emphasis on Islam as a unifying civilizational matrix that would allow Muslims to emancipate and modernize their societies, Islam appeared in reality unable to cope with modernity. His main arguments were to point to the lack of separation between church and state in Islam – an essential component of modern Europe – and the de facto pre-modern nature of Islamic societies, all of which stood out for their fragmentation, feudalism, and impotence. Of course, what Hanotaux assumed – and what Orientalists and neo-Orientalists continue to assume – is that modernity must be Western in all essentials. In response, Abdu articulated what has remained a standard Islamist argument ever since. As for the Western separation of church and state – the disjunction between religious and political life – Abdu argued that this was indeed impossible in Islam, but also undesirable. It was an arbitrary division between the spiritual and temporal that merely served to deprive the social sphere of its spiritual dimension. In Islam, he argued, rather than rendering unto Caesar what is Caesar's and to God what is God's, Caesar must be subordinated to God and held accountable for his actions. In response to accusations that Islam is helplessly backward, Abdu drew a distinction between Islam and Muslims. The beliefs and practices that had constituted the unison march of reason and religion among the pious forebears were not themselves affected by subsequent sociopolitical upheaval, errors, and failures. History is cyclical and subject to the vagaries of man and free will, he argued, and the waxing and waning of the fortunes of Islamic societies was not an argument against the basic correctness of its guiding principles. Moreover, foreign infiltration and encroachment, presently evident in the colonial system, had served to corrupt Islamic governance since the time of the Abbasid caliphate. Thus, a reawakened original Islamic consciousness would be able to restore Islam to political predominance in the modern world and establish Islam as a universal creed, and this was inextricably tied to the purging of Islamic societies from the spiritually and intellectually corrosive elements of Western imperial domination.

Al-Afghani and Abdu thus articulated Islam as a common language for modern political use, through which local grievances and problems could be articulated at a global level. As a rationalist discourse it made use of eminently modern categories of analysis that could be applied to modern sociopolitical and economic concerns. As a traditionalist discourse, it provided sharp ingroup/outgroup boundaries and a matrix for thought and action. It is important to note that, while pan-Islam was an exclusionist identity from a Western perspective – that is, it excluded European culture, if not its technological and scientific achievements – that is only a partial view. From a native perspective, pan-Islam sought to forge a new and enlarged ingroup out of previously fragmented communities. Al-Afghani and Abdu's grand idea and lasting contribution was thus to forge out of Islam a modern political identity that transcended the boundaries of individual tribes, states, and colonial mandates; an idea that bore distinct similarities to Bismarck's attempt to unify the German states and Garibaldi's efforts to unite southern Italy on the basis of shared socio-cultural realities. Pan-Islam ostracized the hegemon – it was, after all, an anti-colonial project – but drew into itself an ethnically disparate and geographically dispersed collection of subaltern peoples laboring under similar structural predicaments (Carrère d'Encausse and Schram 1969: 189–90).

Hassan al-Banna, an Egyptian primary school teacher, founded the MB in 1928 as an attempt to operationalize the ideas of al-Afghani and Abdu. He "transformed an elite intellectual fashion into a popular phenomenon that would profoundly influence the interaction between religion and politics not only in Egypt but throughout the Arab and Muslim world" (Commins 1994: 125). Al-Banna, who had a long history of membership in Islamic charitable and 'moral' societies, was disturbed by British de facto occupation of Egypt and the chronic indebtedness of the Egyptian supply-side economy to European banks. He was also alarmed by Atatürk's abolition of the caliphate in March 1924, and worried that the establishment of a secular university in Cairo in 1925 was a step in the same 'modernization by mimicry' direction as the Turkish government had chosen. The movement that al-Banna went on to found, the MB, saw itself as the intellectual descendant of Afghani, Abdu, and Rashid Rida, one of Abdu's most influential disciples, who would later become a pioneer of Arabism. Following in this lineage, al-Banna was thought of as 'the builder' whose task it was to forge and lead a nation on the basis of the teachings of these intellectual forebears.

Al-Banna was certainly more moved by the Salafi strain in the teachings of al-Afghani and Abdu, than by the rationalist strain. Moreover, the influence of Rida caused al-Banna to mix pan-Islamism with a significant component of Arab nationalism. Al-Banna understood the Arabs as privileged among the Muslim peoples, and natural leaders, in part because the Prophet Muhammad and the pious forebears were Arabs, in part because the Quran had been communicated to humanity, once and for all, in Arabic. Despite his significant intellectual engagement, it was al-Banna's organizational skill and charisma that would form the basis of his legacy.

His establishment of the MB reflected his Salafi inclinations. The MB contained a range of specialized committees, but was headed by a Guide (*murshid*) who was the ultimate and unquestionable authority, advised by a consultative council (*majlis al-shura*). A secret organization was tasked with military training, outwardly appearing as a scouting organization in order to not attract the attention of British and Egyptian officialdom. Mitchell (1969: 5) has described how the MB grew from "modest beginnings" in 1928 to "one of the most important political contestants on the Egyptian scene" by the time of the Second World War. Following a standard pattern of anti-colonial resistance movements, the organization went through three stages of development. First, it devoted itself to "propaganda, communication and information" in order to announce its existence and intentions and establish a popular following. It then moved on to "formation, selection and preparation" whereby it intended to foment a revolutionary consciousness among the people in general, its recruits in particular, and also train the latter for armed combat. The third stage was "execution" or "the active stage out of which the perfected fruits of the mission of the Muslim Brotherhood will appear" (Mitchell 1969: 13–14). This scheme in and of itself demonstrates the modern acuity of the movement. Rather than gathering tribes around a flag and march against the enemy, the MB set itself up as a revolutionary vanguard intent on stimulating mass action through propaganda by the deed. In so doing, the MB applied, not only an organizational model that originated with the European Anarchist movement, but an understanding of mass political action that shared substantial elements with Marxism as well as fascism.

The MB sprung into militant action at the end of the Second World War with the assassination of Prime Minister Ahmad Maher shortly after Egypt's declaration of war on the Axis powers, which the MB had strenuously opposed. The following year, another government minister was assassinated and British soldiers were attacked. Theaters were torched, houses and stores in the Jewish quarter were burned, as well as hotels and restaurants catering to Westerners. Members of the social and economic elite were assassinated, 'immodestly dressed' women were attacked, as were individuals accused of apostasy. The university, where the MB's thought was widely embraced by students, was rocked by riots in December

1948, in protest against Arab impotence to halt the Zionist campaign in Palestine and when Prime Minister Nuqrashi Pasha ordered the MB dissolved in 1949, he too was assassinated. These and other historical factoids of the MB's political activism are themselves relatively uncontroversial among scholars. Dates, personages, and events are not the subjects of significant disputes. What does differ widely, however, is how, if at all, the organization's genesis and militant activities are contextualized. For instance, Murawiec (2008: 34) explains the launch of violence with statements like "Islam was the message; violence was the method...the Muslim Brothers were more effectively violent than other groups on the Egyptian scene...Jihad – war – was the central element." Migaux refers to the internally constructed worldview of the organization as the relevant context for the violent campaign, noting that "al Banna, an excellent speaker, knew how to exacerbate his countrymen's resentment of the English presence and in his speeches he laid all of the Muslim community's problems at the doorstep of Western domination" (2008: 274). In these and other neo-Orientalist narratives, it is as if the colonial powers and its socioeconomic impositions did not exist or, if they did, were not sufficiently bothersome to create popular resentment. The violence is essentially context-less, a product of psychology and emotion detached from social factors and reasons. In such narratives, the MB is its own *primus motor* and *prima causa*, a Shylock utterly bereft of an explanatory Antonio, bursting into violent rage for no apparent reason other than its own fanaticism and penchant for destruction.

Without the anti-colonial context of its actions, neither the secretive nature of the group, nor its organization, selection of targets, or even its foundational ideology can be comprehended. For instance, the MB opposed the Egyptian declaration of war against the Axis, in part because it was understood as yet another sign of national subservience to Britain, in part because the Axis was waging war against Britain, an effort that the MB, from its subaltern perspective, was not unhappy with. Like, for instance, the Irish nationalists and the Boers, the MB's support for the Axis was predicated on enmity against British colonialism, rather than affinity with Nazism, but the MB's critique of un-Islamic societies certainly extended to include the technology-heavy mass societies of the Axis powers. That said, the MB also shared with fascism and National Socialism a post-Enlightenment critique of liberal democracy predicated, to some extent, on similar cultural and linguistic grounds. Put differently, they shared a common enemy and similar idioms, but not a common agenda, in their discontent with Europe's Enlightened liberal democracies.

That the anti-colonial context is essential to understanding the MB becomes even more evident in the work of Sayyid Qutb, whose output reflected Egypt's increasing independence from Britain and the multitude of new post-colonial problems that emerged following the Second World War. Throughout the 1930s and 1940s, Qutb literary production and active life was primarily focused on matters of private and public morality. He was profoundly disturbed by increasing decadence and political turmoil within Egyptian society, but remained content with formulating responses on the individual level. In 1948–1950, Qutb visited the United States on a study trip at the expense of the Egyptian Ministry of Education. Already concerned with the corrosive influence of British colonialism, and deeply anti-colonial in his thinking, Qutb's time in the United States prompted him to re-diagnose his country's ailment. He came to understand the challenge as both more generic and more intrusive, viewing British colonialism as merely an aspect of a secularist, materialist, individualist and capitalist West, a "more wide-ranging and sinister form of collective enmity" (Tripp 1999: 158).

When he returned to Egypt, he launched into a short but intense period of social and political activism in which his earlier individualism was substituted for a pronounced communitarian Islamism. The Islamic critique and Islamic solution he began to propose were directed at both the Islamic and Western worlds, "distinctly influenced by Western historicism and positivism and filtered through Islamic criteria" (Mousalli 1992: 135). Qutb quickly came to understand the MB as an organization dedicated to, not only an intellectually rigorous vision of Islam as political ideology, but also a willingness to act on Islamic principles, notably in the war against the Zionists in Palestine and by attacking British troops in the Suez Canal Zone. Qutb joined the MB in 1952 and was placed in charge of its Section for Propagation of the Call and Publishing. That same year, the Free Officers carried out its *coup d'état*, the British were expelled and the monarchy was abolished the following year. This was a truly revolutionary overhaul of Egyptian politics, creating new hopes, but also new dangers, for the MB.

Nasser's anti-colonial ideology, consisting of the 'concentric circles' of pan-Arabism, pan-Africanism and pan-Islamism, was at least partially underwritten by the MB's ideology. The new regime was initially ambivalent towards the MB, but the latter was far more radical in its Islamic conviction and absolutely rejected the nationalistic and ethnic tenets of the new regime's guiding ideology. The MB was forced to gradually realize "that the government did not intend to live up to the religious image it had promoted" (Kenney 2006: 60), and ambivalent alignment turned into open hostility.

Following an assassination attempt against Nasser, the MB was repressed, its members were imprisoned, and many were sentenced to death. Qutb himself was sentenced to fifteen years hard labor. This turned out to be the most productive years of Qutb's life, and, to the Islamist world at large, the most significant.

In prison, Qutb wrote an extensive commentary on the Quran, *In the Shade of the Quran*, in which he was able to develop his personal understanding of the text. Selections from this work, which appeared in installments throughout his imprisonment, were printed separately in the hugely influential volume *Signposts along the Road*, published and reprinted five times before the Egyptian authorities used its contents to sentence Qutb to death in 1966. *In the Shade of the Quran* was a highly idiosyncratic book, and did not follow the classical pattern of Quranic commentary. Rather than traditional exegesis (*tafsir*), which includes cross-referencing the Quranic text with authoritative commentaries and other writings of established scholars, Qutb simply went ahead to offer his own exegesis of the text. In so doing, Qutb provided the foundation for what may best be thought of as a post-modern, deconstructionist approach to Islamic sacred text and tradition, engaging in a radically modern and individualistic hermeneutic unavoidably informed by personal experiences and aspirations. That is not to imply that he somehow believed that God had lost authorial control of the text, even though his method strongly implied that he understood the way to access God's intent as centered on personal reflection at the expense of collective tradition. Thus, while his ideology and its various spinoffs have come to emphasize the necessity of collective action and 'group think,' it began as an exercise in individualistic reinterpretation. The commentary allowed Qutb to explore the ways in which the original message of Islam, lived by the pious forebears, could now become the foundation for an all-encompassing modern ideology. The operative mechanism in Qutb's reading was not the authority of tradition, but personal faith and the necessity to order one's life in accordance with that faith. According to Qutb, in the Quran, mankind had been given the blueprint for reinventing itself in the mold intended by the Prophet and, thereby, by God. While he agreed with the essential rationality of Islam and the shining example provided by the pious forebears, this was incidental rather than central; faith had to be approached intuitively in a manner that does not depend on reason but, rather, reverses the relationship and makes reason dependent on faith. The emulation of the pious forebears, who had embraced faith and then harnessed its power to transform Meccan society, was an absolutely central aspect of Qutb's thought.

This patently modern reading of the ancient text had radical implications for the existing order in Egypt, the Islamic world, and global society at large. Following al-Atghani, Qutb's key mobilizing analogy was the perennial challenge of *jahiliyya*. In Quranic literature, this term denoted the pre-Islamic state of ignorance that surrounded the pious forebears and was eventually defeated by them. Qutb now argued that contemporary Muslims were duty-bound to struggle against the very same forces in modern guise, in order to re-establish a truly Islamic community and elevate Islam to its divinely appointed status as universal creed. This also meant that Muslims were duty-bound to ensure that Islamic law was the only law governing the community of the faithful, which implied the necessity to eschew man-made laws. This effort, moreover, could only take place by means of jihad, which Qutb understood squarely as militant struggle, following the lead of Mawdudi and Nadawi (Choueiri 1990: 95). Its purpose is to "abolish injustice from the earth, to bring people to the worship of God alone, and to bring them out of servitude to others into the servants of the Lord" (Qutb n.d.: 56). However, the one-on-one relationship between Islamic law and individual freedom was central, "for without such complete freedom, human nature cannot prevail against the force of humiliation and suasiveness and servitude, nor can it lay claim to its rightful share in social justice..." (Qutb 1970: 44).

A hugely significant development during Qutb's prolonged imprisonment lay in his observations of the contradictions contained in Egypt's post-colonial order. The Free Officer regime had, in his view, developed into a nationalist tyranny, yet consisted of Muslims. The Egyptian masses who did nothing to rid themselves of this un-Islamic tyranny also professed to be Muslim. The all-too-common post-colonial disillusionment of true revolutionaries caused Qutb to turn inwards, towards a hard-line nativist position, by concluding that neither the rulers nor the docile population were truly Muslims, but disguised representatives of *jahiliyya*; they were all part of the problem, rather than the solution (Haddad 1983: 85–7). Consequently, Qutb wrote extensively on the distinctions between the Islamic and the *jahili*, in an effort to alert his countrymen to the dangers of their lack of activity. As al-Afghani and Abdu had emphasized the rational as the hallmark of Islam, Qutb, informed by the post-colonial predicament in general and his own imprisonment in particular, came to emphasize its practicality. That is, Islam could no longer be approached merely as a system of beliefs; faith convictions that could be internalized yet not acted upon. A true Muslim must live a truly Islamic life, which in turn is defined as a life of jihad. The structures of the *jahili* order are obstacles to true orthodoxy as well as orthopraxis, and it is therefore incumbent on all true believers to strive to establish an Islamic order in their societies. Muslims have an individual responsibility to ensure that God's law, as revealed through the Quran, becomes the only law governing human conduct. According to traditional scholarship, jihad as military struggle was a collective obligation (*fard kifayah*) with similarities to just war theory in Christianity, governed by strict rules and regulations. In Qutb's reinterpretation, which assumed tyrannical rule and mass inertia by nominal Muslims, the conditions for jihad as collective obligation were utterly absent and thus metamorphosized into an individual obligation (*fard 'ayn*). Jihad was thus incumbent on all the truly faithful, regardless of collective attitudes, dispositions, and capabilities.

In part as a result of Qutb's exhortative writings, the MB, crippled by state repression, was able briefly to reform itself in the early 1960s, appearing this time as study groups and literary circles in which the works of Qutb and others were discussed. Qutb's *Signposts Along the Road* (also referred to as *Milestones*) was central in terms of raising the spirit and hopes of the clandestine activists. In May 1964, Qutb was released from prison and was able to participate in some of these activities himself, but during the summer of 1965, a new wave of mass arrests began. Qutb was arrested in August and charged with involvement in a MB conspiracy to assassinate Nasser. With reference to his literary output – which the state's own censors had allowed him to write and publish from prison – a conspiracy case was constructed. Qutb was hanged on August 29, 1966.

The MB, which in Egypt never fully recovered from the 1966 clampdown, would go on to become the parent organization for a range of Islamist groups, inspired by the analyses and prescriptions of al-Banna and Qutb. The ideas of the latter – his analysis of the imperialist imposition, the pervasive nature of the *jahili* order, and jihad as an individual obligation – would go on to form the corner stone of what has been termed the 'jihadist trend' within Islamism. So too would the Salafi Islamism of al-Afghani and Abdu go on to inform the ideologies of groups far outside the confines of the MB. It becomes a matter of utmost importance, in this context, to understand the Islamic faith community as a multifaceted and above all evolving social organism, or else it becomes impossible to comprehend that its interpretations and applications of Islam are necessarily products of modernity. Modern Muslims, like modern Christians and Jews, cannot escape their modern *Sitz-in-Leben*. For the progenitors of Islamism, this was substantially impacted by the encounter between colonial hegemony and their own subaltern aspirations. Some, however, insist that

Islamism is pre-modern. For instance, Efraim Karsh has argued that Qutb's Islamism was not, in fact a response to the political hegemony and cultural encroachment of European imperialism upon Muslim societies. Rather, according to Karsh, Qutb "traced the 'new jahiliya' to the disintegration of the first umma and the creation of the Umayyad and Abbasid empires" (2006: 215) in which notions of divine sovereignty had been tarnished by the reality of decadent and un-Islamic kingship. To this one must respond that articulating a critique of a contemporary state of affairs and formulating a historical analysis are not mutually exclusive activities. To claim that they are would be akin to arguing that Marx did not respond to capitalism because his analysis harks back to the tensions of feudal society, or that Catholic social teaching does not respond to contemporary issues because they take as their starting point the Sermon on the Mount. The argument rests on a disjunction between contemporary experience and historical awareness that we do not insist on, or even assume to be possible, in analyses of Western contemporary political activity and activism, yet it is proffered as more or less self-evident in analyses of Islamic politics. Qutb shared a broad historiographical perspective with al-Afghani, Abdu, and al-Banna and their analysis of the present predicament was above all a civilizational critique aimed at the emancipation of Islamic societies in the modern era.

It is precisely Islamism's ability to explain features of modernity by means of a modern Islamic historiography that allowed the MB's ideology to spread rapidly throughout the Islamic world. The pan-Islamic call of the MB had broad appeal across the region, and its teachings began to spread across the Islamic world as soon as it was founded. Yet local conditions and developments inevitably impacted and differentiated its growth and development. While the political implications of MB thought are far-reaching, aimed at nothing less than a systemic overhaul, most of its regional branches and affiliates have been active primarily in the social, cultural, and educational spheres. This has perhaps been more out of necessity than choice, since regime control of political space in Islamic countries has invariably been tight. Depending on the level of government tolerance for Islamic politics, and for independent political alternatives in general, the various incarnations of the MB have developed into a disparate collection of groups. Its local manifestations range from the quietist to the violent; from pliant tools in the hands of rulers, to potent oppositionists willing and often capable of mobilizing popular opinion against the forces of *jahiliyya*. In Bahrain, for instance, MB ideology is represented by the Reform Party (Hizb al-islah), whose president and patron is Shaykh 'Issa bin Muhammad al-Kalifah, a member of the ruling family. Consequently, the movement's political wing, the Islamic National Tribune Society (*Jama'iyya al-manbar al-watani al-islami*), combines a pro-regime conservative social agenda with a pro-business economic program. As an agent of the status quo, rather than radical reform, its political thought bears hardly any resemblance to that of the original MB. Instead, it has focused its efforts on social and cultural legislation aimed at asserting the Sunni interpretation of Islam – that of the ruling family – over and above that of the country's majority Shi'a population. So while it is true, as Steve Emerson writes (2002: 63), in an effort to paint the entire global MB network with one brush, that "an offshoot of the Muslim Brotherhood, al-Jihad, had assassinated President Anwar Sadat in 1981," it is equally true that an offshoot of the MB, the Islamic National Tribune Society, underwrites the policies of one of the United States' most loyal and crucial allies in the Middle East. If the intellectual legacy of al-Banna and Qutb was as unified as many commentators pretend, such diversity would not be possible.

In Syria, the local branch of the MB has been one of the most persistent, violent, and popular of the country's political movements in the post-colonial era. It was founded already in the 1930s, under the name Youth of Muhammad (*Shabab Muhammad*) by Syrian students returning from Cairo. Following independence from French mandatory authority in 1946, the MB was an active and legal participant in national politics, actively assisting its Egyptian sister organization as it was struggling against Nasser's regime. In the 1961 parliamentary elections, the organization won ten seats. The rise of the Ba'th Arab Socialist Party (BASP), however, changed its fortunes. Following its 1963 coup, the BASP banned the MB as it conflicted irreconcilably with its secularist (during its first decade in power, even openly atheist) positions. As members of the Alawi religious minority took control of the BASP leadership, the MB became the major player in the underground Sunni based opposition. Conflict with the government grew steadily, and replicated the pattern of insurrectionism set in Egypt, only with greater vehemence and carnage. MB activism was also a catalyst for the activism of other groups and movements disaffected with the regime. Towards the late 1970s, the MB campaign had escalated into entrenched violence, mainly by means of assassinations and car bombs directed against the officials from the ruling party, the government and the military, but also against intellectuals and unaffiliated critics. Crucially, the MB also targeted the Soviet military advisors stationed in Syria following the Syrian–Soviet friendship treaty of 1978. While the alliance with the atheist USSR was repugnant to the MB, it was geopolitically essential to the regime. In 1980, an emergency law made membership of the MB a capital offense. Following escalating confrontations, the regime ended the insurrection by razing sections of the central Syrian city of Hama, the MB's primary stronghold, killing several thousand civilians and imprisoning thousands more. With this, the open activity of the MB in Syria was effectively brought to an end, but the movement has continued to trouble the regime. Headquartered in Paris and Larnaca, Cyprus, the group still maintains a network of supporters in the country. Not only is the regime unable to estimate its size with any degree of certainty, but it also knows that the MB has increased in popularity since it began espousing a reformist agenda after the death of the late president Hafez al-Asad in June 2000. In 2006, the leader of the Syrian MB, Shaykh Ali Sadreddine Bayanouni, stated that his organization seeks to establish a "civil, democratic state" (McCarthy 2006) in Syria, thereby lending its weight to the country's Western-backed, liberal reformist movement. At the same time, this reformist agenda, and its apparent backtracking from a more comprehensive structural overhaul of the patterns of neo-colonial domination, has left a number of its more militant members disaffected, and created an activist gap that is increasingly being filled by Salafi groups affiliated with al-Qa'ida. This will be returned to in the following chapter.

Perhaps the most important metamorphosis of any of the MB branches is that which has taken place in Palestine, where local conditions caused the primarily social and charitable MB branch to establish a military wing, The Islamic Resistance Movement (*Harakah al-muqawwamah al-islamiyyah*, HAMAS) has since its inception in 1987 gone on to not only wage protracted military struggle, but also win national legislative elections. Islamism as an organized political–military force had existed in the Palestinian Occupied Territories since the late 1970s, drawing on the long-standing ability of Islamic charitable and social organizations to effectively interact with the people of the Occupied Territories. The Palestinian MB emerged in 1935 under the guidance of Abd al-Rahman al-Banna, Hassan al-Banna's brother, and quickly attracted popular support. In May 1946 it inaugurated a central office in Jerusalem and local branches proliferated rapidly, but the movement confined itself for the next several decades to social activities. It generally avoided direct confrontation with Israel except for a short period immediately following the 1967 June War, when it set up camps in the Jordan Valley under Fateh's banner and engaged Israel militarily across the border. Its 'quietism' did not mean that the MB was an apolitical or non-political force, however; what has been referred to as its 1967 to 1975 "phase of Mosque building" and the 1975 to 1987 "phase of social institution building" (Hroub 2000: 31) ultimately served to pave the way for the emergence of a generation armed with an Islamic political idiom capable, or so it was thought, of liberating Palestine.

Until the late 1970s, the MB had been the undisputed the hegemon of Islamic activity in Palestine, but the emergence of the Islamic Jihad Movement in Palestine (*Harakah al-jihad al-islami fi filastin*, commonly referred to as the Palestinian Islamic Jihad, PIJ) challenged the status quo and shook the MB's self-perception. The PIJ was originally established in Egypt in 1979 by Palestinian students Fathi Shiqaqi, Abd al-Aziz al-Awdah, and Bashir Musa, drawing on an ideological framework derived from MB thought, but also heavily influenced by the Islamic revolution in Iran (Shiqaqi 1997b: 190–9). After its leaders were expelled from Egypt due to their close relations with those responsible for the assassination of Anwar Sadat, the faction formally announced itself in the Gaza Strip in 1981, under the leadership of Shiqaqi. In contrast to the dominant leftist-nationalist factions of the PLO, which talked variously of Arab unity, variously of class struggle, the PIJ's ideological framework held that the liberation of Palestine is a precondition for the unity of the Islamic world, and that an Islamic vanguard should therefore lead the struggle against Zionist occupation. Situating itself squarely in the Khomeini school of Islamic thought, the PIJ also incorporated a strong commitment to the theme of social justice, egalitarianism and national liberation, and was thereby able to challenge the predominance of the PLO in both the military and sociopolitical arenas (Shiqaqi 1997c: 346–55). That is to say, not only did it signal the ascendancy of Islam as a political language, it also challenged the secular factions within their own national liberation framework, even if it never managed to subvert the PLO factions' dominance. Its position attracted the support of non-Arab Muslim countries and organizations, and broadened the international appeal of the Palestinian struggle. Significantly, its emergence consolidated the interest in Palestine of the newly founded revolutionary Islamic regime in Iran, and the PIJ was awarded Tehran's financial and political support at its inception.

In light of these developments, the MB was forced urgently to examine its positions and question its sense of purpose. The positive social identity it was able to provide its members and supporters stood to be diminished by the emergence of the much more pro-active PIJ. The PIJs challenged the MB in a way that the PLO factions had never been able to because activists did not have to forsake their Islamic identity in order to struggle for the homeland. Quite the contrary, the PIJ provided an avenue for "engaging in resistance activities in the armor of an Islamic identity" (Hroub 2000: 33). When the PIJ was able to recruit members of the MB into some of its cells, this led to intense, and tense dialog within the MB as to whether its priority should be social reform or national liberation. "The leaders had become convinced that [military struggle] not only was the right course of national action, but that it also was the right course to adopt for the sake of organizational interests" (Hroub 2000: 33). That is to say, the MB needed to compete with the PIJ in order shore up its members' positive social identity and stop the potentially disastrous drain of members attracted by the PIJ's pro-active stance.

Social competition with PIJ was thus crucial in compelling the MB to take seriously and begin preparations for military struggle. In the early 1980s, the MB established a small and clandestine military apparatus and an intelligence organization, and set about acquiring arms and the requisite expertise to deploy them. This new resolve was inadvertently demonstrated in 1984 when the leader of the MB in Palestine, Shaykh Ahmad Yassin and some of his colleagues were arrested by the Israelis and charged with possession of arms and planning military operations. The MB also made use of social creativity by effectively taking credit for the establishment and actions of the PIJ, presenting them as the fruit of their decades-long labor to facilitate a struggling Islamic mentality. In the years prior to the intifada, the MB would downplay the organizational affiliation of PIJ members who had been killed in action, stressing instead their Islamic credentials. In the wording of a 1987 MB pamphlet, the fallen militants of the PIJ "are the natural end-product of the Islamist movement" (Hroub 2000: 34). In that period, the MB itself worked to mobilize and organize its cadres while sporadically engaging in military action: planting explosives, firing on Israeli military patrols and killing Palestinians found to be collaborators or agents of Israel.

Active inside the Occupied Territories, neither the MB nor the PIJ were participants in the interfactional wrangling of the leftist-nationalist factions in exile, but decisively challenged, from below, their longstanding monopoly in Palestinian national politics. When the intifada erupted, therefore, many Palestinians turned to them rather than the PLO for leadership and guidance. The PLO program for national liberation, while steeped in the cultural heritage of Palestinian and Arab nationalism, was based on abstract and 'scientific' principles of explicitly Western origin, and the factions' internecine battles were increasingly seen by Palestinians in Palestine as both distant and counterproductive. Islamism, meanwhile, offered an 'authentic' political language; a way of thinking and talking about politics that was grounded in indigenous religious and sociocultural norms and values. Palestinian nationalism in the occupied territories thus took on an increasingly Islamist flavor, dovetailing with Frantz Fanon's observation (1988: 43) that, at some point in every struggle for national liberation, "the customs, traditions, beliefs, formerly denied and passed over in silence are violently valorized and affirmed," and that "the plunge into the chasm of the past is the condition and the source of freedom."

The formation of Hamas almost exactly coincided with the eruption of the intifada, which is why the movement's official historiography dates its establishment to December 8, 1987. Hamas' first communiqué – which was also the first communiqué of the intifada – was distributed in the Gaza Strip on December 11, 1987. As the military wing of the MB in Palestine, Hamas' leadership was virtually identical to the senior echelons of the Palestinian MB, including Shaykh Ahmad Yassin, who became Hamas' spiritual leader, along with Abd al-Aziz al-Rantisi, Salah Shehadeh, Khaled Mishal and Mahmoud al-Zahar. The uprising effectively demanded of the MB leadership to choose whether to "forgo its de facto accommodation with the occupation or lose the Palestinian street, where legitimacy was born less of piety than national resistance" (Usher 1999: 19). Hamas chose resistance and its strikes against Israeli military targets and Jewish settlers in the West Bank proved as popular with the Palestinian people as they were unsettling to the Israeli authorities, which outlawed the movement in June 1989.

Hamas' relationship with the PLO leftists was strained from the very beginning. Hamas regarded them as apostates and atheists while the leftists regarded the Islamists as political primitivists. One PFLP cadre recalled that

> Hamas was rallying around slogans such as 'The people of the book' – the Jews – 'are closer to us than the reds'. There were clashes between our members and theirs, and they killed several cadres from the PFLP. Israel at first turned a blind eye to their rise because they were clashing with us. (Muhammad Issa Abu Khalil to author, June 5, 1999)

Hamas' founding charter, dated August 18, 1988, is replete with Quranic references and religiously tinged hyperbole, and has consistently been used by commentators to demonstrate the movement's fanatically fundamentalist nature. To be sure, Hamas is a religious movement, but as with the language of the secular rejectionists, its statements must be placed in sociopolitical context and weighed against its practical politics and real-world alignments. There was a specific political purpose to the aggressive religious symbolism and rhetoric of Hamas' founding charter, which served to demarcate the advent of something new in Palestinian politics, creating a distinct social identity for the new group. Hamas' indictment of the PLO was based primarily on its abysmal political track record, rather than its secularism. Although the PLO's historic failure to bring about national liberation was seen in part as a consequence of its religious deficiencies, Hamas, by the same token, was created to provide a more effective medium for the same national and nationalist project. Indeed, Hamas placed within an Islamist framework the very same nationalist aspirations that had fuelled the secularist factions since the 1960s, and article twelve of its founding charter accordingly pointed out that "Nationalism from the point of view of the Islamic Resistance Movement is part and parcel of religious ideology" (Hroub 2000: 274).

The process of nationalizing Islamism had begun with the PIJ in the early 1980s (Shiqaqi 1997a: 172–89). Hamas had merely continued in that track, and competed with the leftist and nationalist factions over the ability to define and defend the national cause. The dynamics of the rivalry thus introduced into Palestinian politics was in this respect no different from the long-standing rivalry between the PLO opposition and leadership. In its *Introductory Memorandum*, Hamas argued that the PLO leadership, since the 1970s, had shown signs of being prepared to accept a solution to the Palestinian struggle other than, and inferior to what was indicated in the Palestine National Charter. The 1980s saw the marginalization of the Palestinian struggle on both the regional and international level, Hamas argued, while Israel was emboldened by guarantees of US support. Since the signing of the US–Israeli strategic cooperation agreement in 1981, Israel had annexed the Golan Heights, attacked Iraq's nuclear reactor, invaded Lebanon, and besieged Beirut, "the greatest insult to the umma since the 1967 war." The memorandum continues:

> The Islamic movement in Palestine perceives a great challenge that stems from two factors: First: The retreat of the Palestinian cause to the lower level of Arab priorities. Second: The retreat of the Palestinian revolution [the PLO] from the strategy of armed struggle, to [acceptance of] the political settlement imposed on the Palestinian people. And due to these two retreats, together with the burgeoning ripeness of the resistance of the Palestinian people inside Palestine, but not outside it, a Palestinian Islamic jihad project was inevitable, the first contours of which were found in *Usrat al-Jihad* in 1981, and Sheikh Ahmad Yassin's group in 1983, and others. (Hamas n.d.)

On December 18, 1992, coinciding with the commencement of the secret Oslo dialog, Israel expelled 413 Hamas and PIJ leaders and cadres to Lebanon. The move came in response to the capture and execution of an Israeli border guard by Hamas, and the Israelis hoped that displacement of the Islamists would curtail their operational capabilities inside Palestine. This it temporarily did, but the long-term benefits of their banishment outweighed the disadvantages. Lebanon refused to receive the Islamists, who ended up in the Marj al-Zuhour camp in the southern Lebanon security zone. There, Hamas and the PIJ were not only able to consolidate good working relations with each other, but also with the Hezbollah and Iran, through the presence of Revolutionary Guard units. They moreover came into close contact with two secular Palestinian factions that were very active at the time, Fateh al-Intifada and the Popular Front for the Liberation of Palestine General Command (PFLP-GC), which lead to lasting political rapport and military cooperation. The deportation of the Islamists marked the beginning of significant and robust secularist–Islamist cooperation in the Palestinian political arena, as well as tying the struggle of the Lebanese Hezbollah closer to the Palestinian struggle.

When, in 1993, Yasir Arafat's secret negotiations with Israel led to the Declaration of Principles and the Oslo accord, Hamas and PIJ both joined the Alliance of Palestinian Forces (APF), an inter-factional so-called rejectionist assembly. The other eight members were nationalists and leftists, and each faction had its own understanding of the nature of the challenge posed by Arafat's initiative, and its own view on what could or needed to be done. Nonetheless, the overriding cause around which they all felt compelled to rally was public and demonstrative opposition to the Oslo process and the nascent Palestinian Authority (PA) in order to "undo the damage done by Arafat" (Ramadan Shallah to author, June 10, 1999). "We did not need to debate [among ourselves] whether alcohol should be permitted in a future Palestinian state or whether banks should be allowed to charge interest rates," Imad al-Alami, a member of Hamas politburo, later remarked. "The first step had to be to work together to guide the national movement back onto a correct course" (al-Alami to author, June 2, 1999). Ahmad Jibril, Secretary General of the PFLP-GC explained that the new alliance, "as a front, will not abandon the armed struggle program and we are still in a state of war with the Zionist existence on the land of Palestine" (Jibril 1993). As the alliance reaffirmed the absolute righteousness of the quest to liberate Palestine from the river Jordan to the Mediterranean Sea by force of arms, it also declared that "the present PLO leadership does not represent the Palestinian people, nor does it express its views or aspirations" (Alliance of Palestinian Forces 1994). Hamas' membership of this alliance, far from a violation of its Islamic principles, was in fact a logical extension of its Islamism as a product of its distinctly Palestinian national context. It was also an indicator of the sort of ideological tolerance that would earn it enduring enmity from other parts of the Islamist universe, most notably those within al-Qa'ida's Salafi framework. This will be returned to in the following chapter.

5

Islamists without Borders: Al-Qa'ida and its Affiliates

To many in the West, it seemed as if al-Qa'ida appeared out of nowhere on September 11, 2001. Shortly before 0900 hrs, nineteen al-Qa'ida operatives hijacked three commercial airliners, guided two of them into New York's World Trade Center and the Pentagon in Washington, DC, while the third – likely bound for the White House or the US Capitol – crashed in a field in rural Pennsylvania as the passengers decided to fight the assailants. The attack killed 2,995 people, including the hijackers, caused economic damage to New York City estimated at between $82.8 and $94.8 billion (Thompson 2002: 1) and stock market losses for that week alone estimated at $1.4 trillion (Fernandez 2001). Meanwhile, the cost of the attack itself has been estimated at between $400,000 and $500,000 from beginning to end (National Commission on Terrorist Attacks upon the United States 2004: preface). The attack was as terrifyingly destructive as it was ingeniously simple. Armed with box cutters, pepper spray, and focused dedication to their cause, operatives from an Islamist group based in one of the most 'pre-modern' corners of the world had inflicted a body blow on the world's sole remaining super power. The consequences of this audacity remain incalculable, and have so far included reorganization of the US government, new security legislation throughout the Western hemisphere and beyond, the invasion of two sovereign countries with a staggering associated civilian death toll and anti-Islamic and anti-Arab xenophobia laid bare in numerous Western nations.

The moral outrage and genuine bewilderment experienced by the general public in the West hid from sight the fact that al-Qa'ida's attack did not occur in a vacuum, nor was it a sudden development. One important fact – at the time well known intellectually, but less so emotionally – was that 9/11 was merely the most spectacular in a long series of attacks. The 1996 declaration of war against the United States had not been taken seriously by more than a few analysts in the West 1998, nor had the February 1998 declaration of war on "crusaders and Jews," issued by Osama bin Laden and a half-dozen clerics. The August 1998 attack on the US embassies in

Tanzania and Kenya had highlighted al-Qa'ida as a real problem, but it remained a problem far away, 'over there'; while at least 232 people were killed and over 4,000 injured, only twelve of the dead were US citizens, the rest a nameless mass of natives. Unprepared to respond to this asymmetrical challenge with anything but traditional military means, US President Bill Clinton responded to the attack by ordering Operation Infinite Reach, a series of missile strikes on alleged terrorist targets in Sudan and Afghanistan, killing still more nameless natives. One target of the US retaliatory strikes was al-Shifa medical plant in North Khartoum, which Washington claimed was an al-Qa'ida connected producer of VX nerve gas. This later turned out to be inaccurate (Barletta 1998). What al-Shifa plant did produce, however, was roughly half of Sudan's medicine for both humans and livestock, and the shortage created by the factory's destruction may have caused the silent death of additional tens of thousands of Sudanese (Daum 2001). The embassy bombings as well as the response highlighted an important aspect of the contest between al-Qa'ida and its primary protagonist: the struggle took place in a neo-colonial framework in which the only significant victims for either side were Western, and the only significant threats were those to the Western powers. To the United States as well as al-Qa'ida, the nameless natives were collateral damage in a global struggle.

Western emotional detachment was radically reversed following 9/11, causing a new set of problems. This attack in the US homeland by a non-state actor was of a magnitude that the United States had never before experienced. In fact, as a subaltern attack on an imperial hegemon and its values, the attacks of 9/11 were truly a watershed of world history. The post-Cold War globalization and interconnectedness that had previously been hailed as victories as well as vehicles for liberal democracy and 'Western values' were turned on their head; the very same global patterns of interconnectedness were now employed by the malcontents of the new order, to strike at the heart of the world's sole remaining superpower. To the people and politicians of the United States in particular, the attack was not only an outrage, but seemed a potent challenge for the right to determine the future of the planet.

The new emotional climate was fertile soil for political platitudes such as 'they hate our freedoms' and descriptions of Islamism as a simple, self-contained 'ideology of hate'; phrases aimed to galvanize and mobilize the population, but far too often assumed to have actual analytical content. Such reductionism only served to further distort popular and political perceptions of reality, making the agendas and objectives of the Other even more difficult to grasp than they already were. Al-Qa'ida itself had pursued a similar reductionist approach in its portrayal of an undifferentiated evil

Western hemisphere, but appears to have been considerably more successful. In 2006, Bruce Hoffman (2006a: 1) noted that al-Qa'ida's "portrayal of
America and the West as an aggressive and predatory force waging war on
Islam" continued to resonate among large segments of the Muslim world,
undermining US efforts to "break the cycle of recruitment and regeneration
that sustains al Qaeda and the militant, global jihadi movement it champi-
ons." Al-Qa'ida's relative success in terms of propaganda has in large
measure depended on the fact that the political, social, and economic problems its leaders point to are not isolated figments of fanatical imaginations.
While their methods and prescriptions may be far outside the mainstream
of responses, the neo-colonial reality that they point to has been previously
identified by Third-World liberation movements and militant groups of
various ideological stripes. Despite its outward appearance as a narrow and
extremist, if highly effective niche organization within the Islamist universe,
al-Qa'ida works within a social, cultural, political and economic framework
that allows its message to resonate and enables recruitment and regeneration. In this sense, al-Qa'ida is simply yet another counter-hegemonic movement spawned by the neo-colonial system that the West has created and
enforced. As the adverse effects of that system are most acutely felt in the
developing world, it is perhaps only natural that al-Qa'ida should get more
traction for its reductionist stereotyping than the Western policy makers,
scholars, and pundits have been able to manufacture for their effort in the
same vein. Al-Qa'ida is able to make a plausible case that it is fighting fire
with fire; that is, following Sayyid Qutb in combating what it sees as
the corrosive globalization of Western politics and culture by mobilizing a
salutary, yet equally globalized Islamic response.

What is more, al-Qa'ida's ideological prescriptions may be outside the
mainstream, but its ideology does not constitute a radical departure from
the broader intellectual deposit on which it draws: Islamist thought from
al-Afghani and Abdu, through Qutb and Shariati. Hence, in the eyes of its
constituents, neither al-Qa'ida's diagnosis of the neo-colonial predicament,
nor its adherence to jihad as a permanent individual duty are necessarily
contrived. What is new, however, is the overwhelming focus of al-Qa-ida,
and groups affiliated with it, on directly combating 'the far enemy' (*al-'ado
al-ba'id*), the primarily US imperial taskmasters of local elites, 'the near
enemy' (*al-'ado al-qarib*). This shift in focus will be returned to below.

However, the eruption of the Arab Spring in early 2011 posed a
serious challenge to al-Qa'ida's narrative on several levels. First, unarmed
protestors taking to the streets of Arab capitals were able to deliver a
greater degree of political change in a matter of weeks than al-Qa'ida –
the self-appointed vanguard – had managed in decades. Moreover, the

protestors focused entirely on the 'near enemy', demonstrating clearly that al-Qa'ida's insistence on attacking the 'far enemy' had been unwarranted, or even counter-productive. In addition, the largely secular and democratic objectives of the uprisings bore absolutely no resemblance to the Salafi agenda of al-Qa'ida. Against the backdrop of ongoing and massive popular pro-democracy manifestations throughout the region, the virtually complete absence of protests against the killing of bin Laden in May 2011 placed al-Qa'ida in proper perspective, both in terms of similarities with other political trends, as well as in terms of differences.

As the reality of neo-colonial impositions is experienced by subaltern peoples around the world, al-Qa'ida's is but one among many reactions against it; particularly spectacular and violent, to be sure, but not therefore different in term of its source. The archaic nature of its apparently unshakeable strategic objective – the establishment of a worldwide caliphate – as well as its ongoing criticism of Western imperialism and colonialism, combine to obscure the fact that al-Qa'ida, in essence, is a product of modernity. Its objectives and rhetoric seem to many to be relics of outdated politics, and those whose narratives define Western political discourse are loath to admit that neo-colonialism creates colonial subjects, just as surely as old-style imperial colonialism, but thinking away the problems does not change realities on the ground. The leaders and cadres of al-Qa'ida are twenty-first-century individuals and their worldviews and objectives are the products of the environment in which they exist, and from which they have emerged. Indeed, their very understanding of the caliphate and the first generations of righteous Muslims are a modern conceit, as is their desire to recapture and return to that golden age; as with the intellectual deposit of the MB, echoes of the European counter-Enlightenment and reactions against modernity may be heard. It is important to recognize that these are all expressions of attempts to deal with modern realities and, as such, these expressions are themselves modern. They are not seventh-century people with seventh-century mindsets for the very simple reason that they do not live in the seventh century, and cannot think away the intervening centuries. Nor are they showing any signs of even attempting to think away the historical development of the Islamic community and its relations with the rest of the world – in fact, post-seventh-century developments are part and parcel of their own justification for why political change is needed. As modern people living in the modern world, they are offering a diagnosis of the ills of modernity, and then go on to propose that the remedy lies in the reconstruction of a modern imagining of an ancient religio-political structure. The iconic image of al-Qa'ida as a collection of primitive 'cave dwelling' or 'medieval people' untouched by modernity not only ignores what they say and what they do, but is an anachronism of the highest order.

Organizationally, ideologically, tactically, and strategically al-Qa'ida is not so much nimble as malleable, and what stands out is the modern means by which it is able to mobilize and amplify the grievances of a disparate collection of local groups and movements within an overarching global framework. Ibrahim Abu-Rabi (2004: xvi) has noted that what may be the most important function of al-Qa'ida "is its ability to manage the divisions between *jihadi* groups, and internationalize the *jihadi* movement into one unified organization made of discrete units each with its own leadership." This is reflected in the awareness of US counterterrorism officials. For instance, the 2006 National Strategy for Combating Terrorism (White House 2006: 5) described al Qa'ida as a movement that was neither monolithic, nor "controlled by any single individual, group, or state," but instead united around a "common vision, a common set of ideas." Hoffman (2006a: 3) has similarly noted that, "the current Al Qaeda thus exists more as an ideology than as an identifiable, unitary terrorist organization." In this sense, al-Qa'ida is nothing short of the embodiment of the definition of Islamism, providing above all a common mobilizing discursive framework for a range of otherwise disparate struggles.

Al-Qa'ida is not only adept at modern means of communication and militancy, it is also ideologically modern. Its ideological core stems from the Islamic modernist legacy of al-Afghani and Abdu, which in turn drew on Enlightenment and counter-Enlightenment thought. Tactically, al-Qa'ida bases its understanding of vanguard action in order to stimulate mass political consciousness on the work of al-Banna and Qutb, who in turn had been heavily influenced by European Anarchist, Marxist, and fascist organizational theory. Organizationally, it has been able to create a horizontal structure that gives it relevance in widely dispersed conflict zones by means of modern marketing, chiefly brand name association and extension, which will be returned to below. Moreover, all of this is continually updated; 'lessons learned' and 'best practices' – al-Qa'ida's own as well as those of similar groups – are clearly part of the strategic innovation process. It stands out among Islamist organizations – indeed, among militant organizations generally – for its remarkable ability to adapt in order to sustain its existence. Al-Qa'ida is structurally well-suited to the sort of militant activity it has chosen to wage; the fact that it has been in existence for more than two decades suggests that it is in fact better suited to its chosen theater and mode of conflict than any of its enemies, including, so far, the US military.

Al-Qa'ida has its roots in the Afghan jihad against the Soviet invasion. Fittingly, the first use of the name was not applied to an organization, but to a revolutionary concept derived from the thought of Sayyid Qutb:

> Every principle needs a vanguard to carry it forward that is willing, while integrating into society, to undertake difficult tasks and make tremendous sacrifices. No ideology, celestial or earthly, can do without such a vanguard, which gives its all to ensure victory. It is the standard bearer on an endless and diffi-cult path until it reaches its destination, as it is the will of God that it do so. It is *al-qa'ida al-sulbah* that constitutes this vanguard for the hoped-for society. (Azzam 1988)

Al-Qa'ida al-sulbah, "the solid base," was precisely what the Palestinian Islamic scholar-turned-fighter Abdullah Azzam had in mind when he began to forge the remnants of the Afghan war veterans into a new organization with a new purpose: an international brigade that would confront the corrupt rulers of the Islamic world, beginning with the liberation of Palestine. Following the 1967 war, Azzam – along with his family and some 300,000 other Palestinians – were displaced as a result of the Israeli occupa-tion of the West Bank and Gaza. Once in Jordan, Azzam joined the MB and also participated in militant activism against Israel as well as the Jordanian regime conducted by secular resistance groups. He quickly grew disillusioned with the pitiful state of the leftist and nationalist resistance groups under the PLO umbrella. In the early 1970s, he met the leading intellectuals of the Islamist movement in Egypt, including Umar Abd al-Rahman and Ayman al-Zawahiri – both of whom were influenced by the teachings of Sayyid Qutb and would go on to leadership positions in al-Qa'ida – and Azzam thus became embroiled with, or at least sympatheti-cally cognizant of their efforts to resuscitate the subversive struggle of the emasculated Egyptian MB. After a brief period in Jordan, Azzam took up a position as professor of Islamic jurisprudence at Abdulaziz University in Saudi Arabia. There, his teaching would constitute part of the intellectual formation of a generation of Saudi youth, and, in the late 1970s, bring him into contact with the young Osama bin Laden, who was enrolled as a student (Bergen 2001: 50, 55).

When the Soviet Union invaded Afghanistan in 1979 Azzam authored a fatwa – approved by senior clerics, including Shaykh Abd al-Aziz bin Baz, the Grand Mufti of Saudi Arabia – which decreed the Afghan and Palestinian struggles to be focus points of jihad, and that killing infidels in the course of these struggles was to be considered as the individual obligation, *fard 'ayn*, of every Muslim. The doctrine of Qutb thus received the imprimatur of the Saudi religious hierarchy, and the funding stream that went with it. The result was a massive influx of devout foreign fighters into Afghanistan, volunteering to aid the local mujahedin. When the Soviets withdrew after a decade of fighting, the Islamists could rightly claim victory against one of the worlds super powers; victory in a specific theatre, to be sure; aided and abetted by generous intelligence, financial and material support from the United States, yes; but to the battle hardened veterans who had actually engaged the Soviet forces on the ground and now saw them retreat, the victory belonged to God and them themselves. Importantly, to the general Muslim public it was also a mujahedin victory, endowing these fighters with an air of accomplished heroism that Islamic fighters had not enjoyed for centuries, and which constituted considerable sociopolitical cache.

During the Afghanistan campaign, Azzam had created and headed *Maktab al-Khidmat*, 'Office of Services,' to facilitate the fighting. At the first signs of a pending Soviet retreat, he had begun work to redirect the efforts of the organization to accomplish the second jihad specified in his 1979 fatwa, the liberation of Palestine. The wisdom of this approach was disputed by the cadres from the Egyptian al-Jihad group, who occupied several senior positions in *Maktab al-Khidmat*. These Egyptian cadres instead advocated a broader struggle against corrupt regimes throughout the Islamic world. The Egyptian approach reflected the fact that the Islamic volunteers had come from around the world, not just Palestine, and were now about to return home armed with the experience and expertise gained in Afghanistan. Afghanistan served as a watershed in the history of Islamist mobilization, in that it not only provided combat experience to Islamists from around the world, but also laid the foundation for a network that connected all of their individual local struggles, from Algeria to Indonesia, within an overarching organizational and discursive whole.

In 1989, Azzam was killed by a car bomb in Peshawar by unknown assailants, which brought to the forefront the Egyptians, as well as Osama bin Laden, who was intellectually aligned with them. Following the Soviet withdrawal, *Maktab al-Khidmat* worked to provide logistical support to mujahedin groups on the Afghan–Pakistani border as well as disbursing funds for humanitarian relief. It was also involved in publishing activities through an organization in Islamabad, *Bayt al-Shuhada*. All this was overseen by bin Laden, who, due to his status as 'Islamic hero' following the Afghan war, was able to not only stay in touch with the senior and most dedicated cadres from that war, but to forge new relationships with clerics and statesmen throughout the region. Azzam's 'Palestine first' option was eclipsed by the Egyptian plan for a more comprehensive and systemic jihad.

1991 was a turning-point year for the organization. The invasion of Kuwait by Saddam Hussein's personality cult-oriented secular socialist regime was a clarion call to those who had volunteered in the Afghanistan jihad; the so-called 'Afghanis.' Not because they were enamored with the Gulf monarchies, whose rulers were without exception religiously hypocritical and openly subservient to the neo-colonial order – but because Saddam's regime was the epitome of the sort of enemy that the Afghanis had decided to oppose. Success for Saddam was a loss for Islam, compounded by the fact that the stability of the Kingdom of Saudi Arabia at the very least ensured the safety of the Two Holy Places, Mecca and Medina. Accordingly, Osama bin Laden offered to field his Afghan veterans against the Iraqi military. There is no reason to believe that this offer was an expression either of narcissism, nor megalomania, as Western pundits so often have portrayed it. First, the offer was grounded in a sincere conviction that God had granted the mujahedin victory against the Soviets. Second, the alternative to raising an Islamic brigade was truly hair-raising. That the Kingdom of Saudi Arabia and its neighbors were virtually defenseless on their own was patently obvious, despite the hundreds of millions of US dollars spent on buying state-of-the-art military equipment. Thus, the only alternative to assembling a multinational Islamic brigade would be to invite the United States to fight on behalf of the Kingdom. Indeed, following the invasion, the Arab states themselves sought to formulate a solution that would avoid the loss of ideological credibility that outside assistance would invariably bring (Barnett 1998: 213–21).

A foreign army – that of the uncontested hegemon in the post-Cold War era and principal enforcer of the neo-colonial order – was poised to fight on behalf of Muslims who were too feeble to do it themselves. Islamist ire at this state of affairs has frequently been dismissed as an irrational fear of US occupation of the peninsula in order to plunder its wealth, yet the public humiliation involved in this effort must not be underestimated. In the dominant Western narrative, the United States assisted the Gulf monarchies and protected them from an otherwise overwhelming military threat. In the Islamist narrative, closer to the perceived reality on the ground in the region, the US-led effort exposed the shameful weakness of the Arabs, solidified its own hegemonic position, tightened its grip on the region's resources, and effectively placed it in custody of Mecca and Medina, Islam's holiest shrines. In an honor driven agonistic society, and especially among the Islamists, whose quest for dignity had been frustrated for decades prior to the victory in Afghanistan, this added inestimable insult to the injury already caused by Iraq. Additionally, the structural motivations and implications of US intervention – securing access to oil, strategic control in the region, and lucrative defense contracts – are hardly figments of bin Laden's imagination, but attested to by scholars from a wide range of perspectives. In bin Laden's understanding, these functional and 'objective' power political factors took on religious significance:

> The crusader forces became the main cause of our disastrous condition, particularly in the economical [sic] aspect of it due to the unjustified heavy spending on these forces. As a result of the policy imposed on the country, especially in the field of oil industry where production is restricted or expanded and prices are fixed to suit the American economy ignoring the economy of the country, expensive deals were imposed on the country to purchase arms. People [are] asking what is the justification for the very existence of the regime then? ("Declaration of War" 1996)

Soon after bin Laden's offer of assistance was declined by the Saudi rulers in favor of the US military option, he left Saudi Arabia for Sudan, strategically located on the border of the Arab world and a dynamic environment in terms of militant activism. Astute networking allowed bin Laden to consolidate his efforts at constructing a global network of Islamists, while enjoying the protection of Sudanese authorities. His success unsettled the governments of the Arab world, and when bin Laden made it known that there could be no compromise on the issue of expelling the US armed forces from the region – the only guarantor of the Gulf monarchies' existence – the political break between him and Gulf officialdom was complete (although al-Qa'ida has continued to receive financial assistance from prominent members of the ruling elites in the Gulf). Attempts were made on bin Laden's life, and Sudan came under pressure to expel him. In the 1996 declaration of war, bin Laden explained in some detail why he considered the Islamic struggle against the far enemy and its local representatives as inevitable and urgent:

> It should not be hidden from you that the people of Islam had suffered from aggression, iniquity, and injustice imposed on them by the Zionist-Crusaders alliance and their collaborators; to the extent that the Muslims' blood became the cheapest and their wealth as loot in the hands of the enemies. Their blood was spilled in Palestine and Iraq. The horrifying pictures of the massacre of Qana, in Lebanon are still fresh in our memory. Massacres in Tajakestan, Burma, Cashmere, Assam, Philippine, Fatani, Ogadin, Somalia, Erithria, Chechnia, and in Bosnia-Herzegovina

took place, massacres that send shivers in the body and shake the conscience. All of this and the world watch and hear, and not only didn't respond to these atrocities, but also with a clear conspiracy between the USA and its allies and under the cover of the iniquitous United Nations, the dispossessed people were even prevented from obtaining arms to defend themselves. The people of Islam awakened and realized that they are the main target for the aggression of the Zionist–Crusaders alliance. All false claims and propaganda about 'Human Rights' were hammered down and exposed by the massacres that took place against the Muslims in every part of the world...

From here, today we begin the work, talking and discussing the ways of correcting what had happened to the Islamic world in general, and the Land of the two Holy Places in particular. We wish to study the means that we could follow to return the situation to its normal path. And to return to the people their own rights, particularly after the large damages and the great aggression on the life and the religion of the people. An injustice that had affected every section and group of the people; the civilians, military and security men, government officials and merchants, the young and the old people as well as schools and university students. Hundred of thousands of the unemployed graduates, who became the widest section of the society, were also affected. Injustice had affected the people of the industry and agriculture. It affected the people of the rural and urban areas. And almost everybody complained about something. The situation at the land of the two Holy places became like a huge volcano at the verge of eruption that would destroy the Kufr and the corruption and its sources. The explosion at Riyadh and al-Khobar is a warning of this volcanic eruption emerging as a result of the severe oppression, suffering, excessive iniquity, humiliation and poverty. ("Declaration of War" 1996)

Beginning in the early 1990s, al-Qa'ida underwent a significant organizational renovation, turning its rather traditional network into a complex structure centered on an ideological core. For this reason, al-Qa'ida became organizationally complex to the point that there is considerable disagreement among scholars as to what is and is not properly referred to as al-Qa'ida. One way to bring some order to the debate is Hoffman's observation (2006a: 3–7) that, following additional innovation in the wake of 9/11, there are now four levels, or tiers to the organization; each is distinct, but at the same time intertwined due to adherence to a common ideology. The first tier consists of the pre-9/11 leadership and cadres of al-Qa'ida's network, regenerated with new personnel whenever death or capture creates vacancies. This tier was the totality of al-Qa'ida until its reorganization following 9/11. It constitutes the proverbial band of 'cave dwelling fanatics' who, from their unknown location, or locations, in Afghanistan and Pakistan have reached legendary status by defying US efforts to locate and kill them, and remained at the helm of their organization, at least in terms of coordination, if not direct operational command. "Al-Qa'ida Central" is manned by professional militants, many of whom are graduates of the Afghan war against the Soviet occupation. The second tier consists of al-Qa'ida affiliates and associates, formally established militant groups who have received direct financial, logistical, and operational assistance, as well as spiritual advice, from al-Qa'ida Central. It numbers a geographically and operationally diverse range of groups, from North Africa to Central and South East Asia: the Salafist Group for Call and Combat, the Libyan Islamic Fighting Group, the Islamic Movement of Uzbekistan, al-Qa'ida in Mesopotamia, Jemaah Islamiya, Moro Islamic Liberation Front, and a plethora of groups active in Kashmir, such as Harakat-ul-Mujahidin, Jaish-e-Mohammed, and Lashkar-e-Tayyiba. Outreach to these groups began shortly after the Iraqi invasion of Kuwait, as did increased intensity of dealings with the third tier, which consists of what Hoffman refers to as "al-Qa'ida locals"; a nebulous group of al-Qa'ida sympathizers and adherents who have had some connection with the first tier of al-Qa'ida, even though it may have been brief. They "will have been bloodied in battle as part of some previous jihadi campaign in Algeria, the Balkans, Chechnya, and perhaps more recently in Iraq, and may have trained in some al Qaeda facility before 9/11" (Hoffman 2006a: 6). The fourth tier is the so-called "al-Qa'ida network," individuals who have come to sympathize with al-Qa'ida, but lack any direct connection to, or funding from the organization itself. Energized by any number of locally relevant social and political events, these individuals gravitate towards one another in order to carry out attacks in solidarity with al-Qa'ida's agenda. For these individuals, claims Hoffman, "the relationship with al Qaeda is more inspirational than actual" (2006a: 6). This does not mean, however, that individuals within this tier are not just as dedicated and adept, as evidenced by, for instance, the group of mostly Moroccan immigrants based in Spain who coalesced as a group in order to carry out the March 2004 Madrid train bombings.

The second and third tiers are particularly interesting for the purposes of this chapter. Hoffman notes (2006a: 6) that bin Laden has "sought to co-opt these movements mostly local agendas and channel their efforts towards the cause of global jihad" in an endeavor "to create a jihadi 'critical mass' from these geographically scattered, disparate movements that would one day coalesce into a single, unstoppable force." Part and parcel of this effort has been to create mutual dependency whereby groups receiving support from al-Qa'ida Central would either undertake attacks at the behest of al-Qa'ida, or else provide logistical, intelligence or other support for its operations. This is also where Hoffman's observation about the novel structure of al-Qa'ida becomes most critical: "It has become a vast enterprise – an international franchise with like-minded local representatives, loosely connected to a central ideological or motivational base, but advancing the remaining center's goals at once simultaneously and independently of each other" (Hoffman 2006a: 3).

A network of organizations that share common backgrounds and objectives, but not geographic location, local context, or immediate grievances truly becomes, as the old terrorism studies cliché would have it, a many-headed hydra. Yet this mythological simile also has some important limitations. The Lernean hydra of Greek mythology was a sea creature with nine heads and, for each head cut off, two new heads would grow in its place. As an image of the difficulty in combating Islamist militant groups, this is instructive. Yet all these heads grew from the same body, which is where the utility of the image stops. Islamist struggles, even those carried forward by groups within the al-Qa'ida network, are not products of the central core; they do not grow out of a unified body, but emerge from their own specific local contexts and needs. This can be seen clearly in the development of the al-Qa'ida infrastructure, returned to shortly. This is also the limitation one must place on the common parallel to marketing theory, whereby al-Qa'ida is likened to a franchise, with local representatives buying in to a product line and hawking it in their particular location. Hoffman's point is to distinguish al-Qa'ida from the classic hierarchical pyramid structure of previous generations of militant substate organizations. Such a distinction is certainly in order, as the networked and dispersed aspects of al-Qa'ida do represent something entirely new. Yet like the hydra, the parallel to a franchise relationship between al-Qa'ida's core and its many affiliates focuses explanations of causes and remedies on the core; the provider of the product line that the locals are merely peddling on its behalf. Thus it fails to capture the genius of al-Qa'ida, as well as its thorough comprehension of the means and methods of modern networking. One of the fundamental distinctions between the third-worldist and nativist forms of Islamism delineated in chapter 3 is a territorially bounded struggle. Al-Qa'ida has positioned itself as a symbolic champion of a globalized Islam; of a nativist vision that rejects 'colonially imposed' national boundaries in favor of an idealized Islamic caliphate, albeit revised and updated for the twenty-first century.

There are several advantages to this structure. One is that it not merely allows, but encourages those who wish to access the al-Qa'ida brand to prepare, finance, and conduct their own operations. This, as noted in the 2007 National Intelligence Estimate – the official common statement of the agencies that make up the US intelligence community – enables "even small numbers of alienated people to...mobilize resources to attack all without requiring a centralized terrorist organization, training camp, or leader" (National Intelligence Council 2007: 7). Thus, it puts a minimum of pressure on al-Qa'ida's own resources, and allows it to direct these where it feels they are most needed. Moreover, the loose connection between groups and the core enables it to engage in image management by endorsing or taking credit for successful attacks while distancing itself from less successful ones. Al-Qa'ida can be seen to be anywhere it wants to be, and remain absent if it so chooses. This is especially true when it comes to Hoffman's fourth tier, the self-emerging radicals who are beholden to al-Qa'ida's ideology, but lack any actual organizational linkage to it. In this way, al-Qa'ida's ability to inspire is a greater asset in its struggle than its actual operational capability.

Al-Qa'ida's flat organization, which can cover more ground with fewer people – and, importantly, contains fewer people who are structurally connected to each other – is facilitated by two key mechanisms. One is the use of social capital. The other is an understanding of the importance of brand names and brand name based corporate structures. The product is local, but allowed the use of the al-Qa'ida brand name, which amplifies its appeal and stature. Al-Qa'ida has been cognizant of this, which is reflected in a multi-layered organizational structure that facilitates the amplification of local and parochial grievances by means of a globalized, and thoroughly modern marketing strategy. It is precisely this relationship that makes al-Qa'ida so difficult to pin down conceptually. This is also why the killing of bin Laden was not, as Peter Bergen asserted at the time, "the end of the war on terror" (Bergen, 'Time to move on from war on terror', May 2, 2011): most of the militancy and violence marketed under the al-Qa'ida brand are products of local grievances and struggles, rather than products of Al-Qa'ida Central's transregional ideology. To the militants of the third and fourth tier, bin Laden's death was of no great practical consequence. Moreover, the brand name and the concept are resilient enough precisely because the products are local.

This brand name approach was not bin Laden's vision, but an outcome of his failure to bring about a more cohesive, truly globalized organization. In terms of the cognitive mechanisms underlying al-Qa'ida central's promotion of its struggle, and the means for so doing, the organization has sought to move through the stages of what marketing theory refers to as the EPRG schema, with the acronym standing for Ethnocentrism, Polycentrism, Regiocentrism, Geocentrism (Wind, Douglas, and Perlmutter 1973). Whether or not this is a conscious effort informed by bin Laden's business administration studies at King Abdulaziz University in the late 1970s would be a matter of speculation; it may simply be a matter of natural organizational evolution. EPRG begins with an *ethnocentric* 'home country' orientation and the belief that the central leadership is best suited to make decisions in emerging markets. As the market expands, management moves on to adopt a *polycentric* perspective, a host country orientation, which entails the recognition that local collaborators are more knowledgeable of, and more proficient at interacting with their markets. In its *regiocentric* and *geocentric* phases, the corporation sets policies and organizes activities with a view to the regional and global markets, respectively. National boundaries are now ignored, marketing personnel is drawn from throughout a region, or anywhere in the world, promotional policy is developed in a manner that projects a regionally or universally uniform product image, and regional or global channels of distribution are developed (Wind, Douglas, and Perlmutter 1973: 15).

Importantly, "a key assumption underlying the EPRG framework is that the degree of internationalization to which management is committed (or willing to move toward) affects the specific international strategies and decision rules of the firm" (Wind, Douglas, and Perlmutter 1973: 15). Under bin Laden's leadership, the 'management' was committed to utter transcendence of national concerns and grievances, but many of its key local collaborators, importantly, were not. As noted above, following the assassination of Azzam and the ascendancy of bin Laden and the Egyptian cadres within al-Qa'ida Central, the effort was made to broaden the jihad to include targeting of all unjust and apostate rulers throughout the Islamic world. For bin Laden specifically, however, this was envisaged as an intermediate stage, ultimately leading to the creation of a transnational movement with one single goal – confronting the far enemy, the United States. Indeed, the globalization of the struggle, and a focus on confrontation with the far enemy, appear to have been bin Laden's personal preferences since the early 1980s (Scheuer 2002: 170). Thus, support for local struggles was instrumental, but massive. For instance, in the period 1991–4, the organization stepped in to finance and partially direct the campaign of the Abu Sayyaf Group in the Philippines; 1992–4, al-Qa'ida became heavily embroiled in the Bosnian jihad, with bin Laden financing local militants, as well as establishing training camps that drew Egyptian and other Arab fighters to the Balkans. In the same period, the al-Qa'ida leadership was behind the establishment and early activities of *Jaysh Muhammad* in Jordan, with the intent of toppling the Hashemite monarchy, and also gave seed money to the *Groupe Islamique Armée* (GIA) in Algeria. In 1992–6, senior members of al-Qa'ida led other Arab Afghanis together with local Islamists in attacks on government forces in Eritrea, Uganda, and Ethiopia, and began supporting likeminded groups in Lebanon, Kashmir, Tajikistan and Chechnya. Al-Qa'ida's military chief, Abu Ubayda, participated in Islamists operations in Tajikistan, Burma, Kashmir, Chechnya, Bosnia and Libya (Scheuer 2002: 138–41). This support for extant struggles – struggles that in most cases pre-dated the advent of al-Qa'ida – was an astute confidence and capacity building measure, establishing what Hoffman referred to as mutual dependency between al-Qa'ida Central and various groups and movements across the Muslim world. Yet even as al-Qa'ida supported and promoted such nationally bounded Islamist struggles, bin Laden firmly believed that "geographical boundaries have no importance" and that it is "incumbent on all Muslims to ignore these borders and boundaries, which the *kuffar* have laid down between Muslim lands, the Jews and the Christians, for the sole purpose of dividing us" (Atwan 1996). Thus, the transition from ethnocentricity to polycentricity served to move towards a regiocentric and ultimately geocentric approach; to build local capacity for local struggles drawing on the geographically diverse pool of combat hardened veterans of the Afghanistan campaign; creating a synergy within the unique multi-ethnic Islamic army that bin Laden had been instrumental in assembling.

Yet the reality was that, despite bin Laden's disregard for national boundaries and lack of concern for local grievances, those who made up this transnational fighting force had launched their struggles for local reasons, and remained focused on local solutions. While a new, post-bin Laden leadership may seek to renew or intensify efforts at moving towards geocentricity, such efforts have already failed once because the mobilizing power of local grievances far exceed those of abstract ideals. Bin Laden was a charismatic and unifying leader – membership of al-Qa'ida involved an oath of loyalty to him personally – and his death makes geocentricity an even less viable or probable project. The ascendancy within the al-Qa'ida network of the American-born preacher Anwar al-Awlaki, and of the transnationally active al-Qa'ida in the Arabian Peninsula (AQAP) serving as his base of operations, brought innovation in terms of outreach and marketing. Especially the periodic publication of *Inspire*, a professionally produced English-language magazine for aspiring Salafi jihadists in the West, has exposed a new audience to al-Qa'ida's agenda. So, too, have al-Awlaki's video sermons, delivered in English in a style and tone designed to appeal to the youth, and easily available on the internet. Yet, while such innovations have been effective in reaching new audiences, they do not change the fact that robust and durable struggles continue to be based on local, real world grievances and projects. The Chechens, for instance, had a sense of solidarity for the struggles in the Philippines, Somalia, and Yemen, and were even prepared to exchange lessons learned and so forth, but were ultimately focused on wresting their own country from Russia's grasp. It was a hard sell for bin Laden to convince these local fighters that the real enemy that they needed to confront was the United States. His argument was classical: the United States, a Christian country controlled by Jews, constitutes the power that sustains local despots. Because of the stability this affords the regimes, the only way to foment change locally is by first striking at the United States. Yet even the main Egyptian group within the al-Qa'ida structure, the Egyptian Islamic Jihad (EIJ), bin Laden's closest ally, was extremely reluctant to de-emphasize the local struggle. The EIJ, headed by Ayman al-Zawahiri, was eventually won over to the geocentric perspective, persuaded, however, by an argument about resource management, rather than political principle: attacks on Americans could be conducted effectively at less cost, since they could be conducted with only a few operatives, in contrast to the vast resources that were needed to attack the Egyptian government – smuggling arms, providing safe houses, spiriting operatives out of the country, providing security for their families, and so forth (Salah 1999). After the death of an EIJ fighter who resisted arrest in Albania in 1998, EIJ blamed the United States and thus signaled that it had finally moved towards the geocentric option, stating that the United States "has to bear the bulk of retaliation" (Scheuer 2002: 173) Also in 1998, bin Laden declared the establishment of the World Islamic Front against Jews and Crusaders, intended to serve as an umbrella structure for Salafi jihadi groups willing to engage the far enemy. What is notable is that, despite being a significant event in the evolution of al-Qa'ida, its reception, even from bin Laden's close supporters and allies, was cool. As Michael Scheuer (2002: 175) has noted, although the signatories of the declaration – other than bin Laden and Zawahiri – included representatives of the *Jamaat Islami* of Pakistan, the Jihad Movement in Bangladesh, and the head of Egypt's Islamic Group, there were no representatives from groups in the key nodes of Islamist struggle and activity at the time – Algeria, Bosnia, Chechnya, Somalia, Sudan, Kashmir, Afghanistan. Abu Hamzah al-Masri, head of the UK-based Followers of the Sharia stated that:

> We all agree with bin Laden on the issue of hitting the Americans
> and their bases. But I differ with him over one issue, namely that
> it is the ruling regimes that must be fought first because they
> are the ones letting the Americans run amok in our countries
> and then a war of attrition on the Americans will follow the war
> on the regimes. (Scheuer 2002: 176)

Hafez Muhammad Sa'id, head of the Pakistani group *Lashkar-i-Tayyiba*,
stated that "Holy Quran has set the itinerary for the holy war. It asks
Muslims to start their holy war with those infidels who live nearby. Therefore,
our first target should be India, according to Holy Quran" (Scheuer 2002:
176). Mawlana Masoud Azhar, leader of *Harakat-ul-Mujahedin*, added to this,
"I need mujahedin who can fight for the liberation of Kashmir" noting that
it is "jihad till the cruelty of America and India ends. But India first" (Scheuer
2002: 176). Al-Qa'ida's success at a centrally orchestrated globalization of
the struggle was thus limited, and did not include many of the key Islamist
groups squarely within the al-Qa'ida sphere. This is precisely because,
regardless of theological rigidity and ideological objectives, these groups
are first and foremost to be thought of as movements for national liberation;
nativist and reactionary, to be sure, but nonetheless locally grounded. Yet
again it is instructive to recall Cabral's observation that national liberation
movements are not exportable commodities, but outcomes of local elaboration, formed by the historical reality of each people. This applies no less to
al-Qa'ida's constituent parts than any other group or movement. If injustices
and problems, real or perceived, at the local level are what motivates individuals to join a struggle, then it is extremely difficult to simply redirect
them to fight for a transcendent, global ideological objective.

Despite the fact that Zawahiri's EIJ signed on to the new targeting policy
– and went on to participate in the attacks on the US embassies in Kenya
and Tanzania in 1998 – the bulk of these local struggles remained local.
However, even though it failed to create the geocentric jihadi synergy that
bin Laden had hoped for, his efforts did achieve two extremely significant
things. First, targeting the far enemy was designed to, and indeed did create
publicity for the struggle, for the concept of jihad, in a way that no localized
struggle ever could. Lessons learnt from, for instance, the Palestinian
national struggle clearly demonstrated that as long as the struggle was contained in a developing country and directed against local protagonists, it was
essentially out of sight and out of mind to the world media. Once attacks
moved onto Western soil and involved Western casualties, however, massive
publicity would follow. According to one captured bin Laden operative, bin

Laden firmly believed that "targeting these countries' interests was bound to have massive media value, and this would confirm the organization's capabilities, which some quarters had begun to doubt" (Scheuer 2002: 176). Hoffman (2006b: 3) argues that this means that al-Qa'ida now functions exactly in accordance with bin Laden's vision: on the one hand, serving as a base of operations from which to wage war, while "simultaneously inspiring, motivating, and animating" radicalized Muslims to join the struggle. On the other hand, "continuing to exercise its core operational command and control capabilities" by directing and implementing attacks.

The flurry of attacks either directly organized, or overseen and assisted by al-Qa'ida Central globally, from 1998 onwards, certainly created massive publicity and consolidated its standing as the international vanguard of jihad. This in turn generated tremendous power for the al-Qa'ida brand. Al-Qa'ida became what in corporate contexts is refered to as a "bearer of reputation"; proprietor of a name, a brand that is in and of itself a valuable and tradable asset. It has been shown that the value of acquiring a reputable name is relatively greater for actors who are unable to create one on their own (Tadelis 1999). Clearly, al-Qa'ida has not been in the business of selling its name in the commercial sense, but it has been intensely involved in a political version of the activity known as branding. In fact, while applying the franchise model to al-Qa'ida implies uniformity and central control of activities, the branding model accounts for the dynamic connection between the local and the central; between the agendas and concerns that propel struggles and motivate recruits, and the centrally defined overarching discourse that provides a common language, as well as significance beyond the actual territory that contains the struggle. While franchising refers to the practice of locals selling a non-local product, branding refers to the practice of enhancing the appeal of a local product by marketing it under a reputable brand name. This model for thinking about al-Qa'ida accounts not only for its 'unified multiplicity' of groups and causes, but also tracks more closely with the nature of the "mutual dependency" referred to by Hoffman.

The branding model thus explains why local al-Qa'ida nodes were relatively unaffected by the killing of bin Laden. Moreover, it also provides a good way for al-Qa'ida to deflect the impact of failure by any of its individual affiliates, something of which the Lebanese group *Fateh al-Islam* provides a good example. The group was originally established in Syria in early 2006 by Shaker al-Absi, a Jordanian of Palestinian origin. Its purpose was envisaged as sending fighters to Iraq in order to reinforce the al-Qa'ida movment there, which had just suffered the loss of key leaders, including its leader Abu Musab al-Zarqawi. The Syrian authorities expelled the group's leadership to Lebanon, where it took control of parts of the infrastructure belonging to *Fateh al-Intifada* – a secular Palestinian group – and began clandestine recruitment, attracting both Palestinian and foreign recruits. Following clashes with Palestinian groups in Baddawi refugee camp in northern Lebanon, it moved to take control over Nahr al-Bared camp and announced its existence as *Fateh al-Islam* on November 29, 2006. Behind Absi's choice of setting up the group among the Palestinian refugees lay his conviction that "people here are close to God and feel the same suffering as our brothers in Palestine ... and Iraq" (Mekehennet and Moss 2007). He also argued that fighting US forces in Iraq was no longer enough to convince the American public to alter its government's policy, and they had to be directly confronted with violence.

> Originally, the killing of innocents and children was forbidden ... However, there are situations in which the killing of such is permissible. One of these exceptions is those that kill our women and children. Usama bin Laden does make the fatwas ... Should his fatwas follow the Sunnah, we will carry them out ... We have every legitimate right to do such acts, for isn't it America that comes to our region and kills innocents and children? ... It is our right to hit them in their homes the same as they hit us in our homes. (Mekehennet and Moss 2007)

The group became popular among the local residents as its recruits went to work on funding medical procedures, repairing broken infrastructure and engaging in general bridge building efforts vis-à-vis the population. The journalist Nicholas Blanford (2007: 1) quoted one resident as saying that,

> They marry widows or very poor women to give them a home. They are good people who follow an Islamic way of Life ... Al Qaeda is an ideology only. It is an ideology of opposition to America and to Israel and to live an Islamic life ... we believe in that, therefore we are all al-Qaeda.

However, the notion of an al-Qa'ida affiliation was more than merely philosophical for the *Fateh al-Islam* leadership. A letter sent from Jordan to the leadership of al-Qa'ida in Mesopotamia by Abu Muhammad al-Maqdidi, who had been delegated to obtain al-Qa'ida's endorsement of *Fateh al-Islam*, read in part,

> ... don't ask me to go and tell my brothers to resort to robberies ... did they endorse us or does this activity to [rob] come in the way of Jihad successively ... they endorsed us as Al-Qaeda

> and I was asked several times where are the capacitias, equip-
> ments and weapons and when I replied wait it is on its way to
> us they said didn't we endorse Al-Qaeda? Where are the equip-
> ments...only a few who cannot exit the camp are persuaded
> that robberies are legitimate acts...the rest of them wish to kill
> and fight...please respond clearly...either we remain partners
> or we continue to support you in a brotherly manner. (Haddad
> 2010: 554)

However, Abu Salim Taha, the group's spokesman, gave a contradictory statement, claiming that al-Qa'ida had in fact sent a Saudi emissary to vet *Fateh al-Islam*'s compatibility with al-Qa'ida requirements, but that the envoy's attempts to enforce stricter Islamic standards in the camp had been opposed by Absi. Subsequently, however, Taha stated that

> we are a Salafi-Jihadi movement, linked to Al-Qaeda, sharing
> with al Qaeda its modus operandi and scope of activity; we are
> part of Al-Qaeda now, they send us money and equipments, we
> send them men, we were waiting to wage jihad in Iraq, we
> pledged allegiance to Shaker Al-Absi who in turn pledged alle-
> giance to Abu Hamza Al-Muhajir, the leader of Al-Qaeda in
> Mesopotamia...(Haddad 2010: 554)

On May 19, 2007, the group carried out the sixth in a string of bank rob-
beries that brought it into direct confrontation with the Lebanese security
forces. The latter eventually imposed a siege on the Nahr al-Barid refugee
camp – the Lebanese authorities are prohibited by Lebanese law from
entering the camps – leading to heavy fighting, scores of casualties and
the effective dismantling of the *Fateh al-Islam* infrastructure. Al-Qa'ida
vehemently denounced the actions of the Lebanese government, and
threatened that unless the siege was discontinued, "we will tear out your
hearts with traps and surround your places with explosive canisters, and
target all your businesses, beginning with tourism and ending with other
rotten industries" (al-Hussein 2007). Nevertheless, due to its horizontally
networked organization, the loss of these Lebanese al-Qa'ida loyalists did
not damage al-Qa'ida itself.

It has been persuasively argued that branding has become an important
part of global politics in the post-modern era whereby, as Peter van Ham
(2001: 2) explains, the modern state has become a "brand state" with "geographical and political settings that seem trivial compared to their emotional resonance among an increasingly global audience of consumers."

A brand is perhaps best described as a customer's idea about a product, and a brand state, consequently, comprises the outside world's ideas about a particular country. In this context, the state's brand is essential for the ability to remain competitive in the international arena, and its image and reputation become strategic assets. This postmodern political environment is one in which national territory and other traditional geopolitical demarcations are de-emphasized. Unless one insists that Islamists are incapable of advanced modern thought – which, admittedly, many commentators do claim – there is no reason to deny that the rise of the brand state tracks exactly with the undertaking of al-Qa'ida, both in principle and in practice. In fact, this is one of the main areas in which al-Qa'ida has been able to make its own use of the postmodern globalization phenomenon; to turn this supposed herald of cosmopolitan tolerance on its head and use it as a conceptual tool in its own arsenal. Importantly, van Ham (2001: 3) that the brand state uses its history, geography, and ethnic motifs in a marketing of itself that "lacks the deep-rooted and often antagonistic sense of national identity and uniqueness that can accompany nationalism." In so doing, van Ham argues, the brand state is contributing to political pacification. However, states that lack a brand are impaired in the global arena. "Globalization and the media revolution have made each state more aware of itself, its image, its reputation, and its attitude – in short, its brand" (van Ham 2001: 3).

In this effort, al-Qa'ida has been able to build on an anti-nationalist legacy that predates that of Western politics; as noted in the previous chapter, antagonism against, and marginalization of nationalist chauvinism was part and parcel of the ideological package constructed by Qutb, which in turn drew on the work of Afghani and Abdu, whose works date from a period when the Enlightened democracies of Western Europe remained firmly rooted in their respective nationalist-chauvinist heritages.

The denial of the importance of national and ethnic markers cannot come from outside; it has to be a choice of local actors or else be seen as an imposition, a denial of the ingroup's sociocultural value and status. The local responses to al-Qa'ida's initiative, therefore, has been crucial, but it has also been variable, which accounts for the nebulousness of the movement, and the difficulty of outsiders to define it. As mentioned above, the EIJ reluctantly agreed to the idea for the purposes of resource management, and launched a series of attacks on non-Egyptian targets. The same was true for other affiliates, such as the plethora of groups in Southeast Asia, particularly in the Philippines and Indonesia with its transnational

Jemaah Islamiya network, which al-Qa'ida funded and mentored from its inception in the early 1990s. Elsewhere the response was more variable, and less stable. One example of this is al-Qa'ida in the Islamic Maghreb (AQIM). Formerly known as the *Groupe Salafiste pour la Prédication et le Combat* (GSPC), it split off from the larger GIA ostensibly because it rejected the GIA's mass targeting of civilians in the then ongoing civil war. In 2003, GSPC elected a new leader, Abdelmalik Droukdel, who sought to internationalize the group's agenda. That year, the GSPC declared its allegiance to al-Qa'ida, and three years later, in 2006, it announced that it had united with bin Laden's organization. This led to an increase in its anti-Western rhetoric, as well as calls for jihad against the United States, France, and Spain. Yet the group does not appear to have taken directions or orders from al-Qa'ida's leadership, nor has it brought its localized action into conformity with its globalizing rhetoric. While its attacks increased markedly in 2006, its area of activity remained Algeria and the Sahel; its primary targets remained Algerian government representatives and security forces, as well as foreign workers inside Algeria; and the grievances the group sought to redress remained local. Its affiliation with al-Qa'ida has chiefly been about brand enhancement. As one analyst (Rollins 2010: 14) noted, "a nominal link is probably mutually beneficial, burnishing Al Qaeda's international credentials as it enhances AQIM's legitimacy among radicals to facilitate recruitment." This is not to deny that AQIM has cooperated with al-Qa'ida, or that the two groups have exchanged expertise and aided each other operationally, but the exchange has been predicated on AQIM's own local needs and opportunities.

Also in North Africa, the Libyan Islamic Fighting Group (*al-Jama'ah al-Islamiyyah al-Muqatilah bi Libya*, LIFG) provides additional evidence of brand awareness among Islamists associated with al-Qa'ida; here, an understanding of the potential negative impact associated with the al-Qa'ida brand prompted the group to actively distance itself from the association. Founded in 1995 by Libyans who had fought the Soviet forces in Afghanistan, LIFG has a foundational link to the original al-Qa'ida leadership. Yet it has always emphasized that it is in no way connected, either organizationally or ideologically, to al-Qa'ida, and steadfastly refused to put its operative network at al-Qa'ida's disposal. A reason for this was the view that al-Qa'ida's ideology, especially its emphasis on fighting the far enemy, tarnished all groups engaged in legitimate jihad against oppressive local regimes. Another reason was that al-Qa'ida was draining the LIFG's recruitment base. According to al-Qa'ida documents captured in 2006, Libyans were the single largest national group joining al-Qa'ida. In November 2007, Zawahiri released a tape recording in which he claimed that the LIFG had affiliated with al-Qa'ida. This was strenuously denied by Noman Benotman, a former LIFG leader in an open letter, in which he also exhorted al-Qa'ida "to give up all its operations in the Islamic world and in the West, adding that ordinary Westerners were blameless and should not be attacked" (Taher 2008). Two years later, the matter was decisively resolved when the LIFG released new guidelines for jihad, *Corrective Studies*, which thoroughly repudiated al-Qa'ida's means and methods.

> Jihad has ethics and morals because it is for God. That means it is forbidden to kill women, children, elderly people, priests, messengers, traders and the like. Betrayal is prohibited and it is vital to keep promises and treat prisoners of war in a good way. Standing by those ethics is what distinguishes Muslims' jihad from the wars of other nations. (Robertson and Cruickshank 2009)

In offering a brand that enhances a local product, the service provided by al-Qa'ida is similar to that which was provided by the revolutionary regime in Iran to its various Shi'a clients, differing primarily in terms of its deterritorialization. Whereas the nation-state Iran provided finances, intelligence, arms, and personnel to territorially bounded clients – many of which operated under the Hezbollah brand name – so too al-Qa'ida. While the brand name al-Qa'ida has transcended the nation-state system, and in that sense is an expression of globalization, the 'owner' as well as the 'licensee' remain informed by their particular sociopolitical experiences, environments and assumptions. They are all somewhere, and they all come from somewhere. As has been argued above, Islamist discourse may often appear universal, but its interpretations, uses, and implications are numerous. Nowhere is this truth more completely laid bare than within al-Qa'ida, which is an organizational and ideological paradox. On the one hand, it is an overarching framework for resistance against secular modernity, it acts as a global clearinghouse for a multitude of grievances that knows no territorial boundaries. This de-territorialized vision of a virtual ideal global community is as modern as any globalization effort conceived of in the West. Yet, at the same time, this visionary movement is made up of local nodes of resistance, each one with its own specific local struggle against specific enemies for specific reasons. In terms of these facts on the ground, the grassroots struggles that constitute al-Qa'ida's activities, it is far from a cohesive movement. A group can sign up to the brand, given the right credentials, but it may also opt out once the brand is no longer beneficial. Under Osama bin Laden's leadership, the act of signing up involved an oath of loyalty to him personally as the righteous leader of the Islamic struggle. When he was killed, this opened up for an even looser relationship between the brand owners and licensees, which may ultimately weaken the brand. This does not mean, however, that the actual struggles on the ground will be affected. The touchstone against which the brand's beneficence is measured has almost invariably been its ability to contribute social and political capital for the local struggle. The most significant implication of this is perhaps that we are able to understand that this is not one, but many struggles, and that they are not abstract and theoretical, but acutely local and practical – and therefore capable of redress. Despite its overarching transcendent ideology, the enemy is not one implacable monolith, but numerous pragmatic movements. Moreover, the enemy is not one whose goals are incomprehensible because they are the creatures of a medieval theology; rather the adoption of the theology itself is an expression, a gauge, of sociopolitical circumstances.

The signature acts of violence perpetrated by al-Qa'ida and affiliated movements have tended towards grand spectacles. The 1993 New York World Trade Center attack killed six people, but its planners had anticipated toppling the towers and killing up to 50,000 individuals. The attacks on New York and Washington DC on September 11, 2001, planned and executed by al-Qa'ida's central leadership killed 3,000 individuals and caused economic damages estimated at three trillion US dollars; the bombing of a discothèque in Bali on October 12, 2002, carried out by the al-Qa'ida affiliate *Jeemah Islamiya*, killed 204 and injured 240. On March 2, 2004, the Iraqi affiliate *Jihad wa Tawhid* carried out coordinated suicide attacks in Karbala and Baghdad, killing close to 300 Shi'a pilgrims and wounding almost 400. This is certainly not, as Hamid Dabashi (2008: 12) has suggested, a matter of "intermediary and confused acts of visual anarchism" by a form of Islamism that is merely waiting to die. Rather, this modus operandi is what has created the power of the brand, and is a conscious effort to achieve on a global scale the sort of self-affirmation by means of violent confrontation that other groups attempt on a local level. Concept cars at auto shows or haute couture on the cat walk are not what consumers actually drive or wear. These events are used to unveil ideas and visions that contribute to the overall attraction of the brand, even though they are exceptional, rather than widespread. Al-Qa'ida's spectacular atrocities fill the same purpose. That said, some of this 'violent theater' has been deemed by some within the movement as counterproductive and caused them to leave. Al-Qa'ida itself has noted the tension between maintaining the ferocity of the struggle and adversely impacting the image of the movement. An example of this may be found in Zawahiri's correspondence with Iraqi al-Qa'ida leader Abu Musab al-Zarqawi following the latter's spate of videotaped beheadings of defenseless hostages in Iraq. Zawahiri made clear that Zarqawi was expected to cease and desist from these spectacles because they had begun to hurt the image of al-Qa'ida and affect popular support and recruitment efforts.

The relationship between Hamas and al-Qa'ida has been the subject of ongoing political controversy for much of the past decade, with repeated claims by Israeli sources (Gold 2006; Dahoah-Halevi 2007) that the link is real and robust. Yet the reality of their relationship is that it is one of hostility and rivalry, which has not only led to repeated, sustained and public verbal assaults by each on the other, but also resulted in violent clashes and fatalities. To be sure, both groups have their organizational and intellectual roots in the Egyptian MB, both have incorporated central elements of the thought of Qutb into their political lexicon, both reject secular modernity as an organizing principle of society, and both have engaged in suicide operations against the populations of their respective enemies. Beyond these basics, however, substantial similarities are scarce. Their shared heritage has been nurtured and developed in very different social contexts, and forged to serve different, indeed incompatible political ends. Above all, Hamas' consistent focus on a territorially bounded national liberation struggle contrasts sharply with al-Qa'ida's transnational struggle in the name of the *ummah*. This difference lies at the heart of their enduring enmity. Hamas and al-Qa'ida each have made their own bid to define the meaning and potential of Islam as political discourse. While al-Qa'ida has remained true to the transnational vision of Qutb, Hamas has come to emphasize the more Arabist bent of Hassan al-Banna. Because of this significant, if obscure difference, their distantly common tie to the MB is not only inadequate as a joint platform, but in fact a source of intergroup competition as both Hamas and al-Qa'ida seek to demonstrate that it has made the superior choice. Hamas' adoption of, and incorporation into a national project, effectively creating an Islamic-national 'hybrid' is entirely incompatible with the Salafi 'purism' of al-Qa'ida and its affiliates.

Osama Hamdan, Hamas' representative in Beirut, suggested that the sort of transnational, militantly sectarian tendencies that are embodied by al-Qa'ida "are efforts to create a *fitna* ['brotherly strife'] or crises within this *umma*, which would naturally benefit US interests and contradict the interests of the resistance in the region" (Hamdan to author, April 2004). Conversely, at the time of the World Islamic Front statement in 1998 – bin Laden's "declaration of war" on Jews and crusaders – one Saudi Islamist remarked that Hamas would be a welcome addition to the worldwide jihad if it were prepared to "reject cooperation with those engaged in kufr" – meaning all its secular and nationalist partners in the Palestinian national movement, plus Syria, Iran, and Hezbollah (interview with author, March 1998). Disagreement over tactics, strategy, and scope of struggle has been as public as it has been vitriolic. When, in early 2004, the al-Qa'ida affiliated *Jihad wa Tawhid* ('Holy War and Unity') carried out its coordinated suicide attacks in Kerbala and Baghdad, killing close to three hundred civilian Shi'a pilgrims and wounding almost four hundred, a senior functionary within Hamas' infrastructure in Damascus lambasted the attack as "simply insanity," adding, on the subject of kidnappings and beheadings of foreign civilians in Iraq, that the perpetrators "are committing crimes against humanity and against Islam" (interview with author, March 2004).

The accusation of betrayal against Islam was reciprocated and reached a crescendo in March 2006, ahead of Hamas' participation in elections to Gaza's legislative assembly. Ayman al-Zawahiri released a tape in which "joining those who sold Palestine in one legislative council" and "accepting that the number of votes is the judge between us and them" were described as conflicting with Islam and

> a clear violation of the approach of Koran. That we recognize the legitimacy of their government and system means that we recognize the agreements they signed...Are 80 seats in Gaza municipality worth abandoning the faith of monotheism and abiding by the surrender agreements? (Al-Jazeera, March 4, 2006)

Indeed, this had previously been Hamas' own line of argument, while it was building up its political position in the Occupied Territories. Osama Hamdan fired back by underscoring that the movement would participate in elections in order to bring about social changes conducive to the "jihad and resistance agenda" and that Hamas would "resist the occupation until Palestine is liberated and rights are restored..." (al-Jazeera, March 4, 2006). Accusing "some people wish to offer us advice" of offering nothing concrete to the resistance effort, Hamdan pointed out that a realistic struggle cannot be abstract, but has to revolve around the social realities of the people:

"When we tackle educational, political, economic and social issues, we do so in hopes of achieving our goal of liberating Palestine. But for some people to think that Hamas is waging a political battle and might abandon the resistance or concede parts of Palestine because it is forming the government – well, no such thing is on our agenda" (al-Jazeera, March 4, 2006).

Hamas was a powerful player in Gaza politics long before its landslide victory in the 2006 elections, and had used its position to discourage and suppress Salafi groups sympathetic to, or aligned with al-Qa'ida. This was predicated in part on the desire for political control, in part the knowledge that the existence of al-Qa'ida cells in Gaza would be grist to the mill for Israel's efforts to tag its struggle against the Palestinians on to the US-led war on terror, and in part on a fundamental dislike for Salafi theology. After its election victory, the isolation of Hamas government by Israel and the international community created a power vacuum in Gaza that dissident Salafi activists were able to take advantage of. Moreover, the isolation and impotence of the Hamas government seemed to prove Zawahiri's point, that democracy had been a 'Western trap,' which led not only to increased support for its long standing local rivals, PIJ, but also to a proliferation of Salafi groups.

On August 14, 2009, one of these groups, *Jund Ansar Allah* (the Soldiers of the Partisans of God) headed by a local imam, Abd al-Latif Mousa – also known as Abu Noor – declared Gaza an Islamic emirate. The group had repeatedly praised al-Qa'ida as true heroes of Islam while excoriating Hamas for its abysmal failure to remain true to Islamic principles. In response, Hamas security forces stormed the group's mosque and razed it to the ground, with several fatalities, including Abd al-Latif Mousa, as a result. According to Hamas, Abd al-Latif Musa's connections with Jordanian Salafi Islamists – from whom his group sought a fatwa endorsing the assassination of Hamas leaders and attacks on Hamas security forces – were mediated through Muataz al-Masharawi, a major in the PA's General Intelligence Service and brother of Fateh's strongman in Gaza, Samir al-Masharawi (Hamdan to author, April 2011). For many Western commentators (Wilson 2007; McGirk 2007), already Hamas' election victory had been difficult to comprehend, and the counter-insurgency efforts against Fateh elements that had not accepted the popular vote were often explained as a violent 'takeover' by Hamas, notwithstanding the fact that it was already the legitimate government at the time. Faced with the clashes between Hamas and Salafis, Western analysts and talking heads did not seem to know how to process the events – having been told by Israeli intelligence and pro-Israeli commentators that Hamas and al-Qa'ida were essentially one and the same – and put it down to Hamas simply wanting to ensure control of the territory. The event earned Hamas massive amounts of scorn and further deepened the enmity from Salafi clerics, activists, and bloggers around the world, who accused Hamas of betraying the alleged (perhaps more appropriately, fictional) Salafism of its own founders, including Abd al-Aziz Rantisi and Ahmad Yassin (Hijazi 2009; Siba'i 2009). In any case, the showdown was much more than a turf war for control over Gaza – it was a clash between two incompatible Islamist narratives and yet another example of the fragmented nature of the Islamist monolith.

The emergence of PIJ and Hamas were reactions against the failure of the Fateh-led PLO to wrest dignity and land back from Israel, just as Fateh's ascendancy in the late 1950s had been a reaction against the failure of the Egyptian PLO leadership to do so. Until the outbreak of the Arab Spring, the cadres waiting in the wings, ready to pick up the baton should Hamas prove to be the next in the long line of political and military failures of Palestinian efforts, were the Salafi jihadists. However, the 2011 regional tumult pushed back the Salafi positions in Palestinian politics by regenerating nationalist and leftist agendas. The immediate beneficiaries of this were of the Democratic Front for the Liberation of Palestine (DFLP), the Popular Front for the Liberation of Palestine (PFLP) and the Palestinian People's Party (PPP). The DFLP in particular had long demanded representative democracy and transparency within all Palestinian institutions. According to Suheil Natour, a senior member of the DFLP's central committee and prominent human rights activist, regional developments placed direct demands on the Palestinian factions. "How can we expect to benefit from increased democracy in the region if we ourselves are not democratic? If we want regional democratic support, we have to be democratic also" (Natour to author, April 2011). This view was echoed by other factions, including Hamas, and lent a sense of urgency to the unity talks between Hamas and Fateh. Moreover, at least some of the Salafi jihadi activism in Gaza, such as that of *Jund Ansar Allah*, had been encouraged and supported by Fateh as a proxy in its struggle against Hamas. While efforts at national unity and reconciliation did not make Salafi group disappear, it did make them less relevant, both as an ideological alternative and as a power political instrument.

While leftists, nationalist, third worldist Islamists and Salafists may differ widely in terms of ideology and theology, the Fanonian impulse is at the heart of the thematic repetition of regenerated struggle. It may find new and, to its adversaries, ever-more unpalatable expressions, but that is part and parcel of the dynamic of resistance as self-affirmation: as increased resistance is met with increased force and repression, the resistance will in turn amplify its militancy. The Arab Spring was yet another expression, as regional mass movement, of the very same impulse to resist the very same structures. This ongoing spiral of resistance against an unpalatable status quo has been characterized thus:

> In some places the young are the force of idealism, fire, hunger for justice, thirst for authenticity. In others, with the same enthusiasm, they adopt extremist ideologies and prepare for 'guerilla warfare' in town or country. If there is some corner of the world which has remained peaceful, but with a peace based on injustices – the peace of a swamp with rotten matter fermenting in its depths – we may be sure that that peace is false. Violence attracts violence. Let us repeat fearlessly and ceaselessly· injustices bring revolt, either from the oppressed or from the young, determined to fight for a more just and more human world. (Camara 1971: 33–4)

6

Hezbollah: Islamism as Obligation to Resistance

In September 2002, senior US officials pointed to the Lebanese Hezbollah, rather than al-Qa'ida, as the deadliest and most dangerous of enemies. Perhaps most famously, Deputy Secretary of State Richard Armitage asserted that "Hizbollah may be the A-team of terrorists" and "al-Qaeda is actually the B-team" (Byman 2003: 55). This was a remarkable statement given the events that were unfolding around the world at the time. Al-Qa'ida's attacks on 9/11 had unleashed a massive military response, Operation Enduring Freedom, which began in Afghanistan, was widened to include the Philippines in January 2002 and then the Horn of Africa in October 2002. All these were locations where al-Qa'ida and its affiliates were known to have a presence. It was these groups, not Hezbollah, that were – as a matter of tactical and strategic fact – the primary targets in a global military effort that was exacting a massive civilian death toll, as well as an ever-increasing number of coalition casualties. Yet, despite this strategic and political backdrop, US Senator Bob Graham, Chairman of the Senate Select Committee on Intelligence, described Hezbollah's military training camps in the Lebanese Biqa as places "where the next generation of terrorists are being prepared" (Harb and Leenders 2005: 175) and the Director of the CIA, George Tenet, went on to tell Congress that "Hizbollah, as an organization with capability and worldwide presence, is [al-Qa'ida's] equal, if not a far more capable organization. I actually think they're a notch above in many respects" (Byman 2003: 57).

Few Islamist organizations have captured Western imaginations and amplified Western fears of Islamism to the extent that the Lebanese Hezbollah has done. The movement was part of the initial wave of modern Islamist movements; the 'Islamist awakening' in connection with the Islamic Revolution in Iran that prompted Western scholars to deploy their various threat assessments and theories of crisis management. Yet, despite almost three decades of intense study and commentary, it is also the case that few Islamist movements have been as poorly understood, or as grievously misrepresented, as Hezbollah. In part, this is due to the limitations and agendas that inhere in Western commentary, punditry, and scholarship, delineated in chapter 2. In part, however, there is genuine bewilderment among scholars as they set out to parse the foundations and ambitions of the movement, which appear at times global, at times local.

The reality is that the Lebanese Hezbollah is both an intensely local and global movement. In recent years, it has become equated with so-called 'Islamico-nationalism,' a term that seeks to describe a movement that, despite a claim to solidarity with a transnational *umma*, nevertheless confines its main area of operation to a demarcated national territory (Roy 2003: 1). According to Mohammed Ayoob, this implies that Hezbollah, like Hamas, belongs to a category of Islamists that are very different from more transnationally oriented Islamists, such as the various networks that make up al-Qa'ida's project; whereas Hezbollah "works within the confines of a state system, aiming at liberation or secession," the transnational trend "operates in defiance of such parameters, in near total disregard of national boundaries" (Ayoob 2008: 113). The idea is that, whereas al-Qa'ida operates according to a global and imprecise agenda – which is nevertheless determined by its opposition to global power structures – Hezbollah aims more straightforwardly at liberating a specific territory. Indeed, this is the distinction that Sheikh Naim Qassem, deputy secretary general of Hezbollah, offered when he explained that

> al-Qa'ida has adopted a position against the Americans to go after them directly. They have declared this and expressed that they will confront the American presence wherever the US may be present in the whole world, whereas Hezbollah's choice has been entirely different. Hezbollah perceives that the confrontation must be restricted to the Israelis where they are occupiers of the land, and that does not involve going after all Jews in the world, or even going after the Israelis wherever they may be present in the world. Therefore Hezbollah [and al-Qaida's] projects are poles apart . . . Hezbollah's project has to do with liberating the occupied land whereas al-Qaida's project is about confronting the US directly as an international hegemon. (Qassem to authors, March 2004)

Qassem contends that "those who examine the background closely will find a clear distinction between these movements" (Qassem to authors, March 2004). Hezbollah's position, declared emphatically and delineated repeatedly by numerous Hezbollah officials, has had great popular appeal inside Lebanon and beyond. Rather than being a purely Islamic agenda, it consciously and overtly blends the Islamic and the national – religious and secular concerns – that resonate with people far outside the Islamist sphere. Hezbollah's defiant approach towards the perceived arrogance of US and Israeli policy in the Middle East is not only a genuinely held political position, but a highly effective mechanism for mobilizing support. An analysis of events in Lebanon in the recent past, and the commentary they have generated, may serve to introduce the paradox that has inhered in Hezbollah since its inception in the mid-1980s.

The Israeli invasion of Lebanon in July 2006 and the Hezbollah incursion into west Beirut in May 2008 were grist to the mill of Hezbollah's enemies who claimed that the movement's 'Lebanese credentials' were profoundly discredited and that the party remained today what it had been in the 1980s: a tool serving at the command of the Iranian spiritual leadership, the *welayat al-faqih* ('guardianship of the jurisprudent'). This refers to the guardianship of the jurisprudent, Ayatollah Khomeini concept of how a political order needs to be supervised by a 'deputy' of God, to ensure theological continuity, as long as the twelfth Imam remains in occultation (Algar 1981: 127–66). In a debate on the nature of Islamism in July 2008, Bassam Tibi argued that Hezbollah's intervention into the Sunni sections of Beirut was evidence that Islamism ultimately has serious difficulties in coming to terms with pluralism and democracy because it serves the higher purpose of *nizam islami* ('an Islamic order') which is, in essence, totalitarian. Like the armed Islamists in Palestine and Iraq, Tibi argued, Hezbollah wanted to "have it both ways," being seated in parliament while carrying guns outside. Since Hezbollah "blackmailed" the constitutionally elected Lebanese government and imposed itself by means of violence, he claimed, there was good reason to ask to what extent Islamists can "be trusted even when they avow democracy and run in elections?" (Tibi 2008: 46). However, this argument – which has been a standard concern within the study of Islamism for several decades – fails to take into account the specific context and challenges faced by Hezbollah in particular, and the Lebanese political system in general. It overlooks the constitutional predicament of the Lebanese government following the boycott of its Shi'a ministers that had begun some months earlier. Equally important, it ignores how Hezbollah strategically exploited the 'balance of coexistence' – established by the confessional quota system that continues to define Lebanese national politics – for the sake of preventing the movement's disarmament. Tibi's suggestion also seems to pay insufficient attention to how regional showdowns between major adversaries are a recurring theme in Lebanon's short but turbulent post-independence history. That is, Lebanon has never been left to run itself, but has repeatedly been sucked into the vortex of regional and global power politics. Regional powers have inserted themselves into Lebanese politics and manipulated it; sometimes with the blessing or quiet acquiescence of the West, sometimes meeting with fierce indignation and sudden concern for Lebanon's independence and sovereignty. More generally, commentators tend to overlook the important possibility that the Islamic order that Islamists strive for might have a purpose beyond mere power and control; that rather than being an end in itself, it may serve the purpose of resistance against some other kind of order.

Commentators would do well in eschewing the "theologocentrism" that Maxime Rodinson (1988: 91, 104–7) cautioned against; essentialist explanations of the actions and ideas of Muslims with primary reference to Islam, rather than to the sort of generic social and political factors that shape us all and that may therefore be more readily recognizable. Rather than jumping on the 'Islam is the reason' bandwagon in order to explain the actions and reactions of Hezbollah, it would be instructive to ask how – that is, by means of what social and political mechanisms and dynamics – did the movement get to where it is today? What is the context within which its commitment to Islamism is formed and sustained? And, perhaps most importantly, why this particular commitment? Indeed, Hezbollah's 'roaming the streets' of Beirut in May 2008 had in many ways the same purpose as when it attacked the Multinational Forces (MNF) and the Israeli forces in the same streets twenty-five years earlier: to keep Lebanon out of the Western orbit. The movement's understanding of Lebanese independence remains framed by a third worldist perspective in which the ambitions and designs of the wealthy nations of the West – primarily the United States – pose the gravest challenges to local self-determination. On this reading, countries such as Iran and Syria have been allies and persistent backers of the resistance; resistance as a quest for political autonomy and dignity.

In a speech on May 28, 2008, Nasrallah claimed that Hezbollah guarded the independence and diversity of Lebanon while at the same time declaring his party's affiliation to the *welayat al-faqih*.

> They imagine that they insult us when they call us the party of the *welayat al-faqih*. Absolutely not. Today I declare, and this is nothing new, that I am a proud member of the party of *welayat al-faqih*, the wise *faqih*, the scholar *faqih*, the courageous *faqih* and sincere *faqih*. I tell them: *welayat al-faqih* tells us, its party [Hezbollah], that Lebanon is a diverse and pluralist country that you must preserve. (Al-Manar, May 28, 2008)

Ever since Hezbollah's advent, it has adhered to the *welayat al-faqih*, a concept of which the establishment of the Islamic republic of Iran was the embodiment. Hezbollah subordinated itself to Ayatollah Khomeini in the 1980s and now recognize Ali Khamene'i, his successor, as their *welayat al-faqih*. To Hezbollah, adherence to the *welayat al-faqih* amounts to a religiously sanctioned, but also more generally human course of action. According to Qassem (Qassem 2005: 56–7), the directives of the *welayat al-faqih* do not interfere with domestic concerns, but relate to broader principles and visions. Only if uncertainties emerge on vital issues – such as Hezbollah's participation in Lebanon's parliamentary elections – do they need to turn to the *welayat al-faqih* for direction. Otherwise, the working assumption is that those who live in the local context are also those who are most familiar with its needs and requirements. Importantly, Qassem stresses the centrality of the third worldist dimension of Khomeini's ideal of *welayat al-faqih* and the general norm of opposing injustice:

> As a guardian of Muslims, Imam Khomeini governed the Islamic state in Iran as a guide, leader, and supervisor of the Islamic system on that territory, but defined the general political commandments for all Muslims anywhere they lived in the context of preservation of the resources of Muslim states; enmity towards hegemony; protection of independence from domination and subjugation; work towards unity, especially on common and faithful issues; confrontation with the cancer implanted forcefully in Palestine as represented by the Israeli entity; refusal of all forms of oppression and deflection; caring for the needy and repressed; and strengthening of the practice of joint responsibility amongst people. (Qassem 2005: 55–6)

In this frame, the 'Islamic order' emerged as a path of dignity and self-assertion, provided by the Khomeini school of thought but adopted and adapted in ways suitable to local contexts, conditions, and exigencies. It emerged as a vision of a better, more dignified world, and the mere act of struggling to implement that vision in itself gave the struggler a sense of dignity that he had previously lacked. In the early 1990s, Nasrallah described Islam, besides being "a ritual and faith," also as "a way to organize people's lives until judgement day." Islam, he suggested, possesses the "ability to adapt and respond to changes in time and space ... [Islam] has been the dream of the Muslim people for hundreds of years, and its theory still exists and is still valid."

> Before the Islamic revolution in Iran happened, many Muslim
> scholars and movements adopted this project and worked hard
> to implement it. In the meantime, the Western and Islamic
> worlds were awash in foreign-inspired ideologies poring in from
> East and West. The most distinct achievement of the Iranian
> Revolution was its success in shaking up the world, giving
> a spiritual and moral boost to the already existing ideology,
> crystallizing it, and awakening the Muslims. (Noe 2007: 91)

Hezbollah's early leadership was able to identify with Khomeini's declarations of the US as an arrogant bully in the Middle East to whose schemes the pliant and weak Arab states were all too willing to subordinate themselves. They were able to identify with Khomeini's scolding of Israel as a racist and aggressive entity whose primary purpose was to intimidate its neighbors into submission. Indeed, the Lebanese knew all too well the stonewall of Arab silence during Israeli invasions and occupations – a silence that they felt was not affected by the idealistic, but distant declarations of non-Arab coreligionists. The perspective of the early (and subsequent) leadership of Hezbollah was Fanonian, albeit embedded in a religious idiom and belief system in which there existed no alternative to armed struggle for the liberation of the land and the people. "We cannot rely on rights alone," Qassem charged in the mid-1990s. "It sometimes takes power and force to retain those rights. Sadly, we live in a world where the law of the jungle applies – that is, the stronger will try to dominate the weaker" (Jaber 1997: 87). Hence, it was neither possible nor desirable for Hezbollah in such a context to relinquish the principle of jihad and sacrifice. In fact, the political appropriation and operationalization of these principles have been among the movement's greatest assets.

Hezbollah has persistently rejected the claim that Lebanese territory could be liberated through negotiations, at least negotiations from a position of weakness, since this would make Lebanon vulnerable to Israeli demands for concessions. Instead, force and force alone would offer a realistic chance to oblige the Israelis to withdraw unconditionally. The various failed peace processes, the movement charges have been based on the assumption of Arab weakness, and Hezbollah's guerrilla campaign in Lebanon was an effort to prove this assumption wrong. In addition, the strategic adoption of armed struggle as the primary means of struggle would also bring into the equation an awakening (*istinhaad*) of Arab strength (Hezbollah 1997: 629). Put differently, the Islamic wellspring from which Hezbollah drew its strength would be able to demonstrate that there was an alternative to the defeatist approaches of the emasculated regional regimes. Indeed, this would be the foremost lesson of the triumph of Hezbollah against the Israeli forces in southern Lebanon, when the latter retreated in May 2000. Out of this victory, Hezbollah crafted a confirmation of its ideology, which in turn translated into political currency. This was one reason why the movement would not give away its arms. When the second intifada erupted in Palestine a few months after the Israeli retreat from Lebanon, Nasrallah was able to argue credibly that:

> What is happening in Palestine is the transformation of a specific mind-set that has prevailed for some time now; it is a cultural transformation. When the culture of resistance and uprising becomes dominant instead of that of negotiations and settlements, this is a crucial factor that can determine many things. (*Al-Ahram Weekly*, November 2–8, 2000)

That the armed struggle of Hezbollah – the only military success that Arab arms had wrought against the Israelis – served as a beacon of empowerment among Palestinians was attested by the references and analysis provided by Palestinians themselves. Hezbollah's success was seen as a sign that imbalances of power could be redressed and that subaltern perceptions of their own failures and weaknesses were not the outcome, but the cause of the problem.

Yet Hezbollah's 'Islamico-nationalist' position, its Fanonian outlook, and the ability of both to resonate far beyond its own constituency, stem from the remarkable and widely debated metamorphosis that Hezbollah underwent in the 1990s. After all, the 1980s had experienced a very different Hezbollah as it emerged in the turbulent aftermath of the Israeli invasion of 1982. At that time, it was a clandestine and radically zealous resistance force against the Israeli occupation and the Multinational Finance (MNF) – comprising American, French, and Italian troops – which assisted the pro-Western Lebanese government in restoring its authority over Lebanon. Hezbollah emphasized its transnational credentials, considering itself the extended arm and armed force of the Islamic revolution in Iran. It was in its early days that it pledged allegiance to Ayatollah Khomeini and endorsed the concept of the *welayat al-faqih*. Indeed, in its ideological manifesto of 1985 – *Open letter addressed by Hizb Allah to the downtrodden in Lebanon and in the world* – Hezbollah rejected the legitimacy of the Lebanese borders as the "colonial constructions" of the French, and saw the Lebanese confessional parliamentary system as an "oppressive structure that no reform of patchwork improvement would do any good and that must be changed from the roots"

(Norton 1987: 175). It is important to keep in mind that Lebanon's sectarian political system allots cabinet posts and parliamentary seats according to sectarian quotas based on the most recent comprehensive census, which was conducted by the French mandate authorities in 1932. The constitution determines that the president must be a Maronite Christian and the prime minister a Sunni Muslim. As a gesture to the politically marginalized Shi'a population, following the 1989 Ta'if Accords – the national compact that ended the Lebanese civil war – the speaker of the parliament must be a Shi'a Muslim. Also amended as a result of Ta'if was the division of seats in parliament, from 6 : 5 in favor of the Christians relative to all Muslims, to an equal division of seats. This still fails to reflect demographic realities. In 1986, the United States Central Intelligence Agency estimated that the confessional distribution of the Lebanese population was 16 percent Maronites, 8 percent other Christians, 7 percent Druze, 27 percent Sunni Muslims and 41 percent Shi'a Muslims (Country Studies 2010). To this day, therefore, the Shi'a continue to be structurally marginalized within the Lebanese political system.

As mentioned above, Hezbollah's overall ambition during its formational period in the 1980s was to confront the Israelis and the Western forces deployed on Lebanese soil. And they were successful in that task. After several devastating suicide-attacks and numerous bold ambushes, it managed to oust the MNF from Beirut. The party was also an energetic participant within the broad Lebanese front of resistance groups that eventually forced the Israeli occupation forces to withdraw to the so-called security zone in south Lebanon during the spring of 1985. Despite its fierce militancy, however, Hezbollah prides itself – and also receives outside praise – for its inclusive attitude to other groups and its willingness to create cross-religious and cross-political alliances in an effort to fight the 'Israeli enemy' and US hegemony across the Middle East. Precisely the same ability to cooperate across supposedly rigid boundaries that makes Hezbollah both popular and effective in the region is what makes it a feared enemy in Israel and the capitals of the West. This ability and ambition was evident already in its ideological manifesto of 1985, but more widely recognized during Hezbollah's so-called Lebanonization process in the 1990s, when the movement sought to accommodate the outcomes of the Ta'if Accords that laid the foundation for a process of post-civil war peace and reconciliation.

After significant internal debate and disagreement, the party eventually decided to participate in the Lebanese parliamentary elections in 1992 and thus began an ambitious campaign to prove its Lebanese credentials and shed its image as a mere Iranian proxy (Qassem 2005: 187–91). After the 1992 elections, which won Hezbollah twelve seats in the 128-seat parliament, Nasrallah sought to underline the movement's Lebanese identity: "Be sure that every Islamic entity is part of the particular milieu in which it exists, and each milieu, in turn, has its own specificities. Hezbollah is not an Iranian community in Lebanon, and its fighters and mujahidin are not Iranian citizens" (Noe 2007: 91–2). He also argued that Hezbollah had never proposed the establishment of an Islamic republic in Lebanon as a credible option, and it "will not do so in the future, because the nature of the Islamic republic does not lend itself to forceful action" (Noe 2007: 90). Yet he also pointed out that it was the movement's "wish and desire to see the emergence of an Islamic system because we are first of all Muslims, and not about to give up on our religious identity" (Noe 2007: 91). The Hezbollah struggle for Islam in Lebanon, he suggested, would form part of, and respect the boundaries of a political landscape that served as an open space for all Lebanese:

> We fully understand that a communist would want a communist state, and a Muslim or Christian would want a state that reflects his own faith and ideology. What we do not understand, however, is someone who wants to impose on others by force, or through violent means, his own beliefs and a governance system of his choice. This we will never do. (Noe 2007: 91).

This explicit endorsement of pluralism drew directly from the experience and needs of the war-torn Lebanese population. Such a thoroughly localized Islamism has allowed Hezbollah to criticize, even excoriate Islamist groups who see diversity as a threat, although seldom mentioning their names. Ali Fayyad, a Hezbollah official, has claimed that Islamist movements

> must accept the idea of political pluralism and differences of opinion and give up their habit of transforming them into antagonistic conflicts. They must also stop using violence in the struggle for power and avoid sinking into the logic of civil war that threatens the unity of Arab–Muslim societies. (Le Monde Diplomatique, November 1999)

It is clearly the case, however, that in contrast to other Islamists, Hezbollah has been privileged in its relationship to the state. This privilege was cultivated during the period of Syrian tutelage over Lebanon in the 1990s, during which Hezbollah emerged as a strong enough force to hold its own in national politics. It should also be emphasized that Hezbollah's endorsement of Lebanese pluralism is strictly conditioned and centered on its own imperative to persist in its resistance struggle against Israel. This is the red line that it will not cross, nor allow any other parties to imperil. In fact, the relationship between Hezbollah and the Lebanese government – at least between 1992 and 1998 when Rafiq Hariri was prime minister – was never harmonious but, rather, impacted by intense mutual misgivings and suspicions. These were constantly mediated by Syria, the ultimately power in, and arbiter of Lebanese politics. Syria's ability to enforce this delicate balancing act between Hezbollah and the Hariri government – which in itself was no small feat – is the primary reason for Hezbollah's persistent praise for the years of Syrian presence in Lebanon. Hezbollah knew well, and criticized in private, the staggering corruption within the Syrian security services in Lebanon at the time, but this aspect of Syrian domination always remained secondary to the maintenance of a national equilibrium in which the resistance against Israel was able to continue. For instance, Hezbollah's officials often commend Damascus' obstruction of the Beirut government's decision to deploy the Lebanese army against the resistance, as the former attempted to abide by international demands during Israel's so-called "Operation Accountability" bombing campaign in July 1993 (Qassem 2005: 111–12). Nasrallah grimly recalled years later that had such intervention by the army occurred, "Lebanon would have entered into a dark tunnel, in which the resistance, the army, and all of Lebanon would have been lost" (*As-Safir*, June 26). To Hezbollah, the most important aspect of Syrian intervention was that it protected the resistance from being stabbed in the back by the government in Beirut. Syria, meanwhile, was keen to benefit from both of its alliances: with Hezbollah's resistance in the south, from which it derived military-strategic benefits, and with Hariri's lucrative reconstruction schemes in the capital, an ever-flowing source of capital and contracts. In terms of its public discourse, which reflected its ideological principles, Hezbollah condemned Hariri's neo-liberal restructuring of Lebanese state policy for its neglect of the urban and rural poor. On a pragmatic, strategic level, however, Hezbollah actually benefitted from these state policies. Like many other nationally focused Islamist movements, Hezbollah was able to offer a wide range of welfare services – schools, infirmaries, hospitals, scholarships, agricultural assistance, infrastructure development, and so on – in areas where the state had no interest in, or ability to deliver on its promises and obligations. Thus the shortcomings of the neo-liberal policies of the government have aided

Hezbollah in cultivating popular support and creating robust constituencies (Harik-Palmer 2004: 47–8, 81–94). Indeed, in addition to its acceptance of the parameters of the confessional system, which the party has always maintained are deeply unjust, Hezbollah would also allow itself to be politically curtailed by running on the same parliamentary electoral lists in 1996 and 2000 as its Shi'a rivals in the Amal movement. Hezbollah, it was said, would not be allowed 'to get too big for its boots' but actually acquiesced in this arrangement because its main priorities did not center on parliamentary work or Lebanese domestic politics, but on the promotion of a national endorsement of its resistance project in south Lebanon (Usher 1997: 59–67).

Indeed, some Islamists, even from within its own ranks, were provoked by this 'sell-out' to the Lebanese regime. For instance, in 1997, Sheikh Subhi Tufayli, Hezbollah's secretary general 1989–91, called for civil disobedience and demonstrations against the state's devastating social policies in the eastern Biqa, partly aiming his criticism against the leadership of his own movement. One party official (Abdallah Mortada to author, June 1998) commented that while Hezbollah sympathized with Tufayli's criticism of social policy, he should not provoke the state in a way that threatened the resistance. "For us," the official said, "the resistance is a great concern and a number one priority, and thus we must have a strong and solid base." Such appeasement of the system accomplished what it was designed to do – safeguard the resistance – but also earned Hezbollah significant credit across many layers of Lebanese society. Far from being an unpredictable or unaccountable maverick force, Hezbollah consistently proved itself to be as able to work within the Lebanese system as it would press its own case on matters that it deemed of primary importance. Even communities naturally hostile to an Islamist project began to embrace the resistance as a quest for national dignity and independence.

When the Israelis finally withdrew from Lebanon, Hezbollah was at the peak of its popularity in Lebanon and the Arab world. Its guerrillas were hailed as the first Arab force to ever defeat the mighty Israeli army, which had now been humiliated in Lebanon and forced to withdraw without receiving any political concessions or guarantees for its security by the Lebanese state. As such, it was also the finale to its 1982 invasion of Lebanon, which aimed to strangle the PLO (and to some extent succeeded in doing so) and to turn Lebanon into a 'pro-Western' government ready and able to sign a peace treaty with Israel, as Egypt had in 1979. Nonetheless, Hezbollah's success, some argued, might also be the prelude to its ultimate demise. In the battles in south Lebanon, Hezbollah had proved its credentials through a skilled and proficient guerrilla force that was able to defeat one of the most respected military powers in the world. But now, the argument went, the party was over. With the Israeli withdrawal, Hezbollah had lost the stage from which it had been able to broadcast images of victory via its satellite channel *al-Manar* ('The Lighthouse'). These images were often video taped military skirmishes that showed how Israeli soldiers were ambushed and killed by Hezbollah fighters; an effective and emotionally powerful counterbalance to the steady stream of images from Palestine in which Israeli soldiers punished and humiliated Palestinian civilians. Following the Israeli retreat, the question became, how would Hezbollah face this new reality without the advantages afforded it by its battle field prowess? It had made the resistance its absolute priority, and its fighters were armed, skilled, and prepared – but now there was no occupier to fight. Furthermore, it was argued that the party's 'nationalist credentials' would now be put to the test. Would it abide by its transnational Islamist commitment, pledged by Ayatollah Khomeini and endorsed by the movement itself, to continue to fight Israel in order to liberate Jerusalem, or had its sole concern actually been the liberation of Lebanese territory? Some suggested that Israel might have made a strategically adept move by withdrawing and thereby confronting Hezbollah with such a tricky dilemma. If the retreat was indeed an Israeli 'trick,' it failed when Hezbollah chose a third option: its guerrillas did not withdraw from the border, but remained deployed in the south, further entrenching their positions on the Israeli border. Backed by Beirut, Hezbollah declared that Lebanese territory was not entirely liberated, as Israeli forces remained deployed in the Shebaa farms, on the slope of the Golan Heights. While the Israelis, supported by the United Nations and the United States, claimed that this was Syrian territory and should thus be handled in negotiations with Damascus, the Lebanese regime claimed that it was Lebanese, and the Syrians, the ultimate supervisors of Lebanese politics, were willing to concede to these claims with cryptic formulations about the area being populated by Lebanese. When the Oslo process finally broke down in the late summer of 2000 and the al-Aqsa intifada erupted, Hezbollah also turned up the heat in southern Lebanon by attacking Israeli fortifications around the Shebaa area and capturing three Israeli soldiers (in addition to kidnapping an Israeli citizen, Elhanan Tannenbaum, who had been lured to Beirut). Naim Qassem explained that the capture of the Israeli soldiers was undertaken in order to swap them for "our detainees in Israeli prisons" and

> to show solidarity with the Palestinian intifada, to show that we
> are in the same bunker in the confrontation against the Israeli
> occupation. Also, we wanted to emphasize our right in the
> Lebanese Shebaa farms region. So this operation sent many
> messages, all underlining one essential point: arousal to this
> occupation and aggression in any shape or form. (*Time Magazine*,
> October 16, 2000)

Indeed, as the Palestinian intifada escalated, so did Hezbollah's support for
it. In addition to the Shebaa farms, the Lebanese south again witnessed
significant tensions: attempted cross border raids by Palestinian guerrillas,
allegedly assisted by Hezbollah, a more militant deployment by the movement along the border, and in March 2002, as the Israelis conducted their
raids into the Jenin refugee camp on the West Bank, Hezbollah agents were
captured in Jordan while attempting to smuggle weapons into the West
Bank, something for which the movement proudly accepted responsibility.
Indeed, on the third anniversary of the Israeli withdrawal, on May 25, 2003,
Nasrallah dispelled any notions that the resistance had "abandoned the era
of jihad" by arguing that "our eyes, minds and hearts are now centred on
the land beyond the border... We still exist as the frontline and our eyes
and hearts are present inside Palestine" (*al-Manar*, May 25, 2003).

In a regional environment of despondency, in which no Arab government was willing to assist the Palestinians, such a position earned
Hezbollah widespread accolade and sympathy, if not direct support.
However, increasingly vocal voices inside Lebanon were raised in protest
against the party's willingness – and ability – to in effect formulate
Lebanese foreign and defense policies unilaterally. "Who gave Sayyed
Nasrallah the complete mandate to decide on behalf of the Lebanese
people and throw them into the quick sands they don't want to be thrown
into?" asked Gebran Tueni (*An-Nahar*, June 5, 2004), a columnist at
An-Nahar. The domestic criticism against Hezbollah's militant posture in
the south was accompanied by increasing opposition, both domestic and
international, against the Syrian presence in Lebanon. United Nations
Security Council (UNSC) resolution 1559 was adopted in early September
2004, demanding withdrawal of the Syrian troops and the disarmament
of all militias in the country. This latter provision was aimed exclusively
at Hezbollah and Palestinian factions loyal to Syria. The resolution was
primarily an American–French response to Syria's directives to the pliant
Lebanese parliament to amend the constitution and prolong the mandate
of Lebanon's pro-Syrian President Emile Lahoud. To Hezbollah, however,

the resolution was a recipe for *fitna*, civil strife, and the movement defended the Syrian presence in Lebanon as a bulwark against outside interference. This Western intrusion into Lebanese politics aimed, the movement charged, to weaken the country by attempting to disarm the resistance. In a speech commenting on the resolution, Nasrallah stated that the Security Council had adopted its position against the will of the Lebanese people, claiming that "the vast majority supports the resistance." Therefore, he argued, Hezbollah would accept "a popular referendum" on the resistance "and we accept fair opinion polls if they rely on such fair polls" (*al-Manar*, September 5, 2004). By proposing that the issue of resistance should be decided by a referendum, Nasrallah fired a shot across the bough against the political system that it had thus far acquiesced in for pragmatic reasons; against the façade of democratic propriety that concealed an utterly undemocratic sectarian system. A 'one man one vote' referendum would upset the sectarian arrangement by bringing out in the open the fact that Hezbollah's own constituency, the Shi'a community, were (and remain) systemically discriminated against by the confessional quota system. Astutely maneuvering the system, Hezbollah had accepted confessionalism, and thereby the continued discrimination of the Shi'a community, on condition that its right to keep the resistance under arms would not be infringed. A popular referendum outside the discriminatory confines of sectarian quotas would illuminate the numerical strength of the Shi'a, and hence the deceptiveness of the strength of other communities. This was a sensitive matter. Two days later, following a barrage of criticism in the Lebanese media against Hezbollah's suggestion of a referendum, Hezbollah's media office issued a statement, saying that Nasrallah merely "posed a clear question about the formula that the Lebanese will adopt, should a disagreement [emerge] among them on one of the major internal issues" (BBC Middle East Monitor, September 7, 2004). Hence, Hezbollah backtracked and stuck to its earlier position of embedding itself within a confessional formula that it essentially despised. It had made its point, that the Lebanese political system rests on a fragile formula that cannot withstand actual popular pressures, but also shown that Hezbollah was not about to plunge the country into civil war in order to press its case. For purposes of appeasement and public relations, the movement would describe its position as having been reached out of concern for the various minorities in Lebanon, in particular the anxiety among Lebanon's Christians faced with the prospect of domination by a Muslim majority. As suggested by Hezbollah spokesman Ghaleb Abu Zeinab,

> If we want to get full democracy here we need to have everyone
> persuaded of its benefits, and not afraid that they will be over-
> thrown. Besides, we look at the coexistence we have between
> the different confessions here as an example, and we don't want
> to overthrow it. If it was a 'majority-minority' system here it
> would be explosive. So we'll hang onto this confessional balance
> we have for now. But I don't know what will happen in 20 years.
> (Cobban 2005)

Hezbollah's acceptance of the confessional system appeared as a conces-
sion – and to a certain extent, it was – but it was also a way of exerting
pressure against its adversaries in order to compel them to accept the
bargain: Hezbollah agreed to abide by a system it considered unfair and
discriminatory and in exchange it would maintain its logic of resistance.
Thus, for its own ideological purposes, the movement thrived in this confessional system since its clout and popularity within the Shi'a community
enabled it to wedge a de facto veto into the Lebanese body politic. This
would prove to have been an astute move, since the Syrian troops were
forced to withdraw in March 2005 following domestic and international
pressures on Damascus on account of its alleged involvement in the assassination of former Prime Minister Rafiq Hariri in February 2005. The
withdrawal left Hezbollah exposed, or so it was thought by those desiring
to see the movement weakened and neutralized, if not completely
disarmed.

Hariri's assassination divided Lebanon into two rivaling camps: the so-
called March 8 camp – which takes its name from a massive demonstration
on that date in downtown Beirut, headed by Hezbollah, as a salute to Syria
– and the March 14 coalition, referring to the date of an even larger demonstration a week later by the anti-Syrian parties. Those who hoped that
an era of harmonious independence would follow the Syrian withdrawal
were mistaken, as the country appeared instead to slide towards civil war.
While the March 14 coalition would lean for support towards the West –
especially the United States, France, and Saudi Arabia – the March 8 camp
cultivated its long-standing alliances with Syria and Iran. And while the
March 14 coalition would repeatedly stress the imperative of fully implementing UNSC resolution 1559, Nasrallah warned, at the fifth anniversary
of the Israeli withdrawal on May 25, 2005, that his party would "consider
any arm to reach for our guns as an Israeli arm" and swore that Hezbollah
would "cut it off" (*As-Safir*, May 25, 2005). In March 2006, responding to
an interviewer's claim that there no longer was a popular consensus in
support of armed resistance, Naim Qassem stated that, neither is there

any consensus on the disarmament of the resistance (*Sawt al-Lubnan*, April 1, 2006). The movement was thus digging itself in for a long stand-off.

In July 2006, the country witnessed a destructive 34-day long war as Israel decided to bomb Lebanon comprehensively in retaliation for a Hezbollah cross-border operation during which it abducted two Israeli soldiers. For Hezbollah, the stated objective – in line with its long-standing operational and tactical efforts – was to obtain 'bargaining chips' in its ongoing negotiations for the release of Lebanese prisoners held in Israeli jails (*al-Manar*, July 12, 2006). To Israel, the massive bombing campaign was initially aimed at eliminating Hezbollah. During the campaign, Hezbollah proved a capable adversary, inflicting casualties in Israeli army ranks and pounding Israel with rockets. The Israeli objectives were then revised to a more modest weakening of the movement. The war ended on August 14, 2006, with losses and destruction on both sides. The casualty estimates for the Lebanese side range between 1035 and 1191 dead Lebanese civilians. (United Nations Human Rights Council 2006: 26). On the Israeli side, 43 Israeli civilians were killed, mainly by Hezbollah's rockets, in addition to the 117 Israeli soldiers killed in action (Israeli Ministry of Foreign Affairs 2006). As for casualties in the ranks of Hezbollah itself, the figures are disputed. Israel claims that it killed 400–500 Hezbollah guerrillas, but Alistair Crooke and Mark Perry (2006) argue that evidence suggest that its casualties could be as low as 184. Either way, the war also ended with the adoption of UNSC resolution 1701, which yet again reiterated the imperative to disarm Hezbollah. Yet Hezbollah remained defiant. Even though the party was no longer visually present south of Litani, and despite having suffered huge losses, Nasrallah (2006c) claimed in his 'Divine Victory' speech on September 22 that the war had merely allowed it to strengthen its resolve and accumulate new experiences.

The movement was in no mood to give up its arms. Having rejected the political system in the 1980s and remained detached from it, or aloof, in the 1990s, Hezbollah had accepted cabinet posts following the elections in the summer of 2005, with the stated purpose of safeguarding the arms of the resistance. It had even concluded alliances with domestic adversaries – like Saad Hariri's Future movement and Samir Geagea's Lebanese Forces – in the election campaign, and later also ensured that the cabinet that included these adversaries expressed its support for the resistance. The alliance broke apart some months later, however, over disagreements about whether the International Criminal Court should investigate the assassination of Rafiq Hariri, and Hezbollah and

Amal withdrew their ministers from the cabinet in protest. In early February 2006, Hezbollah announced an alliance with the popular Christian leader Michel Aoun in a bid to counter the March 14 group, which ignored, Hezbollah claimed, the consensus procedures by which the cabinet was supposed to operate. Hezbollah thus guarded its veto, which it saw as the essence of the 1943 National Pact and the 1989 Ta'if Accord.

Such disagreements came to the surface yet again after the war in July 2006, when Hezbollah announced that it did not trust the March 14 camp in government, accusing it of standing with Washington during the war. Therefore, Hezbollah demanded a 'blocking third' (*tilth muatal*) within the cabinet. Hezbollah representatives claimed that the March 14 camp had made a series of political and economic commitments and promises to outside powers, and only a robust counterbalance in the cabinet would be able to obstruct them from delivering on their promises. Hezbollah and its allies chose to boycott the government and impose a picket line on parliament downtown, leading to the standstill of the country for several months. On May 8, 2008, the hamstrung Lebanese government decided to move against Hezbollah by declaring its private telephone network illegal and dismissing the Hezbollah aligned security chief at Beirut International airport. The party responded by furiously lambasting the cabinet decision as a declaration of war and sent its guerrillas into Beirut to seize government buildings, thereby forcing the cabinet to backtrack. At a press conference on May 10, Nasrallah (2008) stressed that the resistance was a 'victim' of directives from abroad, and that the swift move into downtown Beirut was aimed at stopping the implementation of these directives by the army and the security forces. On May 21 in Doha, the parties to the conflict came to an agreement in which the opposition *within* the cabinet, headed by Hezbollah, would receive a 'blocking third.'

For Hezbollah, the implications of the 2006 war were not limited to Lebanon. Nasrallah also addressed the 'pragmatic' Arab elites based on the logic that resistance is strength. What is interesting is that in this geopolitical setting, Hezbollah's logic centered on the value of resistance, not on absolute imperatives. In Nasrallah's (2006b) 'Divine Victory' speech after the war, he told Arab leaders: "I will speak not of removing 'Israel' but of this settlement you seek. How will you acquire an honorable settlement, while you announce day and night that you will not fight for the sake of Lebanon, nor Gaza, the West Bank not even for the sake of al-Quds?". In this regard, the war in 2006 was highly symbolic of Hezbollah's choice of confrontation based on strength, standing out in sharp relief against the Arab states' negotiations based on weakness. When asked in an al-Jazeera interview during the war what end result he would be able to view as a victory, Nasrallah answered:

> To succeed in defence is victory…Victory here does not mean that I will enter and capture northern Palestine and liberate Nahariya, Haifa, and Tiberias…The victory we are talking about is that when the resistance survives. When its will is not broken then this is victory. When Lebanon is not humiliated and its dignity and honor are maintained, and when Lebanon stands fast alone in front of the fiercest military power and does not accept any humiliating conditions regarding a settlement of the issue, then this is victory. When we are not defeated militarily then this is victory. (Bin-Jiddu 2006)

That is, by surviving and by not making any concessions, Hezbollah claimed to expose the flaw inherent in the assumption that Israel is necessarily militarily superior; an assumption that it believes lies at the heart of the political order imposed on the region and most visibly embodied in the various so-called peace processes and the humiliating concessions by the Arabs. For sure, many Lebanese scorned Hezbollah's strategy of confrontation. They deplored the human death toll and massive destruction, and indeed Hezbollah's 'violation' of Lebanese sovereignty by its unilateral maverick decisions. Commenting on Nasrallah's 'Divine Victory' speech in September 2006, the leader of the Lebanese Forces and prominent member of the March 14 coalition, Samir Geagea, probably spoke for many of the movement's adversaries when he remarked that, "We are the victors, and yet we do not feel it was victory but rather that a real catastrophe befell our country, and that our fate and destiny are at the mercy of the wind" (AFP, September 24, 2006).

To Hezbollah, armed struggle is imperative in order to defeat a regional order embedded in the ontology of violence. On this view, the sacrifices of war are painful but necessary in order to confront the challenges inherent in the order. While declaring the war's end in 2006 to be a divine victory, Nasrallah (2006b) expressed awareness of the country's divisions and called for the resumption of a national dialog. Yet Hezbollah's position remained firmly focused on maintaining the resistance in order to confront a national and regional order based on US and Israeli superiority. "Our dignity is above anything else," he declared, and continued:

> We sacrificed our blood for the sake of our dignity. This is how
> we are. What else can we do? This is how things are for us in
> Lebanon...Any talk about surrendering the resistance weapons
> under this state, this authority, this regime, and the existing situ-
> ation means keeping Lebanon exposed to Israel so it can kill as
> it wants, arrest as it wants, bomb as it wants, and plunder
> our land and waters. We certainly cannot accept that...The
> resistance will not end as long as Israel occupies our land, vio-
> lates our honor, undermines our security, and plunders our
> waters and resources. Never! I swear to God.

Throughout the events outlined above, the notion of dignity is central to
Hezbollah's resistance project and it is well aware, and prepared to
absorb, the painful sacrifices that inescapably flows from choosing confrontation over subservience. Yet, the movement also cherishes, and is deeply
dependent upon, the community in which it is rooted and whose identity
and needs it fosters and maintains in the so-called 'resistance society'
(*mujtummah al-moqawamah*) or *al-halah al-Islamiyyah* ('the Islamic domain')
(Harb and Leenders 2005). Like many other Islamist movements, Hezbollah
oversees a vast network of NGOs that offer a range of welfare services to
underprivileged communities, especially in the Shi'a dominated areas in
southern Beirut, south Lebanon, and the Biqa Valley. An important role in
this *halah al-Islamiyyah* is also assigned to the party's media institutions, like
the radio-station *al-Nour* (The Light), the weekly magazine *al-Intiqad* (The
Critique), and perhaps most importantly, its satellite TV-channel, *al-Manar*
(The Lighthouse). According Harb and Leenders (2005: 191), these services
and institutions enable Hezbollah to convey its message through a "material lens" which also is a "symbolic lens" that offers an "identity" and "sense
of belonging" to the Shi'a community. These activities foster a sense of
empowerment and capacity among the Shi'a, who historically, as noted,
have been the most impoverished and politically and socially most marginalized of the Lebanese sectarian communities. Importantly, "the resistance
society modifies the perception of the Shi'a individuals as 'disinherited'
(*mahrumin*) to one of being 'disempowered' (*mustada'fin*)," and this "nuance
is essential, as the latter invokes an opportunity for transformation and
change, whereas the former involves stagnation" (Harb and Leenders 2005:
189).

The integrated and holistic network of this *halah al-Islamiyyah*, or *mujtummah al-moqawamah* affords Hezbollah opportunity to mesh the political
and religious project of the *welayat al-faqih* with the lifeworld of the
Lebanese Shi'a. That is to say, the community's world of meanings projects

a political consciousness in line with Hezbollah's philosophy of resistance and defiance. This is a communitarian identity that carries profound religious depth, similar to other Islamist community formations. With respect to Egypt, for instance, Carol Wickham (2004: 244) describes how the subculture within Islamist communities pointed to ways in which a religiously grounded truth can be forged into a form of psychological empowerment in which the pious Muslims do not fear anything but God. In this regard, she argues that "Islamist ideology challenged the prevailing fear and passivity [towards the regime] by exhorting graduates to obey a higher authority, regardless of the risks they would incur as a result."

Following Khomeini, Hezbollah views the unjust and exploitive world order as an outcome of a materialist worldview that has abandoned faith and submitted to the greedy desires that are always present within the human being. In other words, the very nature of mankind – as problem and as object of transformation – lies at the heart of Hezbollah's religious–political philosophy, and it is not possible to intelligibly reduce it to the components of economic or other rationalist theories. As with Shi'a activism more generally, Hezbollah stresses that the world is 'manmade' and that humans are responsible for making their own choices in this worldly life. According to Nasrallah (2002):

> man makes history and events. All the events that took place in the past, and that are taking place now until the Judgement Day are manmade. They are contingent upon his belief, disbelief, concepts, justice, injustice, righteousness, corruption, goodness and evil. The matter starts with man himself . . . It is the people who create the identity of their society; they can make society just or unjust; they are the ones who create righteousness and corruption.

The prophets, however, were sent by God to guide man onto the right path. While mankind is free to ignore such guidance, Nastrallah noted they do so at their own peril: everybody, believer and non-believer alike, will stand accountable on Judgment Day; there is no way to escape the reckoning of God. "No one can run away from this truth [of death] or this inescapable day. Where to could anyone run away? Is there any place in this universe that does not belong to Allah? Where to can anyone run away from the judgment of Allah and his punishment?" (Nasrallah 2002). On that day, good deeds will be rewarded and bad deeds will be punished. Significantly, good deeds do not only involve praying and fasting. In Hezbollah's highly politicized perspective on Islam, it also involves struggle against injustice. In this context, neutrality is not an option; being neutral in matters of justice versus injustice means that one runs the risk of provoking God's wrath. Taking a stand, however, and willingly committing to the struggle will render great rewards in the afterlife. For a movement with relative modest means (compared to its enemies), this religious dimension is its greatest asset since those who fear God have no reason to fear death and eternity.

Hezbollah's thinking on the subject of martyrdom illustrates this point. The martyrs among the mujahidin are human beings of the highest order. Naim Qassem (Qassem 2005: 28) describes the martyr as a person "who has sold his soul and body to the Lord" and "against whom nothing is a threat." He is prepared to offer his life for the cause, whereas "the enemy" only has weapons that can "inflict danger on life" and are therefore only capable of harming "those who seek life" – and thus it becomes "futile to combat those who believe in martyrdom." Central to Hezbollah's perspective on the redemptive aspects of political struggle is the account of Imam Husayn, a profoundly revered figure within all of Shi'a Islam. In AD 680, Imam Husayn chose to sacrifice his own life and the lives of his men in confrontation with the troops of the corrupt Caliph Yazid outside of Kerbala in Iraq. While Yazid stands as a symbol of corruption and despotic rule in Shi'a cosmology, Imam Husayn stands as an eternal symbol of confrontation against the status quo, said to have challenged the oppressor even though he was outnumbered and aware that this meant certain death. The message of Hussayn as symbol is clear: not even death ought to intimidate and discourage the believer from confronting injustice. As Qassem notes:

> We have learned through Imam al-Hussein that the love of martyrdom is part of the love of God. We have learned to glorify jihad for the sake of Islam. Generations after al-Hussein's resurgence in Kerbala, we still learn from the magnificent accomplishments that materialized through his martyrdom. His vision was not momentary or restricted to the battle: it was directed at the future of Islam and the Muslims. (Qassem 2005: 45)

To die as a martyr for a just cause may not assure a direct victory, but it promises great rewards for the worries in the afterlife. It also generates a value, a sense of justice and dignity, within the community of believers, even in the harshest of circumstances. The struggle, in a sense, validates itself by undermining the enemy's efforts to consolidate and reproduce an unjust order; to fall as a martyr is to point to the paramount importance of living a life in dignity.

Lebanese adversaries of Hezbollah have capitalized on this pledge of death and war. While many Lebanese, especially on the side of the March 14 coalition, voiced criticism against Hezbollah after the July war of 2006 for abiding by a 'philosophy of death' rather than a 'philosophy of life,' Nasrallah responded by conceptualizing Hezbollah's culture of martyrdom as resistance against power structures that are themselves established and maintained by violence, and that compel the weak to live out their lives in humiliation and physical and spiritual poverty. "We all want to live, but *how* do we want to live?" he asked. Would the satisfaction of physical needs be enough, like food and drink? Or does mankind desire more? Healthy human beings who live in harmony, he suggested, regardless of their religious, tribal, or other belonging, abhor a life of humiliation. "Do we want to live humiliated and threatened by the Zionists?" he asked, "To live controlled by the main powers of this world? Do we want to live in Lebanon [in the absence] of a strong army that can defend us against Israel? Do we want to live a life where we are not allowed to build a good economy away from the conditions of the World Bank?" He continued: "We want to live, yes. [But] we want to live with dignity. We are the children of the school that rejects to live humiliated and [our slogan] has always been 'humiliation is rejected by us.'" The sacrifice of martyrdom, he argued, was "to get killed in the battle *for* life."

> Those who are noble will come to defend their parents, people, nation and the dignity of what they cherish... When a nation offers its neck to a tyrant, lots of people will be slaughtered like sheep on the steps of this powerful man. But then it fights and resists, it will give less numbers of victims, but they will be martyrs, and this will change the reality... There is no death in martyrdom. Martyrs creates life for the nation, and protects it... Martyrs thus make life. (Nasrallah 2007b)

Yet besides the comfort given to the dead and their relatives and countrymen, who hail them as martyrs, there is also an obligation (*taklef*) involved in a struggle based on, and serving faith. According to Nasrallah (2005), those fearing the afterlife should commit to the "culture of resistance" and consider that there are "two futures" (*mustaqbalan*) for the *umma* to be concerned about: one in the worldly life and one in the hereafter. This is, he argues, what distinguishes the Islamist ideology – that its adherents cannot ignore how their own fate and that of their families and the nation are intertwined with their deeds in this life, which in turn is the basis for their fate in the hereafter. This is a compelling obligation and it explains, if Hezbollah is correct in its own estimation of the Lebanese political scene, the steadfast support that the movement has received throughout its long and painful struggle. It also conveys an image of Hezbollah's Islamism as communitarian in its approach and strategy. Instead of merely seeking to establish an Islamic state – a prospect that the movement's veteran officials deny has ever been *realistically* entertained – Hezbollah has mobilized a deeply rooted communitarianism within the Shi'a community, which has had a significant impact on Lebanese state politics, especially in terms of obstructing the government's ambitions to acquiesce in and replicate a Western-oriented hegemony. By doing so, Hezbollah rallies a range of sentiments – some Islamist, other secular – that hopes to defy Western ambitions to turn Lebanon into a pliant ally in the Arab world. Importantly, and ironically, this is a strategy that the movement successfully pursues through the contortions of a confessional system that structurally margin-alizes the very Shi'a constituency that constitutes the party's base; a system that Hezbollah essentially despises and – at least on principle, theoretically and rhetorically – would like to see dismantled. Thus, Hezbollah is well described with the word of Rita Abrahamsen (2003: 209), who observed that, among postcolonial opposition forces, "resistance cannot be idealized as pure opposition to the order it opposes, but operates instead inside a structure of power that it both challenges and helps to sustain." As argued above, Hezbollah's choice to persist in its armed struggle actually benefits from the logic of confessional coexistence, the historical and colonial legacy of the Lebanese state that was originally designed to foster the narrow interests of sectarian elites aligned with the West. As Eli El-Hokayem (2006) succinctly puts it:

> In Lebanon's consensus-based politics, monopolizing Shiite rep-resentation guarantees that no combination of political forces can compel Hizbollah to abide by rules or principles it deems contrary to its interests, unless its opponents are willing to risk civil war . . . To be fair, the rest of Lebanon's political elite is also not serious about political reform. Yet the difference between Hizbollah and Lebanon's other politicians is fundamental; the former hijacks the system for ideological reasons and the latter abuse it to promote parochial and economic interests.

Hezbollah has forged a position in which it can remain 'above' the system while promoting its resistance project on the ground; a project that in many ways carries the same ambitions today as when the party emerged it the mid-1980s. According to Nasrallah, this is in fact its intention. Asked whether he feared losing popular support when, in December 2006, the movement chose to confront the Lebanese government and risked provoking further national division, he explained:

> In 1982 when the Zionist enemy occupied our country, we were students. Most of today's leadership of Hezbollah were at the time students, at religious schools or universities, or teachers. Most of us were young... We left our classrooms and our different occupations to join the resistance and we never imagined that we'd stay alive this long and much less that we'd had have any status or popularity in the Arab and Islamic world... or that we'd become MP's or ministers... What was on our mind and what still is on our mind, wasn't the desire to achieve status, it was to fulfill a duty. When the brothers vowed themselves as martyrs, it was not for the desire to achieve status but the desire to fulfill a duty... One of our intermediaries told me lately that if I were to insist on pursuing the opposition's demands and objectives, I might lose my status in the Arab world. [But] we would gladly exchange our status we have achieved in the Arab world for the lives of our children or brethren who died in the name of our cause... We do not seek status. Our fundamental and central cause is that we are fulfilling a duty and that is what governs our conduct. (Nasrallah 2007a)

It was this 'fundamental and central cause' that guided Hezbollah's response to the Arab Spring – support for every uprising in the region except the one taking aim at the Syrian regime. Indeed, Hezbollah's overall response was to not only welcome the uprisings, but encourage them. In late April, Ali Fayyad noted that the events in Tunisia and Egypt were "very important mixtures of democracy and resistance... revolutions based on demands for accountability, transparency" (Fayyad to author, April 2011). Indeed, on March 19, 2011, Nasrallah had given a televised address intended to "boost the morale" of the uprisings in Tunisia, Egypt, Bahrain, Libya and Yemen, stating that "we are with you, we support you ... we call for victory, we pray that you achieve victory, and say that we are ready to extend the hand of assistance ..." He condemned the regimes' refusal to enter into "sincere dialogue" with the protesters and their decisions to resort instead to "killings, to accusation, to humiliation. They said that these honorable people... were sectarian, they were accused of being with al-Qa'ida, other times they were accused of spying for America, and so on ... This cancelled out any possibility of dialogue..." (PressTV, March 19, 2001).

Yet when the uprising in Syria began to gather momentum later that same month, Hezbollah was noticeably silent. The Syrian regime responded to demands for government reform with a mixture of limp reform proposals and extreme brutality, blaming armed gangs and foreign interference as it sought to justify a crackdown that within two months had claimed the lives of over a thousand Syrians. Fayyad commented about the region in general that the people "are creating a new Arab world, it is a historical process... We are only at the beginning of the process, in a transitional stage. We cannot be sure about the future, but we are sure that there is no going backward for any of the regimes" (Fayyad to author, April 2011). Importantly, Syria was specifically included among the regimes that were believed to have passed this point of no return, and Hezbollah officials privately agreed without hesitation that the Syrian system was decrepit, reform had been slow and at least some of the opposition's demands were justified. Yet when Nasrallah broke his silence on the matter, in a speech on Resistance and Liberation Day, May 25, 2011, it was not to offer his support for, and solidarity with the Syrian protesters, but to urge them to be patient and engage in dialogue with the regime. To many commentators, the remarks smacked of hypocrisy and opportunism. A key to understanding the underlying logic is the tactical and strategic, power political aspects of the Fanonian impulse. In his speech, Nasrallah explained that,

> Our position in every Arab square or Arab revolution or popular movement is decided according to two angles. Here I hope that we may be precise. The first angle is the stance of an Arab regime on the Arab–Israeli conflict – its stance, its position, its role... The second angle is the absence of any hope for reform on the domestic level – when the regime has closed all doors, windows and even small gaps for reform, for the benefit of the peoples of these countries. Starting from these two angles we take our position. Our criteria are clear. Our standards are clear. We do not have double standards... Clearly every country knows how to face its situation and solve its problems... However, we take a general stance... that our regimes and governments live up to the aspirations of the nation and the central confrontation that this nation had taken upon itself so far. (Nasrallah 2011)

Thus, the key principle at work in Hezbollah's overall approach was that none of the regimes other than the Syrian were willing to support or participate in the resistance project. The Syrian regime, argued Nasrallah, is a stalwart supporter of the resistance project against Israeli and American designs. Moreover, the majority of the Syrian people still have faith in President Assad, he claimed, and the Syrian regime was the only one that held out the prospect of democratic reforms without the need for revolution; something that he ascribed to the personal character and track record of Bashar al-Asad. Toppling the regime, on the other hand, meant running the risk of replacing it with one that is subservient to the inherently undemocratic neo-colonial order, which, according to Nasrallah, is a clearly discernible objective of Israel and the United States. Two additional considerations, although not stated in the speech, were also at play. One was the specter of a regenerated Syrian Muslim Brotherhood, and the various Saudi funded tribal and Salafi groupings hiding within or behind the democratic movement. Their ascendancy would in itself be a threat to Hezbollah given the deep-seated sectarian enmity between them. Also taken into account was the fact that the Syrian regime and its security forces, faced with an existential threat, would not go down without a fight. A sectarian or clan-based civil war in Syria, manipulated by outside forces, could regenerate similar militancy in Lebanon and risk dragging it into another civil war. These were grim prospects all around, as far as Hezbollah was concerned.

The Syrian situation and its potential scenarios contrasted sharply, in Hezbollah's analysis, with the situations in Tunisia, Egypt, Libya, Bahrain and Yemen. None of these regimes had demonstrated any inclination to support the resistance project. On the contrary, all of them had proven credentials as servants of the neo-colonial order. Since their power and stability depended on the support of Western protectors rather than the assent of their peoples, these regimes were not only emblematic of the region's predicament, but also in a position to refuse calls for reform and crush opposition and protests for as long as the West would allow them to do so. Regardless of the accuracy of this analysis, the decision to call for rapprochement in Syria and revolutions everywhere else was a power political calculation based on the imperative to advance the Fanonian impulse: viewed from the "two angles" that Nasrallah presented in his speech, more could be achieved with the Syrian regime than without it, just as more could be achieved without the other besieged regimes than with them. Presented with a clear choice between democratic aspirations and support for the resistance, Hezbollah chose the latter.

Hezbollah's experience thus demonstrates how an Islamist movement can project its struggle within a society that contains a multitude of confessional and political groups, and in a region that contains a range of threats and challenges. As mentioned above, Syrian tutelage and the confessional system has in this regard privileged the party compared to other Islamist forces around the world, which are often fiercely repressed by incumbent regimes. Indeed, in his May 25, 2011 speech, Nasrallah was explicit about the debt of gratitude that Lebanon in general, and Hezbollah in particular, owes to the Syrian regime, people, and security forces that "helped maintain Lebanon's unity and halted the bloody Lebanese civil war which was about to exterminate Lebanon and the people of Lebanon" (Nasrallah, 2011). Domestically, the Lebanese regime is simply in no position to curb Hezbollah in any meaningful way, even if parts of it may want to do so. And this is the point: Lebanon remains severely divided over the cause that Hezbollah promotes. In that sense, the party's nationalist aspirations may be restricted to Lebanese territory, but the various outcomes of that struggle have a much wider impact on the regional order and beyond, and informs the party's analysis of events throughout the region. This is why Hezbollah's struggle must also be understood as that of a transnational movement, why its local national agenda is part and parcel of its wider ideological aspirations, and vice versa. Indeed, this may also explain why so much effort, especially within the framework of the global war on terror, has been directed at combating Hezbollah's aspirations in Lebanon and beyond.

7

Bitter Harvest: Algerian Islamism

While the democratic adventures of Hezbollah and Hamas have been far from unproblematic, it is to North Africa that we must look for the electoral event that decisively shaped modern Western notions of Islamism's compatibility with democracy. In early January 1992, the Algerian army cancelled the second round of parliamentary elections due to fears of a victory by the Islamist party Front Islamique du Salud (FIS). From that point, the country began a slide into several years of bitter violence and vengeance, as well as a stalled political reform process. The Algerian conflict has in many ways served as an epitome of the dilemma assumed by many Western scholars to be plaguing the Muslim world: that processes of democratization run the risk of being cut short because the most popular and well-organized opposition forces are Islamist parties that – almost by definition – aim to establish 'Islamic states,' which in turn means an end to the democratic project. As Algeria began its descent into chaos, in June 1992, US Assistant Secretary for Near Eastern and South Asian Affairs Edward Djerejian (1992: 37) famously asserted that "those who seek to broaden political participation in the Middle East" will find the United States "supportive," but "we suspect those who would use the democratic process to come to power, only to destroy that very process in order to retain power and political dominance. While we believe in the principle of 'one person, one vote,' we do not support 'one person, one vote, one time.'" This dilemma or at least the perception of such a dilemma, has kept scholars busy studying the nature of Islamism and the various ways in which it might be possible to 'manage' the diversity of its supposed challenges. Sidahmed and Ehteshami (1996: 13) suggest that this means dealing with "an inherent contradiction between the absolutist nature of Islamist ideology and the relativist character of democracy" since there is a "contradiction between a force that sees itself as a custodian of the divine message, hence as having a monopoly on truth, and a system built on relative truths and opinions." John Waterbury (1994: 39) has similarly argued that "religious political groups are non-democrats of a peculiar kind" and when "the

scriptures are both holy and explicit as is the case in Islam, pragmatic compromise will be very difficult." According to the Algerian secular intellectual Latifa Ben Mansour, "no political party founded on the basis of religion
and its instrumental use can be integrated in a republic or democracy. And,
if it takes powers, it is in order to enslave the people and dominate neigh-
bourhood states. These parties only feed on violence and war" (Cavatorta
2009: 135).

Much of this reasoning flows directly from the Algerian experience. But
what exactly does the Algerian case tell us about the Islamist electoral
challenge? Indeed, prominent FIS officials would make no bones about
what they thought of democracy. Ali Belhadj, second in command within
FIS, confirmed perceptions that Islamists see a contradiction between
divine and popular sovereignty, and that they believe the latter to be of a
detrimental nature, when he argued that "Islam sovereignty belongs to the
divine Law; in democracy, sovereignty belongs to the people, to the mob
and the charlatans" (Willis 1996: 198). In May 1991, FIS spokesman Hachemi
Sahnouni claimed that: "In the case of [the FIS achieving] a majority at the
next legislative elections, we suspend the constitution, we ban secular and
socialist parties, we immediately apply the *shari'ah* [and] we immediately
get rid of the President of the republic" (Willis 1996: 199). Of course, on
the basis of comments such as these, Bernard Lewis (1996: 54) would be
able to deduce that Islamists "regard liberal democracy with contempt as
a corrupt and corrupting form of government" and that they are "willing
to see it, at best, as an avenue to power, but an avenue that runs one way
only." But it is possible to advance other ways of understanding Islamist
mobilization and popularity, as well as the nature of their challenge. One
prominent observer of Islamism has suggested that Islamist opposition
forces most often express a critical perspective of the incumbent elites in
power – the political classes as well as military and commercial power
brokers. While the institution of Islamic law (or the absence of it) often is
the main theme within this critical perspective, the central element "to
that critique is the emphasis on corruption, malfeasance, and misbehavior.
The mistreatment at the hand of the government is a constant refrain.
The Islamist critique is persuasive because it rings so true" (Norton 1995).
This statement points to a sociological dimension in the way that Islamists
also must employ a significant degree of pragmatism to sustain their
popular support among constituencies. Beyond their lofty, idealistic appeals
– that often smack of totalitarian utopianism – are the down-to-earth,
social and political concerns of constituents, whose primary need is redress
of social grievances, rather than the creation of some idealized theocratic

state. Lisa Anderson (1997: 24–5) has suggested that the popular impulses of the FIS fed off the general exhaustion that many Algerians felt towards a deeply corrupt, despotic and, in many ways, incompetent regime, pointing out that a survey conducted in Algiers at the end of 1991 showed that "only half of those who claimed to support the FIS declared themselves favourable to the installation of an Islamic republic." Indeed, in the months leading up to the crucial parliamentary elections, decisive changes were also being made within the FIS leadership, as well as the rank and file, as more dogmatic and inflexible officials found themselves as outmaneuvered and left in the cold. Whether these were mere tactics to allay fears within sectors of the Algerian state and society, due to the massive popular support for the FIS, or whether it reflected a more sincere or realistic move towards a role within the existing power structure, will remain a matter of speculation since the FIS was never allowed to gain such a position. Feeling threatened by the popularity of the FIS, the pillars of the regime decided to seek refuge in an authoritarianism that is all too familiar in the region and Algeria pulled back from the brink of representative democracy. The notion that the Algerian army stood as a guarantor of democracy, rather than a defender of the corrupt self-interest embedded in the status quo, was exposed as naive at best.

As Vickie Langohr (2001: 592) has suggested, while the question of the democratic credentials of Islamist parties are important to study and discuss, it is "by and large an inaccurate one," since it "assumes a political context in which democratic politics actually exist and that Islamists choose or decline to try their luck at them. In fact, very few examples of such politics exist in most of the Muslim world . . ." Similarly, Tarek Masoud (2008) answers the question of whether Islamists are democrats with a counter-question: "Does it matter?" He notes that while Islamists' viewpoints vary, and while there is good reason to be cautious – since many Islamists promote ideological schemes that clearly do not accord with Western notions of democracy – a crucial dimension revolves around the institutions and constitutions with and within which they must operate. With respect to the Algerian case, Masoud (2008: 20–21) suggests, for instance, that "a military strong enough to cancel elections between rounds would also have been strong enough to stop a government run by the FIS from enacting a theocratic agenda." Be that as it may, the question is why are robust institutions capable of securing competitive elections not constructed and strengthened?

In the case of Algeria, there is reason to suggest that the primary contest was not Islamism versus democracy (even though that assumed dichotomy is a valid consideration on both practical and theoretical grounds) but the order of power and privilege challenged by new and assertive political elites. Indeed, the challenge of the Algerian elections occurred at a specific moment in time. The Cold War had recently ended and the Western powers triumphantly proclaimed the victory of the cherished ideals of market economy and liberal democracy as Marxist–Leninist alternatives had finally been exposed as corrupt failures. The United States emerged as the ultimate arbiter in many areas of global affairs; in the Middle East, a US-led alliance – notably comprising troops from a range of Arab states (like Syria and Egypt) – had ousted Saddam Hussein's army from Kuwait and irreparably damaged Iraq's regional stature. In November 1991, the Madrid peace conference signaled a comprehensive desire (or so it was thought) to bring the bitter Arab–Israeli conflict to an end. In this context of potentialities and prospects for a new Middle East order, the Islamists emerged as the ultimate 'party-poopers' – alleged anti-democrats as well as diehard enemies of the Jewish state.

The Islamist challenge in Algeria was seen as grave by the Western powers and local elites alike. Conversely, what came to pass in Algeria would be seen by Islamist groups around the Muslim world as exposing an emergent order that comprised serious internal contradictions: the Western world – by consenting to the abortion of the Algerian popular vote – would not abide by and uphold its own declared standards and values. For example, Hassan Nasrallah of the Lebanese Hezbollah, which closely followed the Algerian events since its leadership contemplated participation in the upcoming Lebanese elections, argued that the Western world order would not allow for the electoral success of popular political desires in the Muslim world since this clashed with its own desire to subjugate and control (*Al-Ahd*, January 22, 1992). Tunisian Islamist Rachid Ghannouchi (2000: 103) similarly claimed that Algeria was evidence that Islamists had become victims and that they were

> repressed on the pretext…of saving democracy from themselves. Alleging that if the Islamists were permitted to gain power through the ballot box they would put an end to democracy, the purported supporters of secularism justify for themselves the undermining of what they set forth to protect, and so justify the violation of every human right.

To Ghannouchi, however, the Algerian elites did not target the Islamists "because of their ideology, although admittedly repressing them causes fewer problems, and may even be profitable." That is, they would garner approval and support from the international community by keeping the Islamists at bay. Rather, he suggested, the "repression is practiced against the entire society and is necessitated by the nature of the ruling elite and by its interests and associations" (Ghannouchi 2000: 104). Other observers likewise suggest that the various political processes of liberalization in countries such as Tunisia, Algeria, Jordan and Yemen "were designed not to inaugurate a system of uncertain outcomes – democracy – but to solidify and broaden the base of the elite in power, making possible increased domestic extraction" (Anderson 1997: 20). According to Gudrun Krämer (1992: 24), the process should be thought of as "system maintenance" and reforms as intended to stabilize a political system undergoing acute crises. The purpose, she suggested, was to contain discontent and marginalize, "and if possible delegitimize, all those that refuse to be co-opted into the system or are regarded as too great a threat to the regime to be recognized as a legitimate political actors" (Krämer 1994: 202). Willis (2006) has also described reforms in Maghreb during the last two decades as "regime survival" rather than constructive ways of containing radicalism. In Western Europe, he notes, radical parties and groups – like socialists, unions, women's organizations – were included in the political process in an effort to avoid polarization and radicalization that in itself implied a gradual change of the norms, modalities, and structures of power. The experience in Algeria - as well as Tunisia and Morocco – was of a very different nature. The regime, backed up by external powers (that is, the West) made significant efforts to impede such developments. This can be seen as the main theme that underlies the reforms initiated in Algeria at the end of the 1980s, their abortion in 1992, and the regime's persistent struggle to remain in power, at a gruesome price. From this perspective, the Islamist challenge should rather be understood as directed against certain modalities and structures of power; modalities and structures that consistently generate grievances and militancy, which the Islamists have been able to channel, mobilize and express in its own ideological and theological language.

Thus, while many observers have seen in the Algerian experience both a source and a confirmation of the clash of civilizations narrative there is an alternative reading that situates the mayhem of the 1990s in the country's deeply troubled structures of power and privilege. That is, unyielding centers of power, relying on force rather than popular legitimacy, triggered an equally violent response; a repressive regime faced fierce and increasingly militant resistance; a government that transgressed the law faced equally lawless opponents. Fanon's dictum that the native recognizes himself in the violence of the oppressor – words written as Algerians struggled for national independence from France some decades earlier – have come to describe also the relationship between indigenous post-colonial elites and its discontents. The FIS movement, officially formed in 1989, did not emerge out of nowhere. Islamism was not a new phenomenon in Algeria but had coexisted, in various versions, with other ideological models, idioms and identities for decades. Indeed, there were groups and personalities within the nationalistic FLN (*Front Liberation National*) who also claimed Islamic affiliations during the 1954–62 war of independence. Abbas Madani, the official leader of the FIS, was a veteran of the FLN who spent almost the entire independence struggle in prison. Algerian history bears witness to many strugglers who fought the French under the banner of Islam, from the nineteenth century and onwards. Claire Heristchi (2004: 113) points out that "Islam continued to play an integral part in the evolution of an Algerian political consciousness mixed with the stress on Arabism, while construing an assertive identity and historical belonging within the nationalist camp of the twentieth century." The early 1960s saw the formation of *al-Qiyam* (The Values), a movement headed by the Islamic intellectual Malek Bennabi; Western-educated and francophone, but supportive of a social conservatism embedded in Islamic faith. Benabi developed a profound critique of Western modernity as one that is submerged in moral chaos due to its lack of religious foundations and ethics. As many other Islamist ideologues, he stressed that the greatness of a nation and civilization does not foremost lie in its material wealth, but in its spiritual health and self-esteem. As Muslims had abandoned the strength provided by Islam, he argued, they had become trapped in a persistent inferiority complex towards the West because they adopted modernity on the same materialist basis as the Western powers. In order to redress this predicament, Muslims had first of all to find and mobilize the sources of identity and faith that were authentically their own. Bennabi was the founder of the *Jazari* ('Algerianist') tradition of Islamic ideology, in opposition to many of the Islamist influences of the Middle East, which he considered too theoretical and dogmatic. For Islam to become a popular force, he argued, it be subjected to the life-giving impulses and stimuli of local conditions and traditions. During the civil war in the 1990s, the *Jazari* branch of Algerian Islamism would prove to be more prone to negotiations and settlement with the non-Islamic circles and groups in Algerian society. Other Algerian Islamist currents were more oriented towards the Salafi and Wahhabi norms of Saudi Arabia, or the teachings of Sayyed Qutb and the Egyptian MB.

More generally, Algerian Islamism had begun to grow in strength and popular appeal in the 1970s, in part because the clergy (*ulama*) reacted with resentment against the ways in which it was marginalized by the largely secularist and socialist state. Furthermore, FLN's effort to cultivate a national Arab identity as an antidote to the legacy of French colonial domination caused the state to invest in 'Arabized' education programs. The students schooled in these programs, however, were not only marginalized on the job market, but also subjected to Islamist influences by teachers from Egypt who were often affiliated to the MB, living in exile in Algeria. There was also an international context to this growing popularity. Whereas many Islamist movements in the region had seen their star rising following the Arab nationalists' defeat at the hands of Israel in 1967, the Algerian Islamists experienced their ascendance in 1978 as the Islamic revolution erupted in Iran, and then another push in 1980 as the Muslim guerrillas started to resist the Soviets in Afghanistan. To counterbalance this development, the Algerian regime began to recalibrate its earlier third worldist positions into a more Western-friendly posture. Besides, like many other Arab regimes at the time, the Algerian elites saw the rising tide of Islamists as a convenient bulwark against an assertive left, in a world that was still mired in the polarization of the Cold War. Hence Islamist groups were encouraged to attack leftist gatherings and associations, mainly in the universities, but also within the trade unions. Increasingly, 'Islamic spaces' began to emerge within society, and in certain areas, Islamic groups were able to impose the cultural codes of Islam, so-called *hisham*, on people, mainly women. To benefit from the rising popularity of Islam, the Algerian regime built numerous mosques across the country, but many of those were too transparently under state control and utilized for blatant regime propaganda. In protest, Islamist groups began a blatant process of taking over mosques and religious centres from which they denounced the ways in which the regime imposed its corrupt politics on Islam and thereby tainted its purity. As an alternative, Islamists offered an ideological prism by doing the opposite. By imposing religion on politics, they were able to construct and communicate a critical narrative in which the regime was identified as ultimately corrupt and incompetent. Since this criticism was, in terms of political facticity, essentially correct, it resonated with the reality experienced by many people across Algeria.

The regime's increasing anxiety in the face of Islamist popularity can be seen in, among other things, its efforts at appeasement, such as adopting the Family Code in 1984, a set of regressive laws mainly directed at circumscribing women's rights in matters of marriage, divorce, and inheritance.

Despite such efforts, the regime found it difficult to contain the Islamist opposition, which grew louder and more belligerent, even as the incumbent elites were losing legitimacy. Falling oil prices in the 1980s resulted in deteriorating standards of living for the average Algerian. At the same time, the well-to-do elites faced increasingly vocal accusations of corruption and mismanagement of state resources. To the Islamists, the situation served as proof that Western-style secular models of modernity ultimately ended in rack and ruin for peoples of the Third World. The ruling elites – which, like their colleagues in governments throughout the region, ignored the social pathos and responsibilities demanded by Islam – prioritized their own enrichment over the wellbeing of the people. What Algeria needed, the Islamists argued, was for state and society to embed their national aspirations in Islam, since only religion would be able to guarantee the righteous ethics capable of eliminating the vice and corruption that had penetrated the country's ruling elites and deprived the country and its people of both resources and potential. That is, genuine independence would never be realized as long as Algeria remained subject to Western political models and thought.

The regime's efforts to accommodate Islamists, and then ride on the coat tails of their popular appeal had backfired. Instead of garnering support and creating stability for the elites, these efforts had merely given rise to Islamic spaces where the Islamists' critical discourse could be developed and propagated, and where the regime was powerless to stop them. Moreover, the system as a whole was tightly controlled by the military, which, in the late 1970s and early 1980s, was able to obstruct any efforts by the political leadership that it deemed too inclusive. To the more militant within the Islamist circles, the military's position as a bulwark against meaningful reform indicated the regime's inherent despotism, which could only be confronted and defeated through violence. Most prominent among those who had subscribed to this reading was Mustapha Boyali, a former FLN veteran who developed an idiosyncratic Islamist position, centering on a defiant and harsh criticism of the Algerian regime, especially its socialist leanings and corruption. In 1982, he provoked the state's ever-vigilant intelligence services to the extent that he had to become a fugitive in the mountains. From there he organized a militia, the *Mouvement Islamist Algerien Armée* (MIAA), and launched an armed campaign against the regime, but was killed in an ambush set by the security forces in April 1987. Boyali's death provoked an outrage that – in conjunction with the social unrest that erupted in Algeria in 1987 and 1988 – convinced the more accommodationist circles within the regime, headed by President Chadli Benjedi, to consider greater inclusiveness as a means of accommodating the political opposition. As a result, Benjedi amended the constitution in 1988, allowing for political pluralism and arranging for municipal and parliamentary elections.

When the FIS, in February 1989, was announced as an official political party, this took place partly as a result of the president's ambition to co-opt the Islamists into the system. As Heristchi (2004: 113) notes, it was "the growing crises in the legitimacy of the state that proved to be Islamism's greatest ally, and Chadli's lack of charisma and poor economic performance compounded by growing economic inequalities stemming from clientist networks, rapid demographic growth and accusations of widespread corruption." Hence Benjedi hoped to benefit from the legitimacy generated by the Islamists' presence in parliament while relying on the strong presidential prerogatives granted to him by the constitution (for instance, the president appoints the ministers of the cabinet, to be approved by the assembly). In addition, his accommodation of the FIS stemmed from his ambitions to seek a new powerbase within the regime and the FLN itself. While the FIS leadership welcomed cooperation with Benjedi, it would also, paradoxically, cultivate its own most assertive and radical discourse during this time, drawing on the militant legacy of FLN's struggle against the French. Indeed, its acronym, FIS, was a semantic play (ironically in French) with political connotations, alluding to the French word 'son,' which signified that the movement considered itself to be the 'heir' to (or the 'son' of) a struggle for independence that the FLN was considered to have betrayed.

More populist than intellectual, the ambition of the FIS was to unify the diverse creeds of Islamists in Algeria for the sake of bringing down the regime by the ballot. As such, the central messages of the FIS remained rather general, sometimes confusing, oscillating between the 'rejectionist' discourse of leaders such as Belhadj, and the decidedly more moderate voices of 'accommodationist' leaders such as Madani. According to Roberts (2004: 456), this parallel or dual message resembled FLN's position during the war against the French, when the movement claimed to represent ultimate truth and an absolutely just cause while at the same time leaving room for maneuver and negotiations. The broadness within the FIS also appealed to a broader range of constituencies. Belhadj's uncompromising militancy offered hope to the urban poor who desperately longed for radical change, and his blood curdling threats against corrupt elements within the military and the political elites appealed to those who thought that the regime was beyond redemption. The FIS leadership appeared startlingly bold and brave, thus gaining vast popularity among the marginalized and dispossessed more generally. Taken together, the components of the FIS were able to generate an image of strength and popular depth, and even a sense of invincibility. The FIS' derisive statements against democracy should also be understood, Roberts (2004: 456–7) suggests, as a discourse directed at the country's well-to-do Westernized middle classes, long despised by the *mustadh'afun* (deprived), and as rhetorical efforts to maintain domination over the multitude of Islamist tendencies within the FIS. Moreover, and importantly, the FIS' uncompromising rhetoric dovetailed with Algeria's post-colonial identity marker known as 'unanimism.' Steeped in the legacy of the FLN, unanimism expressed a larger project, a grander struggle demanding the unity of rank and file. That legacy – of struggling for national dignity, independence, and socio-economic betterment – was alive and well in Algeria even though the FLN, as FIS tirelessly claimed, had made a mockery out of it. Heristchi (2004: 127) argues that the Islamists' strategy was to capture the "liberational themes which had underpinned the independence war" and by making use of "essentially the same political discourse as the FLN during and directly after the independence struggle, the FIS aimed at making the regime appear like a moral impostor that had perverted the values of the revolution." In addition to laying claim to this well-established Algerian political discourse, the FIS also delivered on its rhetoric of social pathos and commitment as promised by Islam. Like many other Islamist movements, it cultivated local constituencies through a range of well-organized social welfare services in areas where the state conspicuously failed to meet its obligations to the citizenry. One Algerian female activist explained the popular enthusiasm for the FIS by suggesting that they

> came onto a completely empty field. You had a society that was morose, mired in a kind of lassitude, where people were completely burned out, in despair – and they suggested something. In the electoral campaign, the FIS brought up questions of honesty, of justice. The FLN had a program: housing, work, education. But the FIS said: we won't promise you anything. We'll have a state where we apply Islam, where honesty and justice will reign. And if there's no corruption, there'll be money. If there's justice, there'll be an equitable distribution of housing, and so on. It's a moral contract, not an electoral program. (Bekkar 1997: 290)

This, then, is how to contextualize accusations that the FIS never was able to move beyond the sloganeering of 'Islam is the answer.' The landslide victory of the FIS in the municipal elections of June 1990 stunned the Algerian government and many of those dreading the rise of the FIS, as the party received 54.3 percent of municipal seats (853/1539) and 57.4 percent of *wilaya* (regional) seats (31/48). In a sobering contrast, the FLN received a mere 28.1 percent of the municipal seats and 27.5 percent of *wilaya* seats (Heristchi 2004: 117). From that moment, the regime abandoned its condescending attitude towards the FIS and began to engage it in earnest by a combination of measures for containment and co-optation. In the spring of 1991 it altered the electoral law in order to undermine support for the Islamists, who reacted by calling for a general strike in protest against these measures, which in turn lead to unrest, arrests, and further polarization.

Yet in the parliamentary elections in December 1991, the FIS yet again confounded the regime by claiming victory in the first round of the elections. The movement won 47.3 percent of the votes (231/430 seats in parliament), compared to the FLN's 23.4 percent (Heristchi 2004: 117). This was a tremendous embarrassment for the regime, and especially for Benjedi's strategy of co-opting the Islamist through inclusion. Hence, the army, the real power centre of the regime, 'convinced' Benjedi to step down, after which the generals cancelled the second round of national elections and formed a transitional government, the State High Commission (*Haut Comité d'Etat*, HCE) over which they were in complete control. After the abortion of the election process, the FIS leadership appealed for calm and patience among its furious followers, demanding a constitutional process to restart the second round of the ballot vote. But the centers of power were not interested. The FIS was subsequently banned, its leadership imprisoned and thousands of its cadres were taken off to concentration camps deep in the Saharan desert. While Western terrorism experts and neo-Orientalists may be able to extrapolate from the Algerian elections the lesson that Islamism is incompatible with democracy, the FIS electorate learned that it was the pro-Western elites and the entrenched neo-colonial interests that they serve and enforce, that are incompatible with a popular vote.

As the country subsequently slid into open armed conflict, the regime, just like the Islamists, comprised conflicting centers with conflicting approaches. Some, the so-called *conciliateurs* ('conciliators'), favored some kind of negotiations, while others, the *eradicateurs* ('eradicators'), stressed the need for total confrontation and elimination of the Islamists. As Willis (1996: 245–7) notes, the military leadership had no interest in accommodating or giving legitimacy to the Islamists – however willing to reach a compromise competing centers within the regime might have been – since accommodation would likely entail the military's own gradually diminishing importance and perhaps even its extinction. This rift was mirrored among the Islamists, where the hardliners understood accommodation with the regime as threatening their own position within the broad unanimist spectrum constructed by the FIS. The assassination in June 1992 of President Mohammed Boudiaf, a former veteran of the FLN who had returned to Algeria after decades in exile to restore the authority of the state, suggested that the country was in for a protracted confrontation. Some observers suspect that the infamous Algerian Department of Intelligence and Security (*Département du Renseignement et de la Sécurité*, DRS), was involved in the assassination, since, by going after corruption, Boudiaf had shown that he would not be 'tamed' by the security establishment (Evans and Phillips 2007: 177–81). Even as the *eradicateurs* sought to control the regime's strategy for dealing with the opposition – which was rapidly turning into a counter-insurgency effort – the Islamists' response turned out to be equally callous and brutal. With the moderate leadership imprisoned, younger and angrier Islamist cadres were susceptible to join the militant organizations that had long eschewed accommodation and derided the political processes of inclusion. To them, the lesson and legacy of the martyred Mustapha Boyali – that there could be no alternative to armed confrontation – came across as an essential truth and served as a vehicle for pent up rage and frustration directed against the regime.

The extremely militant and violent Groupe Islamique Armi (GIA) emerged out of the debris of this collapsed political process, drawing on burgeoning sentiments of vengeance. Among its initial leading figures was Mansour Meliani, a former comrade-in-arms of Mustapha Boyali. He had broken away from the MIAA and the leadership of Abdelkader Chebouti – also a close associate to Boyali – after rivalries over leadership. In early 1992, Meliani attempted to gather his armed cells as the election process broke down, but was arrested in July 1992. In January the following year, the GIA group was resurrected by Abdelhak Layada, whose ambition was to form and head a unified command that included all of the country's armed groups (Willis 1996: 280–1). Moreover, the rise of the GIA was connected not only to domestic resentment and anger against the regime, but also to the regional geopolitical situation. The backbone of the GIA would be formed by the groups of so-called Afghans; Algerians who had gained significant combat experience while fighting the Russians in Afghanistan and who, as they returned home, brought with them a more rejectionist and exclusionary brand of Salafi 'jihadism.' This position contrasted sharply against the more accommodating *Jazari* posture within the erst-while FIS leadership. To the GIA, it was evident that armed struggle was the only way to defeat a corrupt regime and erect an Islamic state and establish order. While this perception may well be ascribed to the experi-ences and aptitude for violence of the GIA leadership, it was also, as a matter of fact, a correct analysis of the situation: the supposed guard-ians of Algerian democracy stood as guarantors that there would be no peaceful social change in Algeria.

In December 1992, Layada charged: "We reject the religion of democracy. We affirm that political pluralism is equal to sedition. It has never been our intention to participate in elections or enter parliament. Besides, the right to legislate belongs solely to God" (Willis 1996: 282). The persistent motto reiterated by the GIA was, "no agreement, no truce, no dialogue" (Kepel 2003: 266). In its heyday, the GIA was carving out enclaves within Algiers virtually unopposed, imposing Islamic 'standards' in the neighborhoods. Evans and Phillips (2007: 187) point out that in Blida, for instance, residents received orders to disconnect satellite dishes that broad-cast Western films,women were banned from consulting male physicians, shops selling alcohol, videos, and rai music were shut down, women-only bathhouses and hair-dressers were closed, while butchers who overcharged during the month of Ramadan were threatened with execution. The GIA rarely referred to Algeria as a legitimate entity. Instead, its discourse, also in contrast to the FIS, entailed a vision of a wider Islamic polity, in stark contrast to the Algerian reality. Layada would lament the "collapse of the Caliphate" as the "great tragedy of the Muslim community" since it meant that the Islamic community was "living an abnormal and disharmonious life due to the separation between its high values, ideals and principles in which it believes and the pagan (*jahili*) reality imposed upon it" (Hafez 2004: 49). This sort of rhetoric had previously been marginal and largely foreign to Algerian Islamism. Perhaps such abstract Manichean idealism could be afforded by a movement whose main strategic priority appeared to be violence and vengeance; its mission was more about breaking down an order than establishing one. Put differently, in terms of a Fanonian per-spective: the very process of violent destruction was also a self-asserting remedy for structurally imposed inferiority. Indeed, in the early stages of confrontation, the GIA was remarkably successful in fighting the state as it concentrated its operations against the police forces and regime officials. Willis (1996: 186–8) describes how the regime's inability to stop the GIA' daily attacks gave the group "a religious aura in the eyes of the poor and the young" and points out that its "mystique" derived from its apparent ability to hit whenever and wherever it chose. Beyond the 'mystique,' GIS operations were effective. By the summer of 1993, several police officers were killed every day, resulting in plummeting morale, compromised chains of command and weakened accountability.

The strength of the GIA was the same local embeddedness that had once been the FLN's strength in the struggle against the French. The GIA was taking over urban neighborhoods where its young militants had grown up and where they knew every nook and cranny. Similarly in the mountains, militant guerrillas established their own districts each ruled by an emir, into which the army could enter only at its own peril, subject to ambushes, sniper fire and roadside bombs. Indeed, Evans and Phillips (2007: 189) also attribute the mounting violence to a "curiously strong echo of Frantz Fanon" since it in many ways involved an "assertion of power," in addition to the perception that only violence could bring down the regime. Members of the armed cells realized that "they had the capacity to invert traditional relationships and inspire fear in the regime" which they, in and of itself, found liberating.

> Through bloodshed these young men felt a surge of energy. By killing, they were telling the regime that they, the dispossessed, could no longer be kept in a state of subjugation. The product of rage, rejection and injustice, theirs was a mirror violence, a reply to a regime that had lied, swindled and bullied. It was also a transformative violence. They were standing up and giving vent to their pent-up frustration...In explicitly targeting the men who had hitherto humiliated them on a day-to-day basis they were enjoying the satisfaction of revenge. (Evans and Phillips 2007: 189)

The regime was deeply shaken in these early phases of battle, and it established a counter-terrorist unit consisting of 15,000 troops, which went on to apply extremely heavy-handed measures to suppress the Islamist insurgence. The violence turned more gruesome. One group within the GIA was designated specifically for killing Algerian secular intellectuals, whom the organization considered as representatives of the country's colonial legacy, and whose 'foreign' influences, they argued, corrupted the Algerian potential for submitting to pure Islamic faith. Sid Ahmed Mourad, who took over the leadership after the arrest of Layada, declared in November 1993 that "the journalists who fight against Islam through the pen will perish by the sword" (Willis 1996: 285). The GIA sought to underline the marginality and minority status of the francophone middle class by intimidation and murder. Living in relative luxury, socially and politically cordoned off from the Arabic speaking population, they had enjoyed significant political influence but did not, according to the GIA, represent anyone but themselves. By making the case that the francophone middle class intellectuals were merely regime apologists, the GIA gave its fighters "a feeling of absolute righteousness and allowed them to express their most basic feelings of class hatred" (Evans and Phillips 2007: 191). The FIS was at first grappling uncomfortably with the popular challenge from the GIA and its spokesmen approved some of its attacks against government institutions, but often also condemned attacks against civilians. A watershed event, however, occurred as two prominent FIS leaders, Mohammed Said and Abderrezzak Redjam, changed sides and joined the GIA in May 1994. This was especially significant as Said was known ideologically as a *jazari*, having argued against the polarizing militant positions of the Salafi-jihadi dominated GIA. Some saw this move as seriously weakening the prospects for reconciliation, while others viewed their changing of sides as a strategic maneuver intended to transform the GIA from within and temper its extremely confrontational positions (International Crisis Group [ICG] 2004: 11–13). Simultaneously, in July 1994, the *Armée Islamique du Salute* (AIS) was formed as an armed group affiliated with the FIS. The AIS position was that of the FIS – that armed struggle should be a means to oblige the regime to accept a compromise solution and begin a process of national reconciliation – and was a way for the FIS to compete with the GIA on the GIA's own terms. "We don't have any relations with the GIA because this group is only pursuing the military option," Rabah Kebir, a FIS representative claimed. "They alone are responsible for what they are doing in Algeria" (Willis 1996: 352).

Beyond the mechanics of the struggle, what were the reasons underlying the extreme militancy of the GIA? Hafez (2004: 43) suggests that the group's exclusionary ideological position was able to reap support because it was sown in a climate of "indiscriminate repression" which in turn created a general "environment of brutality and injustice that gives insurgents a shared sense of victimization and legitimacy, which in turn can be used to justify unspeakable acts of terror." He furthermore notes that such an environment affects the internal dynamics of a group through what he refers to as "spirals of encapsulation": groups in a repressive environment suffer from a lack of alternative sources of information, as well as an absence of internal debate. As a consequence, members rely solely on other members for evaluation and increasingly "lose touch with reality" as they ever-more fervently reject the perspectives of non-members.

In such conditions, self-criticism threatens to undermine the very perceptions and theoretical foundations that provide the reason for in-group
coherence and unity, and the struggle and actions of members will rely on
emotive appeals and abstract ideals of retribution and justice. According
to Jason Burke (2004: 205), the events in Algeria conformed to a more
general pattern whereby a more moderate, domestically oriented political
Islamism, "older both ideologically and in the factual age of its cadres,"
came to be supplanted by "a newer, younger (in both senses), international-
ized, more violent Jihadi Salafism." Burke downplays, however, the suggestion of a connection between the GIA and al-Qa'ida, alleged by the Algerian
security services. Rather, he argues, some GIA fighters claim that the movement sought financial assistance from bin Laden in the early days "but
were unhappy with the degree of ideological and operational control that
the Saudi demanded as a condition for any aid" (Burke 2004: 206).

Internal group dynamics and organizational requirements notwithstanding, the vicious cycles of violence and escalating extremism of the GIA
would soon weaken the movement's popular support. There were, for
instance, increasing accusations and rumors that the organization had been
infiltrated by the DRS and that certain local commanders had been
'turned.' Indeed, it was even claimed that some of the more gruesome
and spectacular attacks against civilian Algerians were either manipulated
or directly undertaken by the security services (Evans and Phillips 2007:
240–5; Fisk 2007: 717–19). In addition, the GIA was losing support in many
of the areas where its local commanders, the 'emirs,' had imposed their
authority, which often took place at gunpoint. Between June 1990 and April
1992, the FIS had managed municipal affairs with great care for the local
population as its officials were drawn from the devout middle class and the
intellectuals. Kepel (2003: 262) notes that they "implemented a populist
policy intended to satisfy the social demands of the impoverished urban
young," meaning that they actively opposed corruption and crime and
sought to raise the moral standards among the population. However, when
FIS disintegrated and many of its members were transported to faraway
prison camps in the desert, the younger leaders went on to make a tragic
travesty of local rule by turning Islamic taxes into mere extortion rackets,
often ending up fighting each other over the people's contributions. At the
same time, the army laid down sieges on neighborhoods and villages
that effectively transformed them into ghettoes (Kepel 2003: 263). In addition to the discouraging effect of the relentless and increasingly indiscriminate cycles of violence, ordinary people thus became fed up with this
younger generation of militant Islamists. Unlike their more seasoned and

older colleagues, these young men had no claim to social status and authority other than the force of their arms, and behaved like simple thugs. Far
from freedom fighters or genuine reformers, they exposed themselves as
the leaders of gangs within ghettoes, seeking to profit from their positions
of power, rather than working to ease the people's suffering.

The mid-1990s witnessed the end to a wider armed struggle in Algeria.
By late 1994, even many local emirs within the GIA claimed that the organization was infiltrated by the security services and distanced themselves
from it (ICG 2004: 14). Djamel Zitouni, an exceptionally zealous young
leader who took charge of the GIA in October 1994, was also suspected of
serving the interests of the hard liners within the DRS (Kepel 2003: 206).
While there is little doubt that the Algerian security services in one way or
another were able to infiltrate the Islamist movements, it is more difficult
– and definitely beyond the scope of this chapter – to ascertain the nature
and extent of these efforts. Yet, whatever the case, one may conclude that
the extremism and indiscriminate acts of violence of the GIA served the
interests of the hard liners within the Algerian state, rather than the accommodationist elements on either side. According to Hughes (1994: 436),
Algeria's predicament lies foremost in the fact that the executive dominates
the legislative and the judiciary, and that this executive branch, ever since
the victory against the French in the war of independence, has been dominated by the military. As a consequence, the hard liners of the military have
persistently denied Algerian institutions the possibility of gradual evolution
towards a common national platform with a pluralist identity in which
diverse affiliations are able to coexist in mutual acceptance. Instead, ever
since Algeria's independence, the Algerian political and social fabric has
generated and entrenched and incompatible identities and positions, and
this development has been overseen by the military, which has also been its
primary beneficiary. As opposition politics devolved into an insurgency and
the country moved into a state of civil war, the absence of the very possibility of reconciliation meant that the leadership of the Algerian army and
security services would not be held to account on charges of corruption and
misconduct that had spanned decades. Additionally, tensions, insecurities
and outbreaks of violence further bolstered their position since these
matters required increased budgets as well as sociopolitical control in order
to guarantee the country's 'security arrangement.'

Not just the military, but Algeria's power structures and the elites as a
whole benefitted from the country's deterioration. François Burgat (2003:
107) has pointed out that the "the most gratuitous of the assassinations
and the most sordid of the operations and claims of responsibility actually

proved to be extremely beneficial to the regime, whose international legitimacy grew in proportion to Western disgust at the barbarism of the methods employed by, or attributed to, its political challengers." Firstly, the *eradicateurs* within the Algerian system were able to construct a narrative that revolved around 'evil terrorists' to whom reconciliation and accommodation were entirely foreign; indeed, for the GIA there was no other solution than total war. In that sense, while the hardliners on both sides mirrored each other in unyieldingness, it was nevertheless a battle that the hardened security forces of the regime – given sufficient military and financial resources – was virtually guaranteed to be on top of, at least in the long run. Secondly, the savage attacks of the GIA and its extremist political outlook generated international backing for the Algerian state, which was understood as standing in the frontline in the struggle against 'Islamic terrorism.' The hard liners within the regime would not lose a moment in making that point in their international marketing campaign. In early 1995, for instance, several of the most prominent and important Algerian parties, including the FIS, convened in Rome and agreed to the so-called Rome Accords, which provided an outline for a process of national reconciliation. The accords called for investigations into the ongoing violence in Algeria and the resurrection of a constitutional process in order to arrange for elections according to a pluralist and democratic framework. The regime, however, refused to attend the meeting and ultimately rejected the accords on the grounds that they did not condemn terrorism but instead granted political legitimacy to those responsible for the terror, by which they meant the FIS. While the international community – including Washington and Paris – initially viewed the accords favorably, no one thought it proper to twist the arm of the Algerian regime, and the accords never implemented. In the summer of 1995, a local imam at a Paris mosque, Sheikh Abdelsaki Sahraoui, a prominent figure within the FIS and a contact person between his organization and the French government, was assassinated, which was followed by a number of bomb attacks in the Paris metro. All acts were attributed to the GIA. In this environment it became impossible for the French government to continue dialog and cooperation with Islamists – even though the first victim of the string of attacks in Paris was their FIS interlocutor – and Paris instead chose full cooperation with the Algerian regime in its 'war on terror.'

Meanwhile, the GIA under Zitouni's command, would purge its own ranks of those considered 'unreliable.' In December 1994, the ex-FIS members Mohammed Said and Abderrezzak Redjam, along with several hundred other members of the GIA, were executed by Zitouni's men, accused of trying to transform the organization towards a more accom-modationist position (ICG 2004: 13). Zitouni also released a pamphlet in which he declared that the GIA adopted the Salafi tradition and that members should 'repent' in case of earlier affiliations with the FIS or other Islamist or secular organizations. Anyone attempting to leave the GIA would be condemned to death (Hafez 2004: 47–8). In November 1995, Zitouni declared Algerian society in its entirety as *takfir*, having abandoned Islam. In January 1996, he declared war against the AIS when the FIS refused to abandon its demand to resurrect the electoral process, and in June that year the guerrillas of the AIS responded by killing him in a gun battle. His successor, Antar Zouabri, was equally, if not more extreme in his positions. He reiterated the verdict that Algerian society was *takfir* and went on to perpetrate some of the most gruesome massacres of the entire civil war.

As ordinary Algerians responded to these excesses in violence by turning away in disgust, the AIS halted its armed struggle and negotiated a truce with the military establishment in 1997. The regime thus triumphed since it had to make none of the political concessions that had been the standing demand of the AIS during its armed struggle. Most importantly, there was no political recognition of the FIS. In short, the armed struggle of the Algerian Islamists ended in failure and political marginalization, as well as severe internal divisions and hostilities. The popular mobilization and hopes that the FIS had generated some years before lay in tatters. The population was fatigued and therefore welcomed the presidency of Abdelaziz Bouteflika in April 1999, who was also approved by the military leadership. With Bouteflika a process of amnesty was initiated for those members of militant Islamist groups who decided to lay down their arms, although members of the GIA's successor groups – the *Groupe Salafiste pour la Prédication et le Combat* (GSPC) and the *Houmat Daawa Salafia* (HDS) – were not offered such amnesty. Bouteflika further improved relations with the outside world, although the regime had enjoyed grudging but solid international backing ever since its decision to cancel the election process in early 1992. As Francesco Cavatorta (2009: 139) notes about the French position, "while officially worried about the 'abnormality' of the actions the generals undertook, Mitterrand had already given the green light to the coup and French politicians, from both left and right, publicly expressed their support for the coup."

The range of anxieties surrounding the FIS victory must be qualified and problematized. While there is no reason to doubt the fear among secular democrats in Algeria, the apprehensions of the international community, as Cavatorta notes, were different; especially those of the Western powers. To them, democracy as such was not a top priority. After all, Western countries have long been aligned with a range of dictatorships, not least of which is the profoundly repressive regime in Saudi Arabia. Rather, in Algeria, the FIS posed a challenge to the new order envisaged by Western policy makers and their intellectual mentors in the early 1990s; the post-Cold War triumph of secular, liberal democracy in and for the West, and the neo-colonial order it required in and of the Third World. Western governments, primarily France and the US, were also deeply concerned with the FIS' assertive support for Saddam Hussein in the Gulf war, and did not take lightly the movement's support for the Palestinian cause, all of which evoked a third worldist sense of defiance. In addition, Western allies in northern Africa, such as Morocco and Tunisia, were no less apprehensive of what an Islamist-oriented Algerian regime might augur for their own assertive Islamist opposition forces. In short, ever since its abortion of the democratic process, the Algerian regime has been able to convey an image of itself as confronting the evil seed of Islamism at home while deepening its ties with the EU and the US in the formation of the post-Cold War order.

In this regard, the primary ambition of Western and local elites seems to have been the fostering of the transnational integration of open markets and flow of capital, rather than the cultivation of viable democratic institutions. Indeed, the political order taking form in Algeria – and in the Sahel more generally – has been predicated with security and stability and its main purpose has been to provide a protective shield to this economic cooperation (Hill 2009: 39–56). In 1994, Algeria was invited as a partner in the NATO-led Mediterranean Dialogue (although it did not join until 2000), which comprised the US-aligned Arab governments of North Africa, plus Israel and Jordan. The invitation suggests that the regime in Algiers was considered a close ally of the existing order, and that the linchpin of its relationship with the West was shared concern for security and stability. This concern had direct and significant domestic impact. Cavatorta suggests that, since the abortion of the 1992 elections, the regime has been able to benefit from increases in development, military and other financial forms of aid, which has allowed it to consolidate stability, rather than move towards democracy. Both state and non-state actors, he argues, have contributed to the regime's financial solvency and, "crucially, to the setting-up of a 'liberal' economy, which would benefit foreign investors and a number of pro-regime businessmen" (Cavatorta 2009: 151). As long as the regime satisfied the requirements of the international community – supplying the global economy with a steady flow of oil and gas and secure the International Monetary Fund (IMF) outline of budget balances, privatization, and foreign investment – it would receive considerable leeway to handle its internal affairs. The more uncompromising circles within the regime, who feared a pending struggle for survival if reforms of any type were implemented, were thus able to impose repressive measures against the opposition without having to be overly concerned about objections from the international community. This persistent failure of the international community to commit the Algerian regime to serious investigations and political reforms, even as it suggested rhetorically that it would, is a result of Algeria's disciplined dedication to abide by the canons of a prospering economic order of integration in the region; of the willingness of the Algerian regime to abide by the Structural Adjustment Programs outlined by the IMF and the World Bank, rather than committing to meaningful political reform. This is suggested by, among other things, the EU granting Algeria membership of the Barcelona process and the Euro-Mediterranean Partnership in 1995, and EU's generous financial assistance to Algeria throughout the 1990s. In addition, whereas the Algerian regime began to reform its economy already in the 1980s and enacted the Petrol Code in 1990, which opened up its lucrative hydrocarbon market to outside investors, this economic reform process deepened significantly in the mid-1990s. The main objectives of the IMF and World Bank was to see to it that Algeria's economy conformed with the neo-liberal principles of low inflation, stable exchange rates, a balanced budget, and reduced public spending which they considered "essential to revive growth" (Hill 2009: 516). Despite a few deficiencies, the IMF was content with Algeria's performance in the 1990s, and as Cavatorta (2009: 159) notes, amid these outlines of economic reforms, it is "interesting to note that there was no mention of democracy and democratization."

As is often the case with such austerity programs, livings standards declined among ordinary Algerians, in parallel with perceptions of the legitimacy of the regime. As the process of economic reforms generated funds and international backing for the regime, it enabled it to cling to power by imposing a stability that relied on heavy 'security measures.' Ironically, the cut backs in state expenditure and decreased standards of living – including diminishing state subsidies and escalating unemployment – enabled the growth of an informal economy in which militant groups were able to gain a foothold and thrive, and replenish its ranks from a steady stream of angry men.

8

Western Europe: Islamism as Mirror Image

Islamism in Europe today cannot be comprehended without two conceptually distinct, yet very much intertwined inquiries: into the structural situation of Muslim communities in Europe on the one hand, and into the motivational injects into these communities by Islamist groups and movements located in or based beyond Europe's borders on the other. That is, we need to look at the sociopolitical reasons why significant numbers of permanently resident second- and third-generation Muslim Europeans are discontented and disaffected, and at the tactical-strategic targeting of these individuals by Islamist organizations seeking to capitalize on discontent. At this intersection of an essentially European immigrant phenomenon and an essentially extra-European effort to exert influence, neither aspect is primarily about Islam's 'core' or 'essence,' which in the European context constitutes a dangerous myth. Nor are they primarily about the specific groups and attacks that have grabbed so much attention in the past decade, which are epiphenomenal to understanding the dynamic. Rather, Islamism in Europe, like Islamism elsewhere, is first and foremost a matter of generic human efforts to reconstruct and affirm collective identities in a context of social and cultural marginalization.

Despite the fact that the crushing majority of the European Union's seventeen million Muslims have never been involved in any kind of violence and are loyal citizens of the countries in which they reside, and despite the fact that most Muslim preachers and community organizers in Europe reject violence and terrorism, the 'Muslim question' in the public square has come to be framed primarily in terms of cultural incompatibility and terrorism. In Western Europe in the post-9/11 period, Islamist terrorism has been negligible compared to the number of attacks from other types of groups. In 2007, Europol member countries experienced two "failed, foiled or successful" Islamist attacks, none in 2008, and a single attack in 2009. This may be compared to 532 nationalist-separatist attacks in 2007, 397 in 2008 and 237 in 2009, or the leftist attacks that in those three years numbered 21, 28, and 40, respectively (Europol 2010: 50). National guidelines for reporting terrorism related incidents to EUROPOL vary to the extent that these figures can only be considered approximate, and the Islamist plots that have come to the attention of authorities have tended to aim for greater casualties than those hatched by other types of groups. Moreover, the major Islamist attacks that have taken place have been highly significant, politically as well as in terms of casualties and media coverage. It is important to note, however, that over the last few decades, Europe has experienced far more acts of violence and far worse protracted carnage at the hands of various ethno-nationalist sub-state groups such as the Irish Republican Army (IRA), the Basque *Euskadi ta Askatasuna* (ETA), and the Corsican *Fronte di Liberazione Naziunale Corsu* (FLNC). Yet these sustained campaigns of violence have not given rise to claims that Irish and Basque culture or 'Corsican values' are somehow incompatible with European standards and norms. In fact, it is known that neither their means, nor their ends, are representative of the entire populations in whose names these groups struggle. The violence perpetrated by Islamists, however, has elicited exactly opposite responses. Whether among populist politicians, the media or in the 'blogosphere,' the debate about 'homegrown terrorism' feeds into "the occasionally hysterical discussion about the presence of Islam in Western societies," has fuelled Islamophobia, and "amplified an atmosphere of distrust" in which a majority of Muslims simply do not recognize themselves, and feel maligned and excluded (Laurence and Strum 2008: 8). Thus, the militant radicals that emerge from the fulcrum of disaffection and radicalization have been allowed to frame the debate about the entire Muslim presence in Europe, which in turn creates further intergroup separation in a downward spiral of mutual prejudice and friction.

One obvious reason that IRA or FLNC violence does not raise question marks around the compatibility of Irish or Corsican, and European values is that these nationalities are part of the European ingroup. Ingroup vision enables a greater recognition of nuances and aberrations than tends to be exercised when one examines an outgroup, especially one that is perceived as threatening (Moghaddam 2008b: 93). The equally obvious corollary of this blurred vision is that Europe's Muslim communities are indeed conceptualized – repeatedly and publicly – as an outgroup; an alien and threatening presence. The widespread use of the term 'homegrown terrorism' for violence perpetrated by European Muslims, but 'domestic terrorism' for the violence of Irish or Basque groups, makes it clear: the latter belongs, the former is a fifth column.

Research suggests that negative perceptions of the Other on both sides are not correlated to personal negative encounters. In a 2006 poll, 51 percent of Muslim immigrants in Germany said that Europeans are hostile to Muslims, but only 19 percent reported a "bad personal experience." In some other countries, the numbers tracked more closely, in others they did not. In France, for instance, 39 percent believed Europeans to be hostile and 37 percent reported bad personal experiences, while in the United Kingdom, those figure were 42 and 28 percent respectively. This suggests the creation of stereotypical, identity-based group narratives that center, but are not dependent on actual experience of the outgroup (Pew Research Center 2006).

The relationship between the European and Islamic cultural spheres has, for over a millennium, contained much adversity and mutual suspicion. The historian Herodotus referred to Europe as a geographic region already in the fifth century BC, but in response the emergence of Islam and the papacy's burgeoning controversy with Byzantine Christianity, Europe began to be thought of as 'the sphere of Latin Christendom.' While its precise geographic boundaries as well as its cultural and political substance have changed over the centuries, this foundational exclusion of the Oriental Other has remained at the heart of the European *esprit*. As Edward Said (1979: 3) noted, "European culture gained in strength and identity by setting itself off against the Orient as a sort of surrogate and even underground self." To be sure, there has also been much positive cross-cultural exchange – ranging from philosophy and military strategy to the culinary arts and fashion – and enmity has been far less cohesive than traditional historians have tended to admit. Yet in the creation of European and Islamic cultural and political narratives, the meetings of minds have tended to be overshadowed the clashes of armies, and the most enduring cognitive impact on both sides seems to have been exerted by episodes such as the expansion of Islam into Christian areas, the crusades, the battle between Christians and Moors in the Iberian Peninsula, the incorporation of the Balkans into the Ottoman Empire, the siege on Vienna, and so forth. This is not in itself odd, since the creation of narratives about oneself and one's ingroup invariably rely, to some extent, on comparisons with outgroups; a tendency that is exaggerated in national historiographies specifically intended to galvanize ingroup solidarity, cohesion, and sense of mission.

Thus, the development of ideas about what it means to be European has in some measure been predicated on ideas about what it means to not be Muslim, and anxieties about Islam in general predate and give depth and context to current anxieties about Islamism and Islamic terrorism specifically. Thus the construction of Europe's dominant historical narratives, rather than the reality on which they are based, have contributed to what Justin Vaisse (2008: 1) refers to as the "popular myth" that "Muslims in Europe are, in one way or the other, inherently foreign, the equivalent of visiting Middle-Easterners who are alien to the 'native' culture." One of the clearest examples of this is the popular concern with European Muslim demographics. It has spawned a multitude of books and articles that extrapolate from the idea that high Muslim fertility rates threaten to drown out the less procreative natives, and thereby ultimately destroy European culture. The very notion that the fertility of European Muslims is a threat illustrates a view of Muslims as an alien and dangerous presence; 'demographic concerns' simply do not emerge other than as a response to the presence of racial or cultural undesirables. In addition, it is statistical nonsense. The implicit underlying assumption is that Muslims form a distinct and rigidly bounded demographic block defined solely by religion; a block that is incapable of change and will therefore never blend into the rest of society. Yet cultures and faiths do not function like that, and the significant rates of intermarriage, conversions (both to and from Islam), and the reality of integration contradict such assumptions, as does a larger view of the evolution and integration of cultures more generally (Westoff and Frejka 2007). So, too, do the numbers: while European birthrates are generally low relative to those of non-European immigrants, the newcomers' birthrates fall rapidly after arrival and among subsequent generations, and tend to level out at national averages (Vaisse 2008: 2). It could be added that genetic biological ideas about how to maintain the health, balance, and vigor of Europe's cultural stock are steeped in a totalitarian and exclusionary intellectual heritage, which ought to worry Muslims and non-Muslims alike. However, this has not stopped authors and commentators – alarmist populists as well as serious scholars – from connecting the supposed incompatibility of European and Islamic culture to the birthrate issue, and constructing arguments about the looming 'erosion' or 'distortion' of Europe's authentic ideals, values and policy (Ye'or 2005; Bawer 2006).

Those who today point to essential cultural incompatibility tend to do so with reference to the monolithic and nebulous nature of Islam, and the challenge posed by the religious–political holism of Islam to Europe's secularized, post-Enlightenment state–church arrangements (Laurence and Strum 2008: 1, 9; Fetzer and Soper 2005: 9). As for European Islam as a monolith, this notion is clearly related to the European ingroup's inability to see differences and nuances in the Muslim outgroup, which is less a community than it is a collection of many communities divided along sectarian, linguistic, cultural and ethnic lines, as well as their being in the process of developing national differences depending on where in Europe they have become rooted. At the same time as the supposedly monolithic nature of Islam is a frightening Other to populist politicians and those they influence, the fragmented reality of these communities is used by government authorities across Europe as a way of "refusing to respond to Muslims' sociopolitical overtures" (Vertovek and Peach 1997: 30). The reality of Islamism in Europe is far more generic, but also far more complex, than meta-cultural arguments about essences and compatibilities. Rather, at the heart of the issue lies, on the European side, the desire to preserve a specific sociocultural heritage – be it religious or secular – viewing Muslims in general as a threat to social cohesion and cultural survival, and Islamism in particular as the spearhead of undesired social change. On the Muslim side we find the desire for socioeconomic equality of immigrant communities in the countries to which they have been admitted, and views of the dominant European cultural narrative as a bulwark against equality and therefore a threat against their own sociocultural cohesion and survival. None of this, however, hinges on some essential incompatibility of Europe and Islam. Instead, this dynamic is the outcome of generic patterns of intergroup relations between established hegemonic communities, on the one hand, and marginalized communities, on the other. These are patterns of competing or conflicting social identities, the narratives they create, the actions they lead to, and the political positions that develop around them.

Bhikhu Parekh (2008: 6) notes that although Muslim immigrants had begun arriving in Europe as guest workers from the 1950s onwards, "they were culturally invisible until the 1970s and politically invisible until the late 1980s." Once migratory patterns and the composition of the population changed from being primarily a migrant labor pool to primarily immigrants, refugees, and citizens, the attempts by Europe's Muslim communities to transmit their own identity and value systems to their children caused them "to press for appropriate provisions in workplaces, hospitals, etc. for themselves and especially for their women" (Parekh 2008: 7). Parekh also notes that the European states' understandings of themselves as nation-states based on a homogeneous national culture, on which earlier immigrants had made no similar demands, "led to tensions, court cases, public debates and protests" and, as a result, "Muslims now became an unmistakable *cultural* presence and a source of public anxiety" (Parekh 2008: 7). Different national models for dealing with the issue were developed, with France opting for assimilation, Britain for integration and the Netherlands for multiculturalism, with the rest of Europe adopting one or more of these models. Yet fundamental problems of belonging and attachment did not go away, because they were not adequately addressed. As Tahir Abbas (2007: 440) has noted about Muslim communities in the United Kingdom, they continued to experience "pernicious socio-economic and ethnocultural exclusion" due to a lack of "structural pre-conditions" capable of dealing with their cultural concerns and aspirations. This, he suggests, effectively prevents Muslims from having a real stake in society; from "becoming engaged citizens in the context of an ever-evolving national politico-cultural framework."

Without a firm sense of belonging in Europe, developments in their native countries, rather than their new countries of residence, remained a main point of reference for the Muslim communities' understanding of who they were. The Iranian revolution in 1979 and the Israeli invasion of Lebanon in 1982 were two formative events that contributed to a burgeoning process of politicization of Muslim identity, albeit in vastly different ways. In the former case, the revolution afforded them a vicarious sense of accomplishment (at least initially) as a Muslim nation rose to overthrow a repressive, Western-backed regime. In the latter case, it created a sense of exasperation as another Western-backed regime invaded a country with a majority Muslim population and effectively crippled it, with full impunity. Other events in the Muslim world that unfolded during the 1980s, with direct effect on many European Muslims' sense of self, and sense of how to relate to the perceived hostility of the Western nations that had admitted, but not accepted them, included the outbreak of the first intifada – the popular uprising in Palestine – and the mujahedin victory over the Soviet invaders in Afghanistan. If the 1980s demonstrated anything, it was that while peaceful coexistence gained Europe's Muslims very little social, cultural, and political headway, revolts, revolutions, and insurgencies in the Muslim world were recreating a new kind of non-subservient Muslim self; a self that forcefully made itself equal to the Westerner. To some, this was a powerful and attractive reaffirmation as the value of their own collective identity was being called into question.

It is important to note that Islamic fervor among European Muslims throughout the 1980s translated primarily into social and cultural movements, such as the *Tablighi Jemaat*, "an a-political, quietist movement of internal grassroots missionary renewal" (Metcalf 2001). Political fervor was still channeled into support for groups identified with national or ethnic struggles in their various countries of parental origin, such as the groups within the Palestinian national movement or the Kurdish *Parti Kerkerani Kurdistan* (PKK). One important addition to the menu of movements and causes of the 1970s was the international brigade of volunteers who joined together as Muslims to fight the Soviet invaders in Afghanistan. While volunteers from Europe were relatively few, the war in Afghanistan provided a new model for thinking about how to identify and mobilize. The portrayal of the *mujahedin* in Western news media and movies was one of nobility and heroism, and they were directly supported by Western European countries, as well as the United States – a far cry from portrayals and attitudes towards the 'traditional' struggles of the various ethnic and national movements.

For many European Muslims, however, the 1992–5 Bosnian War was the most impactful. It was an entirely European atrocity in which the indubitably European Muslims of Bosnia were subjected to ethnic cleansing and attempted genocide by fellow Europeans, primarily the Bosnian Serbs. To be sure, atrocities were carried out by all sides in the conflict, but according to the best-documented research to date, conducted by the Research and Documentation Center in Sarajevo, Bosnian Muslims constituted 83 percent of the war's circa 97,000 civilian casualties (Hoare 2008). Muslim refugees in large numbers poured into Western Europe, especially to Germany, directly impacting the awareness and fuelling the fears of a European Muslim population that had already begun reconstructing its fragmented sense of self and its place in Europe. The war in Bosnia constituted a watershed in terms of popular opinion among significant segments of European Muslims, towards Europe as well as the United States. Zeyno Baran (2004: 8) notes that, "even secular, non-political Muslims were furious about Western indifference to the mass killings of their co-religionists. While the United States (unlike major European countries) did finally come to the help of the Muslims, the damage to the US reputation had already been done." Perhaps not surprisingly, Bosnia was the first military campaign in which significant numbers of European Muslims volunteered to fight alongside their co-religionists. Importantly, it was also one of the first conflicts outside Central Asia and the Middle East into which the emergent al-Qa'ida injected financial assistance as well as training and leadership. Not only did contingents of Arab–Afghan veterans from the Gulf emirates and Jordan – who for various reasons were unable to return home – arrive to take up arms in Bosnia, but at war's end, in 1995, al-Qa'ida also began actively to recruit European Muslims and send them to training camps in Bosnia (Lia 2008: 107, 141).

The Bosnian War as a radicalization event – due both to conditions in Europe and motivational injects from al-Qa'ida – was part and parcel of a politicization process that had already gone on for about a decade. The pursuit of cultural rights by the first generation of Muslim immigrants to arrive in Europe and the resistance they encountered had been inherited by a new generation who had grown up in Europe. Less diffident than their parents, they also knew their way around the political system. Throughout the late 1980s, an emerging tendency was in evidence among this new generation towards positing Islam, rather than national or ethnic heritage as the primary determinant of identity. Vaisse (2008: 1) is certainly correct in noting that, "when it comes to Muslims, people wrongly assume that religion – rather than nationality, gender, social class, etc. – necessarily trumps other identities." Indeed, this common fallacy, an outstanding example of theologocentric reasoning, is the foundation of two of the most powerful misperceptions about Islam in Europe, namely that "being Muslim constitutes a fixed identity, sufficient to fully characterize a person" and that this cohesive and static identity, to quote a 2005 *Foreign Affairs* article, makes Europe's Muslims a "distinct, cohesive and bitter group" (Leiken 2005: 122). To argue that there was a tendency towards Islam as a primary source of identity is not to suggest that this identity was either simple, all-encompassing or static. Quite the contrary: this reconstructed identity was a response to complex social factors and therefore by its very nature not static. Nor does any type of self-identification encompass all European Muslims. For instance, Olivier Roy (2006: 117) has written about "dynamic and fluctuating subcultures" that emerge because "the Muslim population of foreign descent living in Europe displays tensions between five levels of identity." Without validating Roy's typology, it is worth noting that all of the "levels" that he posits are social identifications – that is, references to some larger group as a means of describing oneself – and one is what Roy calls "a Muslim identity based exclusively on religious patterns, with no reference to a specific culture and language" (Roy 2006: 117). It is this 'level' that became increasingly prominent beginning in the late 1980s, giving rise to Soroush's observation, quoted in an earlier chapter, that some Muslims are gradually coming to understand Islam as a source of identity rather than truth, "one of the greatest theoretical plagues in the Islamic world" (Soroush 2000: 34).

In addition to the reasons for this turn mentioned above, Parekh suggests that the reasons for the increased salience of Islam as identity among second-generation immigrants to Europe included their limited contacts with their parental homeland, rejection of parental constraints, and being embarrassed by aspects of their parental culture. Importantly, he goes on to note that, "since the wider society, too, had begun to refer to them as Muslims and associated negative ideas with the term, Muslim youth in the spirit of 'black is beautiful' asserted their Islamic identity with pride" (Parekh 2008: 8). This observation is of paramount importance. While Muslims fighters in Afghanistan were viewed as noble and heroic – that is, subject to positive stereotypes – Muslims in Europe were still laboring under overwhelmingly negative stereotypes. As discussed in chapter 3, social identity formation depends on knowledge of one's membership in a group, evaluation of the positive and negative aspects of that membership, and an emotional reaction. Fathali Moghaddam (2008b: 90) points out that the salience of any given group identity is contextual, and that the more 'distinctive in context' a characteristic is – such as being African-American in a predominantly White school – the more likely that characteristic is to be internalized and emphasized as a salient group identification. What took place among Muslim youths in Europe in the 1980s was thus neither new, nor specific to, nor dependent on some features essential to Islam; the very same, well documented dynamics had already given rise to, among others, the feminist movement and the black power movement, whereby a collective identity that served as reference point for discrimination was internalized and turned into a badge of honor around which to rally. Note the words of French Islamist author Farid Abdelkarim:

> Before going further, we are going to put an end to all the names that are used...to designate young people 'emerging from immigration.' Whether you are white, tanned or black, you have to reject slurs and pet names that put you in the category of 'we don't know who you are.' You are not a North African or an Arab...You are neither an Islamist or a fundamentalist...whether you apply the precepts of Islam or you are non-practising, if you do not renounce the faith in your heart, you are Muslim. Therefore, you are: a young Muslim. Respect starts here! With the way you see yourself, and who you want to be. Then you will be able to demand respect from the others. (Kepel 2004: 268–9)

This dynamic of increasing polarization between Muslim and 'native' European communities, and the concomitant politicization and 'purification' of Muslim identity, was fertile soil for radical Islamist organizations. One of the most prolific, Hizb al-Tahrir ('Liberation Party'), a radical Salafi movement, was founded in Jerusalem in 1953. It spread rapidly throughout the Muslim world, but made no inroads into Western Europe until 1986, when it was established in the United Kingdom by a recent asylum seeker of Syrian origin, Omar Bakri. Breaking with the movement's clandestine and elitist modus operandi, Bakri sought to forge his UK branch into a populist and activist movement. Sensing that Europe had become ripe for the mobilization of a reconstructed Muslim identity, the UK branch held rallies, demonstrations, and public conversions (Taji-Farouki 2000: 31). While this was criticized by the movement's central leadership as more advanced stages of the party's strategy that were only appropriate in Muslim societies, Bakri contended that "the attempt to engage with society to change its ideas must be linked with action: The struggle to pitch the party's ideas against those that underpin society creates an obligation to enter a direct political struggle in Britain as in any Arab or Muslim country" (Taji-Farouki 2000: 31). These differences led to Bakri's eventual dismissal as head of Hizb al-Tahrir's UK branch, but he had already set up a splinter group, al-Muhajiroun ('The Emigrants') – formally established in 1996 – which would emerge as more radical and uncompromising in its rejection of the West.

Hizb al-Tahrir and al-Muhajiroun's ability to proliferate were direct consequences of the structural situation of Muslim communities, and in turn came to serve as facilitators of militant action, even though they generally stayed well clear of perpetrating violence themselves. They reinforced the radicalized discourse, further deepening the misgivings and hostility against Muslims of the host society, which in turn fed further frustration and radicalization. In this role, they served as conveyor belts of militants for al-Qa'ida and other groups. In a letter published on al-Muhajiroun's website on July 15, 1999, Bakri called on Osama bin Laden to attack the West. Following US pressure, it was removed from the website, "but it was later read aloud in mosques in North London, Bradford, Sheffield and Leicester" (Siddiqui 2004: 55).

> The Islamic Movements have not used the real weapon yet. . . . Oh Osama . . . you and your brothers are now breathing life and dignity into the body of the *umma*. Our main mission as Muslims is to carry the Islamic message to the entire world . . . We are an *umma* of jihad and beyond doubt, we have been chosen by Allah to lead the whole world if we hold to his command . . . The opportunity is here and we must not pass it by . . . Our Muslim brothers are firm in their jihad so we must not lose time aimlessly and [we must] act now. The *umma* is our *umma*, the war is our war, and the enemy is our enemy, the *mujaheddin* are our brothers, the victory or defeat is our victory or defeat, and the *Khilafah* is our *Khilafah*. Oh Osama . . . Let us hear the good news from you and your brothers, for a new dawn is near at hand. (Siddiqui 2004: 55)

In October 2000, Bakri stated that, "we collect funds [for the International Islamic Front for Jihad against Crusaders and Jews] to be able to carry on the struggle, we recruit militiamen, and sometimes we take care of these groups' propaganda requirements in Europe" (Siddiqui 2004: 24). Groups such as Hizb al-Tahrir and al-Muhajiroun – including splinters from these two – proliferated throughout Europe from the late 1980s onwards and have served two important functions: to facilitate contact between recruits and groups engaged in armed struggle, and to continually reinforce the discursive framework that sustained radicalization of European Muslim identities in the first place. It is important, in order to retain some sense of perspective, that, just as violent or pro-violence Islamist groups do not require blanket or even majority popular support in order to function in the Muslim world, neither do they require it in Europe. And just as local Islamist militants in the Muslim world tend to persist in their local national struggles – even as they legitimate, and are in turn legitimated by al-Qa'ida's globalist narrative – so too in Europe. Roy (2009: 18) correctly notes that, "a dominant characteristic of al-Qaeda's type of violence is de-territorialization," yet incorrectly goes on to assume that this is internalized by the activists it attracts, suggesting that "specific conflicts play a role only as narratives and not as geo-strategic factors; the radicals are not involved in actual conflicts, but in an imaginary perception of the conflicts." As demonstrated elsewhere in this volume, however, al-Qa'ida has generally failed to raise the gaze of local militants from focus on their own local struggles. And this has been true also in Europe. Notwithstanding their emphasis on a global solution to a global challenge, the various European Islamist groups have remained for the most part conspicuously parochial, taking on the national focus of the communities in which they operated. Thus, the Islamist groups active in France – primarily the *Groupe Islamique Armé* (GIA) and *Groupe Salafiste pour la Prédication et le Combat* (GSPC) – have remained entirely Algerian both in terms of demographics and targeting, while France has been used for fundraising and recruitment among radical-ized segments of the French Algerian population, and as a safe haven from Algerian government counter efforts. The GIA was responsible for much of the carnage during the Algerian civil war beginning in 1991. In the second half of 1995 it carried out a series of bomb attacks in Paris, killing eight and wounding 157. This string of attacks, however, was a direct result of French cooperation with the Algerian authorities and thus also part of the GIA's Algerian campaign. The GSPC, founded by Islamists who rejected the GIA's indiscriminate murder of Algerian civilians, has never carried out a major attack outside the Sahel, despite the fact that it is considered one of the most capable militant Salafi groups in the world. In September 2006, Ayman al-Zawahiri announced a union between al-Qa'ida and the GSPC, with the French and Algerian governments as a common enemy, and in January 2007 the group changed its name to al-Qa'ida in the Islamic

Maghreb (AQIM). Despite these lofty statements, its participation in al-Qa'ida's deterritorialized jihad has not gone beyond exchanges of logistical, financial and intelligence support with other Islamist groups. Likewise in the United Kingdom, the struggles engaged in by radicalized Muslims are predominantly ones that relate to their own families' countries of origin. With a preponderance of Muslims from the Subcontinent, the struggles that have agitated them, and to which they have gravitated, have over whelmingly been located there. The pattern is replicated throughout Europe. Even in the most 'purified' and globalized version of Islamism, then, is it possible to see the difficulty of al-Qa'ida's internationalism to eclipse more localized grievances. Although militants find a source of identity, validation, and comfort in the abstract globalist narrative of al-Qa'ida, they persist for the most part in more socially meaningful struggles.

The difference for European Muslims ought to be, given that it is their marginalization in Europe that prompted the process of politicization and radicalization, that the 'near enemy' and the 'far enemy' are one and the same. Yet, with some notable exceptions – including the so-called 7/7 bombings in London – actions in Europe by European Muslims have almost entirely consisted of legal forms of protest. The majority of truly internationalist attacks that have been planned in Europe or used Europe as staging ground – including 9/11 and various subsequent attempts to blow up transatlantic airliners – have not depended on local activism, but on the financing, training and leadership from the central leadership of al-Qa'ida. James Brandon points to the concern with "homegrown Islamic terrorism" that flares up, "usually following an attempted or successful bombing," as a significant misunderstanding. Brandon suggests that the public discourse ignores that fact that a steady stream of information is emerging from terrorism trials in the United Kingdom that increasingly brings the whole concept of 'self-starters' and 'leaderless jihad' into question. Recent British trials, Brandon (2009: 10) argues, indicate that a majority of major terrorist plots formulated in the United Kingdom since 2001 have been "at least partly directed by major al-Qa'ida figures in the Afghanistan and Pakistan border region. Indeed, without the training supplied by al-Qa'ida members, it is likely that few of these plots would ever have become viable." Looking at a range of attacks and plots – including the so-called 7/7 and 7/21 bombings, the 'crevice plotters' and a number of cells dismantled by the authorities – Brandon points out that "each of the major terrorist plots affecting the United Kingdom since the 9/11 attacks in the United States have had ties back to al-Qa'ida's central organization in Afghanistan and Pakistan" and that, without direct external involvement, "many of these plots would never have become remotely viable" (Brandon 2009: 10, 12).

Who, then, are the Islamists of Europe? Certainly the vicious circle of social marginalization and politicization of Muslim identity continues. The attacks of 9/11 and other 'Muslim atrocities' have galvanized the pattern. In the words of Parekh (2008: 11), the terrorist attacks that took place in New York, Madrid, London and elsewhere have had "a traumatic effect on Europeans. Hitherto they had seen Muslims as a culturally threatening but manageable presence; they now developed a morbid fear of them. Furthermore, this fear was transformed into the fear of Islam as a religion in whose name the attacks were believed to have been perpetrated."

The sociopolitical foundations of marginalization and radicalization thus continue to replicate themselves, with socially adverse consequences for all involved. In the words of Tahir Abbas (2007: 440), "the nation-state stigmatizing young Muslims...further disenfranchises the young who are already susceptible to poor leadership" and leads "to the complete vilification of all things Islamic." Parekh notes that, "in almost all European societies, young Muslims underachieve educationally and are among the poorest members" (2008: 2), which is an effect of social stigma and thus a cause of identity reconstruction (Crocker and Quinn 2004). However, it has already been noted that while there are patterns of social behavior, there is rarely if ever uniformity. Thus, not all Muslims are religious, not all religious Muslims are Islamists, not all Islamists are militant, and not all militant Islamists are violent. Yet stigmatization and marginalization call for counter-strategies; they destabilize the social identity of the marginalized and create a "cognitive opening" towards groups and individuals who would supply an alternative source of social identification (Wiktorowicz 2005: 5). "Because social comparison processes have such a powerful influence in intergroup relations, the ability to influence social comparison targets is of the highest importance" (Moghaddam 2008b: 96–7). It is precisely in this cognitive opening, then, that the battle for Muslim identity takes place, and where various responses crystallize. The vast majority of Europe's Muslims have pursued 'normative' or individualistic strategies; that is, avenues towards improving one's situation that do not challenge society's dominant normative assumptions and arrangements (Moghaddam 2008b: 98). Justification for these assumptions and arrangements are typically provided by authority figures, the media, and so forth, and "it is in the interest of majority groups to direct minority group members" towards this option. The 'psychological citizen' in Europe is fostered to support and sustain a thriving democracy. However, in a situation where the European narrative and those who supply it have often been experienced as hostile – where Muslims have been given little reason to feel European – many have not derived their identity from society at large, but, rather, from their sense of standing outside it. They have sought alternative authorities as they have gone about recreating their 'psychological citizenship.' Some of the alternatives that have made themselves available have been Islamist groups of various levels of radicalism, which have directed their followers towards 'collective strategies,' which are challenges against the status quo in order to alter it. Within this subset of the population, then, some challenges have been radical and violent, others have not.

This analysis of the causes and dynamics of Islamism in Europe is certainly not uncontroversial, even among those who reject the binary arguments about cultural essences and historical enmity. Olivier Roy, for instance, has explicitly rejected alienation as an explanation of the radicalization process because it entails apparently insurmountable definitional problems, and because, he claims, "the socio-economic definition (deprivation, poverty, racism, social exclusion) is not supported by data. We find people from all backgrounds in al-Qaeda: engineers, former drug-addicts, social workers..." (Roy 2009: 20). If one's focus is the individual, then he is surely correct but if one's focus is the larger group that provides the individual with a positively valued social identity, then he is not. According to Roy, al-Qa'ida in the West should be understood as a "youth movement" that builds on a narrative, rather than ideology or theology. He contends that this narrative has three elements: the suffering of a virtual *ummah*, the role of the individual activist "who is suddenly put in the situation of becoming a hero who would avenge the sufferings of the community" and comes to understand jihad as the individual duty of every Muslim, and "the enactment of the fight against the global order" (2009: 24–5). Roy argues that it is more productive to understand al-Qa'ida in Europe as a youth movement that shares some of its political features with the dissent of the "ultra-left" and some of its behavioral features – especially its "fascination for sudden suicidal violence" – with the perpetrators of school shootings (2009: 21). He furthermore argues that, "ideology plays little role in the radicalization of the jihadist internationalist youth: they are attracted by a narrative not an ideology" (2009: 14) and that "here, traditional anti-imperialism merges with Islamism" (2009: 17). But traditional anti-imperialism *is* ideological, as well as territorial and directly related to realities on the ground. Moreover, ideologies are *nothing but* narratives, and sociopolitical narratives are *by their very nature* ideological – model accounts of the nature and shortcomings of society, prescriptions for human behavior in order to improve it and, importantly, why they ought to do so. What remains absent is an explanation of the processes whereby these narratives gain credibility and become attractive. As noted by one scholar (Kepel 2004: 4), it is initially perplexing that radical Islam is so attractive, given that it operates in an environment that contains, not only law-enforcement constraints and anti-terrorism legislation, but also largely hostile Muslim communities "determined to marginalize the radical fringe." Roy (2009: 25) concedes that "the fact that AQ is constantly presented by Western leaders as the biggest threat gives more value to the decision to join it. The narrative is substantiated by the Western reaction to it." If this is the case, then he is tacitly agreeing that Islamists are seeking a distinctive and positive social identity in reaction against Europe's dominant narratives, which is central to the processes of alienation and marginalization. He is surely correct in asserting that there is a foundational element of anti-imperialism in al-Qa'ida's ideology that replicates that of the struggles of previous generations – which is precisely what makes al-Qa'ida a supplier of an ideological narrative. But the link Roy attempts to establish between radicalization and youth delinquency as well as individual suicidal violence obfuscates that point. While possibly descriptive of some, it is a diagnosis that utterly fails to capture the essentially social nature of Islamist activism. Roy (2009: 24) writes that among the troubled youth who engage in individual suicidal violence, "there are many patterns in common with radical terrorists: a possible history of drug addiction, a lack of social life, the fabrication of a narrative through the internet, the recording of a video before taking action, search for fame, use of the internet, the attribution of a collective responsibility to the targeted random victims." This reduces activism to social dysfunction, and effectively denies that Islamist activists have real social and political concerns; it also fails to explain, yet again – why this choice? Why now? Why in Europe? While Roy supplies anecdotal incidents of radicalized individuals that match his description, they are not a representative sample.

Roy suggests a tripartite counter-radicalization strategy: First, "we should stop speaking of Muslims through the lens of terrorism"; second, "we should stress the real nature of the radicals: not powerful devils, but petty and often unsuccessful delinquents, in a word, losers, who have no future"; and third, "we should stop promoting 'good' versus 'bad' Islam, because it supports the idea that AQ is a religious organization" (Roy 2009: 26). This is all fine as far as it goes, although the characterization of Islamist radicals as petty delinquents and "losers" seems to contradict his earlier assertion that alienation is not at the heart of the problem. More significant is the fact that this strategy does not come close to addressing actual issues in the real world. None of Roy's points are anything but semiotic changes. In a manner that has been typical of Enlightened Europeans throughout the twentieth-century encounter with Islam, Roy advocates no concrete social reform or actual political change. Thus, all the underlying structural issues that facilitate politicization and radicalization in the first place remain unaddressed. As Moghaddam (2008b: 93) puts it, "group-based inequalities are not being overcome through positive psychology processes." The problem posed by radicalization cannot be confronted merely by altering how it is spoken of, but requires actual revisions to the actual treatment of Europe's Muslim populations.

9

Conclusion: Islamism and a Fragmented Quest for Dignity

This book has sought to challenge the persistent and powerful myth, proffered by those whose narratives define the Western political discourse, that Islamism is a monolith; a monolith, moreover, that is somehow detached from the various sociopolitical and historical contexts that surround it. Dispelling the image of Islamism as a self-contained *sui generis* evil requires only a brief critical examination of the environments in which it has emerged and been sustained. As we have seen, colonialism did indeed sow division, creating and maintaining borders and propping up subservient local elites that served to enforce Western edicts. These local elites and their imperial taskmasters constructed political cultures that brought modernity to the Islamic world by means of mimicry and subservience, and many in the Muslim world felt betrayed, humiliated, and exploited. When Islamism emerged in the late eighteenth century, it was one of many political and intellectual currents born in the centrifuge of modernity as a means of dealing with its challenges. Many of its earliest thinkers – like Jamal al-Din al-Afghani and Muhammad Abdu – both admired and objected to modernity as it was represented and promoted by the West. While certain modern methods of politics, economics, administration, science and technology were inspiring and attractive, there was also a 'darker side' to modernity: Western efforts and ambitions to subjugate and dominate much of the Muslim world, which, in the age of empires and colonies was no mere fantasy, but a clearly discernible fact. Islamic political thinkers at this stage pioneered the idea that the Muslims in general suffered from an inferiority complex vis-à-vis Western models of modernity, which weakened their ability to withstand the Western onslaught. Islam was forged into Islamism, serving both as a source of identity capable of reaffirming the dignity of the native, as well as a lens through which the native was able to analyze the structures, requirements, and weaknesses of the world order, especially as it was implemented in Muslim lands.

To al-Afghani, for instance, the 'authenticity' of Islam was conceived as a contrast to, and counterbalance against a widespread native acceptance of

Western superiority that effectively concealed the self-serving schemes of Western imperialism. Keddie (1983: 42) writes of the "self-strengthening" effort that permeated al-Afghani's project and which was shared by many Muslims who "did not wish simply to continue borrowing from the West or bowing to growing Western domination, but wished rather to find in indigenous traditions, both Islamic and national, precedents for the reforms and self-strengthening they wanted to undertake." To al-Afghani, she notes, "it was important not to lay undue stress on the Western origin of what he was borrowing, as this might encourage the trend of admiration for the West and feelings of Islamic inferiority and helplessness" (Keddie 1983: 42). Such self-images – of inferiority, helplessness, and impotence – were the strength of imperialism. Hence, the image of the Muslim Self was objectified as a target also in the burgeoning Islamist struggles. As Albert Hourani (1983: 113–14) points out, al-Afghani rejected the idea that the European powers were "innately stronger than the Muslim states," and "the prevalent idea that the English were superior" should be considered a dangerous "illusion (*wahm*)" since "such illusions make men cowardly, and so tend to bring about what they fear."

In this context, Islam became both a barricade and a staging ground in the struggle to reassert the native Self and native dignity by means of resistance. Yet Islamism would also go on to develop into a matrix for governance, giving rise to various conceptions of Islamic statehood as an objective of the struggle. That is, Islamist thinkers came to view revealed religion as an essential ingredient, not only in the struggle against current forms of hegemony but also in their own alternative forms of governance. It is of course possible to object that this emphasis on transcendence, faith, and so forth makes the point that Islamism is indeed a 'pre-modern' reaction against the conditions of modernity; that Islamism is merely a mobilization of religion as a means to subvert the position of reason, materialism and secularism as central to the ordering of modern societies. The answer is that this view is clearly correct, other than the very important fact that religion and religious politics are not pre-modern, but part and parcel of modernity for a vast majority of human beings around the world. 'Pre-modern' is a pejorative word loaded with normative content; content derived from a belief in linear social progress that has seen materialist secularism eclipse religion as the central organizing principle of social life, ipso facto establishing it as more advanced, superior, and preferable. As Berger (1999: 1–4) has pointed out, this is a powerful delusion about the way in which the world actually works, which fails to take into account that the fashions forged by Western elites are by no means universal. Indeed, as peoples around the world have grappled with secular materialist modernity as it relates to their own colonial and neo-colonial predicaments, established religious frames of reference have often been part and parcel of their own formulations of modern alternatives – recognized, recognizable and eminently powerful in terms of their ability to motivate and mobilize. They constitute a rejection of Western assumptions of intellectual superiority that are upsetting to Western intellectual elites – and that is precisely the point. They also constitute a rejection of the idea that the native needs to mimic the West in order to be modern – and that is also precisely the point. But rather than thinking of this as a pre-modern rejection of modernity, it is a rejection of modernity as Western, and therefore a rejection of the assumption that the West has a right, by virtue of its intellectual superiority, to define social, political, and economic propriety for the rest of the world.

As the previous chapters have demonstrated, different Islamist groups and movements have taken very different paths in their particular struggles, translating the faith dimension in different and often conflicting ways, in part depending on whether they have come to emphasize the process of liberation or its objectives – resistance or statehood. However, before summarizing these differences and their implications, one first needs to say something about underlying commonalities. These relate primarily to a critique – or, perhaps better, rejection – of what Roxanne L. Euben (1999: 155) has referred to as "post-Enlightenment rationalism." While this rejection of the corner-stone of modernity would eventually be translated into quests for Islamic statehood as an *ideal* model of governance, the assumptions that underpin the critique are themselves exceptionally important: Islamism promotes transcendence as constitutive of all spheres of life, and desires it to permeate and govern all spheres of life. Hence, the source of all laws governing human conduct should be God. In making her point, Euben cites Khomeini and suggests that Qutb would easily have agreed that

> in Islam the legislative power and competence to establish laws belongs exclusively to God almighty. The Sacred Legislator of Islam is the sole legislative power. No one has the right to legislate and no law may be executed except the law of the Divine Legislator. (Euben 1999: 118)

This transcendence should guide individuals, societies, and the states that oversee them precisely because the human struggle for justice, as well as the administration of a just society, are contained in sacred Scripture. Perhaps the most important implication of this scriptural code of conduct is that the political dimension of faith goes beyond, or is more basic than Islamic statehood. In their struggle for a just society (according to their own standards), also the believers themselves are subordinated to the idea of justice and accountability, in this life and the hereafter. Thus, Islamism cannot be understood only as a struggle to establish a certain kind of statehood or governance, but as a critique of the conditions of materialist modernity and the assumptions of rationalism, with its all-eclipsing emphasis on the power of human reason.

Islamists offer a diagnosis of post-Enlightenment modernity as a disastrous and deluded effort. Human nature, in the Islamist view, is essentially animalistic and bereft of a firm normative system of ethics. A non-relativistic system can only be grounded in religious belief in transcendence and revelation. The task of the prophets, as Khomeini stated, was to guide humans on a path of salvation that involved social justice as a crucial dimension; a dimension forgotten or ignored by an arrogant humanity that had been seized by materialist desires. That is, beyond that imperative of an Islamic state, Khomeini saw Islam as *guidance* or what he referred to as a 'thesis' that involved the human being's striving for perfection whereby a sense of self-assertion, self-actualization, and empowerment could be realized. The Islamic thesis, he argued:

> to make the complete human being out of man. It has come to upgrade man from his current status. Man has natural aspects – Islam helps him to develop them. Man has psychological needs – Islam provides for those. Man has spiritual wants – Islam has a cure for that. Man has a rational aspect – Islam helps him develop that. And man has a divine aspect – Islam provides for that. Islam and other religions have come to help this underdeveloped man, with all his aspects, to grow and develop. (Rajaee 1983: 47)

This is the 'constitutive' aspect of Khomeini's Islamism. Its aim is to shape a new mentality and to create a 'new man' who is self-assertive and ready to make sacrifices in the struggle for his fellow human beings, against oppressive social structures that obstruct them from developing their divinely appointed potential. This struggle is an ambition that goes beyond that of establishing an Islamic state. Beyond the means of the state itself (in the Weberian sense) lies an element of faith and religious duty that permeates and compels mankind to strive for perfection. As Khomeini stated, "Man has what is 'with himself' [animal aspect] and he also has what is 'with God' [divine aspect]. As long as he is preoccupied with what is 'with himself' he will perish but if he turns to the other aspect he will live forever" (Rajaee 1983: 47). This aspect of the afterlife builds on a number of religious convictions that have been deeply politicized within Islamist thought, for a range of reasons discussed in the previous chapters. As the Muslim Brotherhood, Hezbollah, Hamas, al-Qa'ida and others have stressed, each in their own way and within their own contexts: to take a stand in order to challenge and contest an unjust order is not only a right but also an obligation for the believers. This is what Hezbollah's secretary-general Sayyed Hassan Nasrallah refered to as *al-mustaqbalayn*, 'the two futures' that combine to compel the believer to struggle in the here-and-now with a view to both earthly and eternal consequences.

An individual's political positions, especially heroism for the sake of justice and resistance against oppression, will be greatly rewarded. It follows from this that martyrs are individuals of the highest order. In Islamist narratives, the exalted status of the martyr points to the superiority of Islamic ideological convictions based on their being embedded in a transcendence of materialist assumptions. This is the background against which Hamas' statement that 'we love death more than they love life,' and various variations thereof, must be understood – not as morbid fascination with self-destruction, but as a statement of the superior life-force inherent in their own transcendental ideology. This ought not be so alien to the West as is often pretended. Although largely forgotten or ignored in the modern and Enlightened West, the Christian tradition knows well – beginning with the description of the martyrdom of Stephen in the seventh chapter of the Acts of the Apostles – that the 'crown of martyrdom' is considered as the ultimate affirmation of the value of life. Subsequently, the notion that a believer affirms life by choosing death over surrender has had direct political application; religious and political struggles have often fused, producing martyrs such as Jean d'Arc and Oscar Romero, and countless others. In the run-up to the American Revolution, for instance, Presbyterian pastor and proto-revolutionary Samuel Davis, described torture and martyrdom explaining that:

> Victory and triumph sound strange when thus ascribed; but the gospel helps us to understand this mystery. By these sufferings they obtained the illustrious crown of martyrdom...Their death was but a short transition from the lowest

> and more remote regions of their Redeemer's kingdom into his
> immediate presence and glorious court in heaven. (Sandoz 1998:
> 91)

That the specifics of creed, conduct, method, and paradisical expectations
of Christian and Islamic martyrs may differ does not change the fact that
the ontological assumption – that choosing death over submission is an
affirmation of life – is essentially similar.

The present volume has also argued emphatically that the Islamist
struggle must also be understood as a third worldist struggle for independence against foreign intrusion and domination, past and present. Thus,
Khomeini's conception of the *welayat al faqih* must not be thought of as
an end in itself, but as an ideal strategy and model of governance capable
of withstanding the pressures of an essentially hostile world order; a world
order in which Muslims find themselves under persistent duress and faced
with constant challenges from the outside. Moreover, as Sami Zubaida
points out, the Islamic revolution as it unfolded in Iran was an expression
of a specific historical trajectory that involved both the particular exigencies of its parochial Iranian context and the conditions of a more general
third worldist struggle. This latter element has emerged in many countries
and territories around the world in which populations grapple with trou-
blesome aspects of independence and foreign intervention (Zubaida 1989).
For this reason, one must recognize the very significant difference between
its anti-imperialist and nativist expressions; between the Islamic revolution
itself and the structures that generated it, on the one hand, and the
outcome of establishing of the *welayat al-faqih*, on the other. That is to
say, it is possible and necessary to parse Islamism as endorsement of faith
as a framework for the process of liberation, on the one hand, and as
endorsement of a framework for the administrative institutionalization of
Islamic rule by a Muslim clergy, on the other. Indeed, many Islamic scholars as well as non-Muslim activists opposed to the global order and US
hegemony have expressed their admiration for the achievement of the
Islamic revolution in toppling the regime of the Shah, but then voiced
their abhorrence at the authoritarian character of the Islamic republic that
followed. Like other ideological constructs, the third worldist impulse with
its faith-based dimension that drove the Iranian revolution is capable of
serving to mobilize both for and against reform and revolution. In the
aftermath of the Iranian revolution, the revolutionary impulses were
eclipsed by statist objectives, but both were represented by Islamist clergy
and intellectuals.

As mentioned above, the constitutive aspect of faith inherent in Islamism goes beyond statist aspirations, and involves a dimension that might be termed a 'new mentality' or 'new consciousness.' The politicized aspects of faith, its attendant obligations towards the community, and the eternal rewards of the hereafter, have converged to create an ideology that, according to Islamist thinkers, cannot be tampered with or compromised. As the Tunisian Islamist thinker Rachid Ghannouchi (2000: 104) has asserted, from within an Islamic framework, pragmatism could never be given priority over principles based on and demanded by faith. Likewise, with respect to Middle East 'peace process,' Amr Sabet (2008) contends that Islamists simply cannot consent to relinquishing rights or duties in the name of cost-benefit analyses based on materialist assumptions. Cost-benefit reasoning is championed by the West and continuously foisted on the Arab side as 'what needs to happen in order to solve problems.' The Islamists response is to re-configure the power structures in which this argument is made, and which make this argument normative, in order to maintain rights in the face of materialist cost-benefit analyses. Thus, propagating the notion of an Arab–Islamic 'sacred right' to reclaim occupied land is a concrete rhetorical step intended to guarantee the Palestinian people's right of return to what is 'rightfully theirs.' If one takes this Islamist conviction seriously, talk of the 'sacredness' of occupied land is not mere hyperbole, but a primary indicator of how belief in the precepts of revealed religion become politicized. That is, Islamists' political accountability contains a dimension of eternity where secular and 'Enlightened' Westerners see only the present here-and-now. Western and Islamist cost-benefit analyses are simply configured differently. Both sets of perceptions of reality inform actions and principles; neither recognizes the other as adequate or relevant.

On the Islamist side, this perspective feeds directly into the revolutionary enterprise of attempting to mould a new mentality. This is far from unique to Islamists. Indeed, it has been most common among radical visionaries on the anti-imperialist left. In his portrait of Che Guevara, Michel Löwy suggests, that "a revolution is authentic only if it can create this 'new man'" and notes that Che's ambition was to shape a new mindset – "communist man" – within the alienated worker who had internalized the canons of capitalist society and become "a wolf in a wolf community" (1973: 17).

> Communist man must necessarily be a man of greater inner resources and a greater sense of responsibility, bound to others by a relationship of real solidarity, of concrete universal

brotherhood; he must be a man who recognizes himself in his work and who, once the chains of alienation have been broken, 'will achieve total awareness of his social being which is equivalent to his full realization as a human creature.' (Löwy 1973: 19)

The difference is that Islamists see the constitutive aspect of this 'new man' as grounded in faith and revelation, rather than materialist ideology. In this context, it is instructive to note Ghannouchi's comment that one of the objectives of "Westernization in Muslim lands" has been to

> super-impose the values of Western liberalism on Muslim society with the result that the grip of traditional values was weakened; *but no new morality could develop to fill the gap*. It is in this moral vacuum that personal aggrandizement and socio-economic exploitation have become rampant, mostly in the name of economic development and material progress. Islamic resurgence represents a rebellion against this state of affairs. (Ghannouchi 2000: 117)

While this difference is significant in terms of epistemology and teleology, the basic functional similarity of the 'Islamic man' and 'Communist man' should serve to remove some of the exotic qualities that have attached to conceptions of the former. As with the idea that martyrdom is life-affirming, the project to forge a 'new man' through struggle is by no means limited to Islam but also present within ideological constructs known well within Western history.

It has been the contention of the preceding chapters that this 'conscious-making' of Islamism – affirming and strengthening Self, dignity, and steadfastness in a context of externally imposed and internally consumed humiliation – accounts for a significant part of the Islamist project. In this sense, Islamist militancy is yet another expression of a range of revolutionary positions; ways of thinking that have emerged in different forms and in different contexts in the turbulent process of de-colonization and the ongoing struggle against neo-colonialism. But it is nevertheless important, as this volume has sought to illustrate, to recognize that common basic features necessarily take different trajectories, and therefore produce different struggles and visions, depending on social, cultural, economic and political context. Often, idealized constructs – conceptions of what ought to be – are adapted, rethought, moderated or indeed compromised as its proponents seek to navigate the terrain of reality. Gledhill (1994: 81) stresses the need to grasp the content of resistance strategies in order to identify "what kind of impact they have on power relations, accepting *that they do not pose an immediate threat to the stability* of existing forms of social and political domination." He emphasizes the importance of not approaching radical efforts of resistance against the status quo through a lens of "stability versus totalizing 'revolution'," even when "we are dealing with a counter-hegemonic culture whose tone is apocalyptic in creating the societies of their imagination. After all, even 'real' social revolutionaries like Lenin and the Bolsheviks did not succeed in creating the societies of their imagination" (Gledhill 1994: 81).

The effect of differentiated local contexts and challenges is that groups and movements labeled 'Islamist' have formulated disparate and sometimes flatly contradictory understandings of Islamist ideology and strategy. Islamist movements and thinkers articulate and advocate an array of shifting ideas and tendencies; some inclusive and accommodating of those not like themselves; others implacably hostile and absolutist to everyone outside a narrowly conceived ingroup. Some, like Hamas, have chosen a territorially bounded national path while others, like the jihadists of al-Qa'ida, have developed a transnational narrative and methodology in order to promote their struggle. In some cases, even the commonalities may be deceptive. While they all reject the assumptions of the post-Enlightenment ethos and all in their own way struggle against the various dimensions of foreign intervention into the Muslim world, the 'Western identity' of their enemy has not been constant. While most colonial and neo-colonial interventions have been and remain 'Western,' it is important to remember that a significant part of the Islamist movement was forged in a struggle against Soviet intervention in Afghanistan, as well as Soviet influence in countries like Syria, Iraq, and Egypt. To be sure, the origins of Marxism and Marxism–Leninism are decidedly Western in terms of geographic origins. However, the pervasive idea that Islamism is founded on some hatred of Western liberalism and democracy is patently false given that the current leadership of many of the most effective and militant Islamist movements cut their teeth in the struggle against an utterly illiberal and undemocratic communist dictatorship. The underlying commonality between the Soviet Union and the capitalist West, as far as Islamist resistance movements are concerned, is the post-Enlightenment ethos of superiority, secularism, and materialism, on the one hand, and their attempts to enforce an exploitative imperial hegemony over Muslim lands, on the other.

In this context, one must neither ignore nor forget that Islamist parties, especially during the Cold War, were manipulated by Arab and 'Islamic' regimes to counterbalance against the threats and challenges posed by leftist and secular nationalist movements, and that Islamist groups were an effective and therefore frequently used weapon in the armory of those who sought to maintain the systemic order, including Western powers. While the encouragement of foreign powers and local elites did its part to foster Islamist militancy, it is also important to see how more uncompromising forms of Islamism – expressed by, for instance, Sayyed Qutb and subsequent generations of Salafi-jihadists – were shaped, not by tacit support from regimes, but by brutal repression. It is easy to detect the third worldist bond that Islamists share with many Arab nationalist and secular currents, but it is also easy to see where those bonds break. In Egypt, for instance, the MB cooperated with the Free Officers around Gamal Abdul Nasser in opposing the British and their allies within the Egyptian sociopolitical elite, and following the revolution in 1952, the MB made cautious overtures towards the new post-colonial government. Yet for ideological reasons, fear of the power of Islamism, and reluctance to imperil its newfound power over the Egyptian body politic, cooperation turned into confrontation. It was the Free Officers' brutal repression and persecution of the MB that served as the midwife of Qutb's brand of radicalism, and it was the shared experience of this repression, and the crushed post-colonial dreams of many devout Muslims that went with it, that made Qutb's ideas popular. Qutb provided a narrative that outlined what would go on to become the received view among a multitude of Islamists around the world: that the cruelty of Nasser's regime and others like it were due to abandonment of God. Rather than creating a 'new man,' the post-colonial regimes merely replicated the self-serving greed and repression of their erstwhile colonial masters. As noted above, this is analogous to the criticism voiced by the progressives that had supported or even participated in the Islamic revolution in Iran and then watched in horror as the Islamists outmaneuvered, expelled, or executed all who would threaten its power. Hence, the Islamist contest was not only against Western colonialism but against materialism and secularism as such; whether it was Western, Soviet or indigenous mattered little, as these labels merely described different bottles containing the same poison.

As Islamist narratives and aspirations went from clashing with colonialism to confrontation with neo-colonialism, it also moved to challenge local post-colonial elites in a struggle for power framed by the turbulence of de-colonization and state building. Local differences in these levels of confrontation have had significant impact on the way Islamist movements have positioned themselves towards the regimes, and affected their priorities and ambitions. For instance, while many Islamist movements have been subject to harsh and persistent repression, marginalization and exclusion by local regimes, Hezbollah in Lebanon has been relatively privileged. There is no way of knowing how Hezbollah would have reacted if the Lebanese regime had decided to move against the movement's guerrillas, but there is reason to believe that the clash would not have been insignificant. Indeed, in the 1980s, Hezbollah was even prepared to fight its Syrian benefactors in order to safeguard its 'right' to conduct resistance against Israel (Goodarzi 2006). It was the overarching imperative to maintain the resistance against Israel that eventually prompted, or enabled Hezbollah to develop a doctrine and philosophy of 'national resistance' that, to its mind, in no way contradicted the idea of an Islamic resistance. Similarly, Hamas accommodated power political reality when it participated in the legislative elections in Gaza 2006, abandoning its earlier rejection of all Oslo derived institutions of Palestinian governance. Since 1993, it has offered Israel a series of long-term truces, based on preconditions that Israel has not been able or willing to accept. What Hamas has not done, however, is to renounce its moral, transcendental right to struggle for the rights of the Palestinian people.

Hezbollah and Hamas' perspective on resistance highlights another commonality among many Islamist militants: armed struggle as self-affirmation of human value and dignity; what has been referred to earlier in this book as the 'Fanonian impulse.' As noted above, this view rests on the conviction that the world and human relations are not shaped by the universal values of Western civilization, human rights, or natural law, but are instead created by the use of force. Historically, this force has been wrought by colonialism and is currently reproduced by neo-colonialism. Hence, Islamists, like many other 'liberation movements' or 'resistance forces' in the Third World, perceive themselves as engaged in a struggle against the persistent greed of Western hegemony, on the one hand, and the ignorance of the subalterns, on the other. Put differently, in the Islamist perspective, the world order is embedded in an ontology of violence; the strong establish norms that guide and define acceptable human conduct and the weak consume and internalize these norms. As argued earlier, this was also the Fanonian analysis of the colonial condition, and to Fanon the remedy was violence. Not only was violence necessary in order to break down an order built and maintained through violence – violence as instrument – but violence was also necessary as a means to reify a sense of Self among the subalterns of the system. Just as Islam is capable of enhancing self-esteem and thereby shatter the sense of inferiority that cripples the subjugated, violence is cathartic for those who are subjected to an overpowering structure that has been created and consolidated by violence. In fact, as we have seen with Hezbollah, a central component of the movement's emphasis on resistance is to obliterate the idea of Arab weakness and Israeli superiority. The Fanonian impulse is very much crucial to the movement's strategies of defiance and resistance.

The other movements and groups treated in this volume have, each in its own way, come up with a similar analysis in their own context. The Algerian Islamists have not been as privileged as Hezbollah; neither in terms of cooperation with the regime, nor in terms of being able to develop its influence and prioritize objectives in an orderly fashion. In Algeria, the Islamist struggle that emerged with a great popular following in the late 1980s but was stalled in 1992 would soon revolve around mere survival – and in this regard, the Islamists of the FIS lost. They did not survive the Algerian regime's onslaught, or the repressive and brutal strategies of the hard line elements, the *eradicateurs*, of the military and security establishment. Rather, the quest for dignity among many Islamist cadres, especially the young, triggered a Fanonian impulse that propelled them into bitterly violent cycles of vendettas with the regime, which took the country close to a chaotic civil war throughout the 1990s. As we have seen, the more accommodationist and pragmatic elements both within the regime and the Islamist movement were forced to step back in the ongoing showdown and witness how their popularity and legitimacy slowly eroded as public despair and alienation prevailed. Algeria turned a corner at the end of the 1990s and there were real prospects for national reconciliation, as well as international pressure for some regime elements to be held accountable for human rights abuses. The process was slow, however, and the events of September 11, 2001 and the subsequent US war on terror provided an opportunity for Algerian elites to jump on the bandwagon and contribute their on-the-ground expertise in the fight against Islamic terrorism. According to Jeremy Keenan (2009), the United States viewed its ability to control the Sahel, including southern Algeria, as a strategic asset. Hence, a way to get a foot hold in the region was to cooperate with the Algerian regime and even turn a blind eye to its fabrication of some of some of the many terrorist operations (Keenan 2009: 269–96). Paradoxically, the ongoing instabilities in Algeria, the real and the fabricated has provided a rationale for Western military assistance to, and close political relations with the Algerian regime; assistance and relations that in turn have benefitted the economic interest of foreign governments and transnational corporations (TNCs). Gregory White and Scott Taylor have argued with respect to the disturbances in Algeria and Nigeria that one must take into account the possibility that domestic conflict may in fact serve the interests of TNCs and the West because "a society divided against itself, living amidst a steady level of 'ordered chaos' and civil war, cannot unite to exert pressure against the TNC operation. Such instability, in turn, provides the justification for ongoing support for a military regime by external actors" (White and Taylor 2001: 340).

In this context, scholars have described how Western powers, both the United States and the European Union, consider Algeria important primarily in terms of its economic stability and that, as a result of this focus and despite official rhetoric, issues related to democracy and human rights are given less priority (Cavatorta 2009: 185). This has been an important element in Algeria's feedback loop of investment, repression, austerity and resistance. Indeed, Algerian elites have been keen to abide by the guidelines of the IMF and the World Bank, and living up to European expectations of economic stability in the region. As a result, the regime has largely been left alone with respect to human rights abuses and the effective strangling of the Algerian Islamist opposition. Far-reaching and harsh Structural Adjustment Programs (SAPs) have prompted an emphasis on stability and security and thus virtually required repression of those who would disturb the balance. While these programs may have solved many macroeconomic burdens for the regime and the country, they have also exacerbated many of Algeria's social and political tensions, leading to a series of crises – from strikes and demonstrations to assassinations and civil war. The support that the Algerian regime gained from subordinating itself to the SAPs was a great help in its fight against the Islamist insurgents throughout the 1990s. Ironically, the austerity measures required by the SAPs have also radicalized the marginalized strata of the population and given rise to an informal economy in which various Islamist networks have been able to thrive, and in which corrupt elements of the security services have frequently been implicated. Authoritarianism has followed and Washington and Brussels have often looked the other way. Thomas Carothers (2003) has argued that this is evidence of the 'split personality' of US policy, which is officially committed to promoting democracy while in reality it buttresses, directly or indirectly, a number of authoritarian regimes. The reality is that the requirements for good governance placed on Arab regimes by investor nations often involve an expectation of repressive conduct; securing investments and keeping radicals at bay. Hill (2009) also contends that while France would occasionally admonish the Algerian regime for its human rights abuses, it would also support the *eradicateurs* in their brutal fight against the Islamists. As was noted in chapter 7, direct

French intervention in Algerian affairs has been the sole trigger of Algerian Islamist terrorism on the French mainland.

Another more diffuse consequence of the experiences in Algeria in the 1990s was that many Islamist groups and networks viewed the civil war as emblematic of national struggle; there was no hope for change, either by ballot or bullet. Confronting the local regime thus served no purpose since these regimes are situated within, and benefit from larger power structures centered on European capitals and Washington, DC. This is part of the reason why transnational groups like al-Qa'ida and the range of Salafi-jihadist networks directly or indirectly connected to it were able to market their modality of struggle with such success. In a context where the local despots are virtually untouchable due to the support they receive from foreign backers, it would seem natural to some that those foreign backers are the problem that needs to be confronted first. Switching the focus from the 'near enemy' to the 'far enemy' was thus not merely a matter of inclination, but a direct outcome of structural realities.

However, the rapid political change achieved by the popular uprisings in Tunisia and Egypt in early 2011 – where presidents bin Ali and Mubarak were forced to resign within a month of the onset of protests in their respective countries – called into question, not only the need for al-Qa'ida as a militant vanguard for regional change, but also the appropriateness of al-Qa'ida's focus on the far enemy.

Gilles Kepel coined the term 'Salafi jihadism' to describe a school of thought within Salafism that emerged in the 1990s and distinguished itself from mainstream Salafism by commitment to violent jihad. It combines "respect for the sacred texts in their most literal form" with an "absolute commitment to jihad, whose number-one target had to be America, perceived as the greatest enemy of the faith" (Kepel 2003: 220). While rooted in its faith, filtered through the writings of Qutb and others, as a transnational social phenomenon, the movement was something new; yet another response to the failure of previous attempts to resist and restructure the prevailing order. By transnational, rather than international, Devji suggests that their network has no particular territorial rooting, unlike nationally focused Islamists like Hamas and Hezbollah, and that their membership and support base are identified with the Islamic *umma*, rather than with the people of a particular nation-state. The Salafi jihadist trend therefore believes that "territory serves *only as a temporary base for some greater project, not as an object of desire or control in its own right*" (Devji 2005: 153).

To this transnationalism, however, is commonly attached a fiercely militant purism in relation to Islamic orthodoxy as well as jihadi orthopraxis.

The level of abstraction at which the 'Islamic man,' his actions and objectives are set – bereft of specific constituency, boundaries, and limitations – enables and exaggerates nativist ideas of purity. As we have seen, this is a nativism of which Fanon warned, and which stands in sharp contrast to the third worldist agenda of those whose struggles are dedicated to specific constituencies in specific territories. Both approaches are expressions of Islamism and both are a resistance struggle – but they are not the same resistance struggle. Hezbollah's Ali Fayyad has argued that the difference lies in the ability to parse between the political and religious spheres, and apply the appropriate concepts. Commenting on Lebanon and the region at large, he argued that,

> Extremist Salafi takfiri organizations deal on religious criteria with the international community. We do not, and this is a big difference. Christians here are our brothers ... I feel that the Christian groups fighting the Israelis and resisting the US hegemony are closer to us than Salafi takfiri Muslims. We want to build our alliances with a political rather than religious focus ... To fight the Christians because they are Christians, Jews because they are Jews – this has no basis in Islam and has never happened in our history. Conflict has happened for political reasons ... Ignorance of context is not just a problem of Christians reading the Quran, but also of Muslims. A literal understanding of Quran is very dangerous. It is the first step towards Salafism. (Fayyad to author, April 2011)

To Fayyad, the cooperation between Coptic Christians and Muslims in the context of the Egyptian uprising was therefore a sign of health; placing the imperatives of resistance in a political rather than religious context. To Salafi groups, by contrast, that same development was extremely troubling. As a consequence of nativism – applying exclusionary religious principles to the resistance project – Egyptian Salafis were quick to attack Coptic Christians and churches in order to sow division and force an end to the new 'interfaith' modus vivendi.

The angry exchange, recounted in chapter 5, between al-Qa'ida and Hamas regarding the latter's participation in the 2006 elections is another case in point. While many Islamist movements formed political parties during the 1990s and participated in elections (if they were permitted to do so by the authorities), jihadi currents in places like Egypt and Algeria were more or less eradicated during their bloody vendettas with their respective regimes. This led some of them, most notably perhaps the Egyptian Islamic Jihad headed by al-Zawahiri, to tie themselves to a transnational network that would involve them in politics in far-flung places like Afghanistan and Sudan. To al-Zawahiri, widely regarded as the chief ideologue of al-Qa'ida and the elected successor of bin Laden after the latter's death in May 2011, any accommodation with any political system that does not stem from his own understanding of Islam would imply the neutralization of the cause of Islam. Thus, in March 2006, he scolded Hamas for participating in the parliamentary elections for the Palestinian Authority, since "joining those who sold Palestine in one legislative council…as a constructive religious judgment and accepting that the number of votes is the judge between us and them is a clear violation of the approach of the Koran" (IntelCenter 2008: 91). He continued:

> That we recognize the legitimacy of their government and system means that we recognize the agreements they signed. It also means that, should these criminals receive a majority in any upcoming elections, then we will have to accept their right to sell Palestine. However, nobody, be he Palestinian or not, has the right to relinquish a grain of the Palestinian soil. This was an Islamic country, which the infidels occupied. It is the duty of every Muslim to seek to regain it. This is the dangerous meaning of accepting to join these secular councils on the basis of a secular constitution and on the basis of the Madrid and Oslo accords, the road map, and other agreements of surrender that violate and even clash with the sharia. (IntelCenter 2008: 91)

Al-Zawahiri warned all his "Muslim brothers" in Palestine and Iraq and elsewhere that the various political processes including elections was part of a deceptive "American game" that involved four objectives; first, abandonment of Islamic law; second, recognition of various agreements "imposed by the enemy"; third, the relinquishing of arms and jihad; and fourth, recognition of the enemy's military superiority and recognition of the presence of US military bases across the region. As al-Zawahiri concluded, "the Crusader–Zionist enemy lures some of us into approving part of the game's rules with promises of power and freedom of movement, but then resorts to pressure and siege to force them to accept the remaining rules" (IntelCenter 2008: 92). That is, even partial acceptance of, or inclusion in extant political systems will force abandonment of the greater transcendent struggle that lies at the heart of the Islamist project.

Similarly, in May 2006, Syrian-born Salafi preacher Abu Basir al-Tartusi (2006) published a tract denouncing Hezbollah by describing it as an ally of "infidelity and apostasy" since it had subordinated itself to the Syrian regime, governed by the secular Ba'th party. The tract contended that Hezbollah "does not even conceal its ignorant, nationalist orientation" and has "sullied itself" by adjusting to the Maronite controlled regime in Lebanon, accepting a political system that is ultimately secular, and embracing concepts like "national unity" and state law. "It is a Lebanese party protecting nothing but Lebanese lands," the tract went on, excoriating Hezbollah for aligning itself with other groups and movements on the basis of territorial boundaries "regardless of religion, virtue, and ideological orientation", rather than ignoring those same boundaries. To al-Tartusi, this plainly meant "that Hezbollah is not an Islamic Jihadi movement, striving to establish a world of Allah and his rule; rather it is a Lebanese national *rafidite* [apostate] movement whose only concern is spreading Shi'ite Islam." In this way, Hezbollah's pragmatic alliances with other political parties were portrayed as alignments with "criminal gangs" aimed only at protecting the party from domestic confrontation and conflict. Hezbollah's stated solidarity with the Palestinian cause was lambasted as a sham since, in reality, the groups served the interests of both Syria and Israel by "preventing the armed Palestinian groups present in Lebanon from practicing their legitimate right of protecting Palestine...The Jewish Zionists are interested in their security, and they do not care about the type or colour of the dog that guards them, be it a Syrian from among the Ba'th-Ansaries, or a Lebanese from among the Shi'ite *rafidite* soldiers." The Israeli withdrawal had thus been conducted because the Israelis shrewdly regarded Hezbollah as a "better guard against the Palestinian mujahidin than the SLA" (al-Tartusi 2006).

In June 2006, Abu Musab al-Zarqawi, head of the Iraqi branch of al-Qa'ida at the time, similary claimed that Hezbollah "puts forth lying slogans about Palestinian liberation when in fact its serves as a security wall (for Israel) and prevents Sunnis from crossing its border" (AFP June 1, 2006). To Hezbollah, increasingly embedded within the Lebanese system, such attacks were naturally disturbing, especially as Salafi jihadist groups had already established a presence in Lebanon, inside the Palestinian refugee camps as well as in traditional Sunni areas throughout Lebanon. In late December 2005, an obscure group widely believed to have ties to al-Zarqawi's Iraqi al-Qa'ida branch, launched a number of katyuscha rockets against Israel from south Lebanon. In an interview with *al-Hayat*, published January 20 the following year, Nasrallah expressed concern because Hezbollah itself regarded the launching of katyuschas against Israel as part of its carefully calibrated 'balance of terror' with Israel; these rockets should under no circumstances be launched randomly. Yet the movement remained extremely cautious in responding to what it recognized as a potent challenge. In April 2006, a cell was uncovered and arrested by the Lebanese Army Intelligence Directorate in Beirut, suspected of plotting to assassinate Nasrallah. When rumors surfaced that this group was part of a Salafi jihadist current known as *al-Da'wah wa al-Tabligh* (the Call and Dissemination of Faith), Nasrallah immediately stressed that the foiled plot should not be used to criticize Salafism or Sunni Islam in Lebanon. "Do we not always say [that] no man shall have the burden of another man's actions?" (BBC World Summary, April 15, 2006), Nasrallah asked in order to forestall sectarian confrontation, and continued:

> This should be the case not only when a group is discovered before implementation or while planning, but also upon implementation. Who will be held responsible if the group implements its plan? Will the Sunnis in Lebanon be responsible merely because these youths are Sunni? Never. This will be injustice and betrayal of blood and disavowal of the Koranic logic and our religious commitment. If a group belonging to the Shi'ites, Sunnis or Christians plans to kill or kills someone, no-one should accuse all Shi'ites, Sunnis or Christians in Lebanon. This is incorrect, illogical, insensible, illegal, unethical and inhuman. We must warn against any exploitation of such incidents for sectarian incitement purposes. (BBC World Summary, April 15, 2006)

Similar attention to the importance of nuance – purposively deployed in order to avoid division in Muslim ranks – was evident even in the wake of the attacks on September 11, when, on September 16, US President George W. Bush referred to the looming counter-effort as a 'crusade.' In sharp contrast against the Salafi jihadists (and many other less radical tendencies and movements), Nasrallah responded by saying that, "no Muslim should believe that the war waged against the Arabs and Muslims is Christianity's war against Islam." Indeed, misreading the conflict by taking the US president at his words would, according to Nasrallah, cause a catastrophe by creating civil strife within the *umma* and ultimately weaken it in the face of real enemies:

> O brothers and Sisters, O Arab and Islamic peoples: You should know that the Zionists want to see a war between Christianity and Islam and a war between Christians and Muslims all over

the world. Would you fulfill that desire for them? Many Christians and Muslims reject terrorism whatever its source might be. They adopt great positions in fighting Israel and Zionism, and have offered martyrs who defended Lebanon, Palestine, Syria, the Arab homeland, and the Islamic states. By all standards, no one should be drawn to sedition of this kind. (BBC World Summary, April 15, 2006)

Senseless abstraction and inattention to nuance would, to Nasrallah and his movement, cause nothing but harm to the overarching priority of remaining under arms in confrontation with Israel. Al-Qa'ida's Quixotic struggle against an abstract enemy was no substitute for Hezbollah and the Palestinians' socially grounded struggle against a very real enemy – and Nasrallah would make this point abundantly clear. After the al-Qa'ida affiliated *Jihad wa Tawhid* ('Holy War and Unity') had carried out its coordinated suicide attacks in Kerbala and Baghdad in March 2004, which killed close to 300 Shi'a pilgrims and wounded almost 400, Nasrallah (2004a) furiously lambasted the "fanatic, radical, and tyrannical groups that still live in the Middle Ages, lacking brain, mind, religion, morals, but that are Muslims or claim their affiliation to Islam." To him, the sectarian sedition sown by these groups would be reaped as victory by the enemy. "If we can surmount, isolate, and besiege this [intra-Muslim] sedition, we will bring down the gravest weapon possessed by America and Israel" (Nasrallah 2004a).

The feud with al-Qa'ida, its affiliates and their modus operandi allowed Nasrallah to point to the difference between third worldist Islamism and nativist Islamism. In 2004, with reference to the targeting of Iraqi civilians, he asked:

What does it mean when someone sets booby traps in the markets, cities, and in front of the police stations in Basra at 0730 am, the time when the streets are jammed with students, people, merchants and customers?...I cannot say that this is ignorance, it is treason...Yes, frankly, these are the crimes that must be condemned and rejected by each fighter in the Islamic world...The freedom fighters in Lebanon, Palestine, Iraq, Syria, and the entire region are refusing to recognize these perpetrators as part of their ranks...Those who kill and target the occupiers can be classified as Islamic fighters and loyal patriots. On the other hand, those who target the Iraqis are assassins belonging to the American caravan. They are accomplices in the American crime. (Nasrallah 2004b)

Similarly, when a large-scale bomb attack against one of the holiest Shi'a shrines in Iraq – the 1,000-year-old Imam Ali al-Hadi mausoleum – ignited a new round of sectarian violence in Iraq, Nasrallah called for calm at a mass rally in Beirut. The first to benefit from any such attacks, he claimed, is the US occupation, by creating the illusion that continued occupation is their only guarantee for security. The occupation, he suggested, is afraid of popular unity, and the prospects for such unity is actively undermined by those *takfiriyun* – those who accuse other Muslims of apostasy – who are now provoking civil war between the Shi'a and Sunni Muslims (Nasrallah 2006a). It is interesting to note that, even as sectarian tensions simmered in Lebanon following Hezbollah's takeover of Sunni-dominated parts of Western Beirut in May 2008, Sunni Islamist groups in the country have repeatedly affirmed their solidarity with Hezbollah's resistance project against Israel (ICG 2009). Lines of hostility and solidarity are almost never clear-cut or formulaic.

Islamism is a multidimensional paradox that does not neatly conform to Western models of political behavior. Schwarzmantel (2008: 126) has argued that what distinguishes the politics of identity from the politics of ideology is that "the latter seek to bring people together for broad projects of social transformation, while the former accepts the irreducible differences in society and is more skeptical of broad programs of social action." Groups asserting an identity, he suggests, are more inclined "to create a space for the growth or at least preservation of the particular identity in question, and its recognition by and respect from the wider society" Schwarzmantel (2008: 126). In a some ways, this is the core of Islamism – a position that asserts a native identity in confrontation with those who would subjugate it; using that assertion to elevate native consciousness and create an 'Islamic man' where previously there was only a subaltern wretch. Yet Islamism is also ideology, it does seek to build further on this assertion of Self, to replace the current unjust hegemony with an arrangement that it understands as a more just, equitable, and moral society guided and framed by Islam.

Thus, Islamism is both identity and ideology, it is simultaneously process and objective, tactic and strategy, reality and ideal. It is a totalizing ambition grounded in the diffusion between the public and private spheres, between the present and the transcendent. At the same time, the multitude of local contexts out of which Islamism has emerged have forced each individual group and movement to socially construct its own distinct emphases, its own focus and priorities, its own level of sociopolitical groundedness or abstraction. They are all attempting to break with a condition that they can no longer tolerate, to jolt the native out of consuming and internalizing the myth that his inferiority vis-à-vis the hegemonic powers is natural, to reify the faith that he is told holds him back and prevents his progress, to make himself the equal of the hegemon by the same force that has been used to impose his inferiority, and to create an Islamic man in place of the subaltern. The modalities by which that new reality is sought, however, are diverse and divided. In the words of Mirza Asadullah Khan Ghalib (Jalal 2008: 4):

> Alas, not all things in life are easy;
> Even man struggles to be human.

References

Abbas, T. (2007). Ethno-religious identities and Islamic political radicalism in the UK: A case study. *Journal of Muslim Minority Affairs*, 27(3).

Abrahamsen, R. (2003). African studies and the postcolonial challenge. *African Affairs*, 102, 89–210.

Abu-Rabi, I. M. (2004). Preface. In al-Zayyat, M. *The Road to Al-Qaeda: The Story of Bin Laden's Right-Hand Man*. London and Ann Arbor, MI, Pluto Press.

Adams, C. C. (1933). *Islam and Modernism in Egypt: A Study of the Modern Reform Movement Inaugurated by Muhammad Abduh*. London, Russell and Russell.

Ahmad, K. (1983). The nature of Islamic resurgence. In Esposito, J. L. (ed.) *Voices of Resurgent Islam*. New York, Oxford University Press.

Ajami, F. (2004, March 22). The Moor's last laugh. *Wall Street Journal*.

Albertini, T. (2003). The seductiveness of certainty: The destruction of Islam's intellectual legacy by the fundamentalists. *Philosophy East and West*, 53(4), 455–70.

Algar, H. (1981). *Islam and Revolution 1: Writings and Declarations of Imam Khomeini*. Berkeley, Mizan Press.

Al-Hussein, R. (2007, May 26). Lebanon will never let the terrorists win. *Ya Libnan*. Retrieved January 3, 2011, from http://yalibnan.com/site/archives/2007/05/lebanon_will_ne.php.

Alliance of Palestinian Forces (1994). Al-Mahamm al-siyasiyah li-tahaluf al-quwah al-filastiniyah [The political mission of the Alliance of Palestinian Force] *Majallah Fateh*, 307, 18–19.

Almond, G. A., Appleby, R. S., and Sivan, E. (2003). *Strong Religion: The Rise of Fundamentalisms Around The World*. Chicago and London, University of Chicago Press.

Al-Tartusi, A. (2006, May 23). The Lebanese Hezbollah and the exportation of the Shi'ite ideology. [Arabic tract] Lebanon. Retrieved December 8, 2010, from https://www.siteintelgroup.com/_layouts/SiteIntel/Application Pages/Document.aspx?ID=14652

Anderson, B. (1993). *Imagined Communities: Reflections on the Origin and Spread of Nationalism*. London, Verso.

Anderson, L. (1995). Democracy in the Arab world: A critique of the political culture approach. In Brynen, R., Korany, B., and Noble, P. (eds) *Political*

Liberalization and Democratization in the Arab World. Vol. 1, *Theoretical Perspectives*. Boulder, CO, Lynne Rienner Publishers.

Anderson, L. (1997). Fulfilling prophecies: State policy and radical Islamism. In Esposito, J. L. (ed.) *Political Islam: Revolution, Radicalism or Reform?* London, Lynne Rienner Publishers, Inc.

Arendt, H. (1958). *The Human Condition*. Chicago and London, University of Chicago Press.

Asad, T. (1986). *The Idea of an Anthropology of Islam*. Washington, DC, Center for Contemporary Arab Studies, Georgetown University.

Atwan, A. (1996, November 27). Interview with Saudi oppositionist Osama bin Laden. *Al-Quds al-Arabi*.

Salah, M. (1999, March 8–14). The secret of the relationship between al-Zawahiri and bin Laden: The jihad leader turned bin Laden into a mujahid. *Al-Wasat*.

Ayoob, M. (2008). *The Many Faces of Political Islam*. Ann Arbor, MI, University of Michigan Press.

'Azzam, A. (1988, April). The Solid Base. *Al-Jihad*, 41.

Bahtia, M. (2005). Fighting words: Naming terrorists, rebels, bandits and other violent actors. *Third World Quarterly*, 26(1).

Baran, Z. (2004). *Hizb ut-Tahrir: Islam's Political Insurgency*. Washington, DC, The Nixon Center.

Barletta, M. (1998). Chemical weapons in the Sudan: Allegations and evidence. *Monterey Institute of International Studies Nonproliferation Review*, 6(1).

Barnett, M. N. (1998). *Dialogues in Arab Politics*. New York, Columbia University Press.

Bawer, B. (2006). *While Europe Slept: How Radical Islam is Destroying the West from Within*. New York, Broadway Books.

Beinin, J. and Stork, J. (1997). On the modernity, historical specificity, and international context of political Islam. In Beinin, J. and Stork, J. (eds) *Political Islam: Essays from Middle East Report*. London, IB Tauris and Co.

Beiser, F. C. (ed.) (1993). *The Cambridge Companion to Hegel*. Cambridge, Cambridge University Press.

Bekkar, R. (1997). Taking up space in Tlemcen: The Islamist occupation of urban Algeria. In Beinin, J. and Stork, J. (eds) *Political Islam: Essays from Middle East Report*. London, IB Tauris and Co.

Ben-Dor, G. (1977). Political Culture Approach to Middle East Politics. *International Journal of Middle East Studies*, 8(1).

Benjamin, D. and Simon, S. (2002). *The Age of Sacred Terror*. New York, Random House.

Bergen, P. (2001). *Holy War, Inc*. New York, Touchstone.

Bergen, P. (2011). 'Time to move on from war on terror.' CNN Online. Retrieved June 3, 2011, from http://news.blogs.cnn.com/2011/05/02/bergen-time-to-move-on-from-war-on-terror/

Berger, P. L. (ed.) (1999). *The Desecularization of the World: Resurgent Religion and World Politics.* Grand Rapids, MI, Wm. B. Eerdman's Publishing Co.

Berman, P. (2004). *Terror and Liberalism.* New York, W. W. Norton.

Berman, S. (2003). Islamism, revolution, and civil society. *Perspectives on Politics*, 1(2).

Bin-Jiddu, G. (2006, July 20). Interview with Hezbollah Secretary General Hassan Nasrallah. Al-Jazeera. Retrieved January 3, 2011, from http://www.globalresearch.ca/index.php?context=va&aid=2790

Blanford, N. (2007, May 22). New fight rips at a fragile Lebanon. *The Christian Science Monitor*, 1.

Boroujerdi, M. (1996). *Iranian Intellectuals and the West.* New York, Syracuse University Press.

Boehmer, E. (2002). *Empire, The National and the Postcolonial: Resistance in Interaction.* Oxford, Oxford University Press.

Boyd, K. (ed.) (1999). *Encyclopedia of Historians and Historical Writing Vol. 1.* London and Chicago, Fitzroy Publishers.

Brandon, J. (2009). Al Qa'ida's involvement in Britain's "homegrown" terrorist plots. *CTC Sentinel*, 2(3).

Brannan, D. W., Esler, P. F., and Strindberg, A. (2001). "Talking to 'terrorists': Towards an independent analytical framework for the study of violent sub-state activism." *Studies in Conflict and Terrorism*, 24(1).

Browers, M. L. (2005). The secular bias in ideology studies and the case of Islamism. *Journal of Political Ideologies*, 10(1).

Brown, R. (1988). *Group Processes: Dynamics Within and Between Groups.* Oxford, Basil Blackwell.

Bulliet, R. (2004). *The Case for Islamo-Christian Civilization.* New York, Columbia University Press.

Burgat, F. (2003). *Face to Face with Political Islam.* London, IB Tauris.

Burke, J. (2004). *Al-Qaida: The True Story of Radical Islam.* London, Penguin Books.

Buruma, I. and Margalit, A. (2002, January 17). Occidentalism. *New York Review of Books*, 49(1). Retrieved January 3, 2011, from http://www.travelbrochure-graphics.com/extra/occidentalism_ian_buruma.htm

Buruma, I. and Margalit, A. (2004). *Occidentalism: The West in the Eyes of its Enemies.* New York, Penguin.

Byman, D. (2003). Should Hezbollah be next? *Foreign Affairs* 82(6), 54–66.

Cabral, A. (1969). *Revolution in Guinea: An African People's Struggle.* London, Stage 1.

Cabral, A. (1973). *Return to the Source: Selected Speeches by Amilcar Cabral.* New York and London, Monthly Review Press.

Camara, H. (1971). *Spiral of Violence.* London, Sheed and Ward,

Carothers, T. (2003). Promoting Democracy and Fighting Terror. *Foreign Affairs*, 82(1), 84–97.

Carrère d'Encausse, H. and Schram, S. R. (1969). *Marxism and Asia: An Introduction and Readings*. London, Allen Lane.

Cavatorta, F. (2009). *The International Dimension of the Failed Algerian Transition*. Manchester and New York, Manchester University Press.

Choueiri, Y. M. (1990). *Islamic Fundamentalism*. London, Pinter Publishers.

Cobban, H. (2005). Hizbullah's New Face. *Boston Review*, April/May. Retrieved January 3, 2011, from http://bostonreview.net/BR30.2/cobban.php

Commins, D. (1994). 'Hassan al-Banna'. In Rahnema, A. (ed.) *Pioneers of Islamic Revival*. London and New York, Zed Books.

Coury, R. M. (2005). The demonization of pan-Arab nationalims. *Race and Class* 46(4), 1–19.

Country Studies (2010). Retrieved December 11, 2010, from http://www.country-studies.com/lebanon/population.html

Crocker, J. and Quinn, D. M. (2004). Psychological consequences of devalued identities. In Brewer, M. and Hewstone, M. (eds) *Self and Social Identity*. London, Blackwell Publishing.

Crooke, A. and Perry, M. (2006, October 13). How Hezbollah defeated Israel Part II: Winning the ground war. *Asia Times*. Retrieved January 3, 2011, from http://conflictsforum.org/2006/how-hezbollah-defeated-israel-2/

Curtis, N. (2004). Nihilism, Liberalism and Terror. *Theory, Culture and Society*, 21(3).

Dabashi, H. (2008). *Islamic Liberation Theology: Resisting the Empire*. Abingdon, Oxon, and New York, Routledge.

Dahoah-Halevi, J. (2007, May 17). The Growing Hamas-Al Qaeda Connection. *Jerusalem Viewpoints*, 7(1).

Daum, W. (2001). Universalism and the West. *The Future of War*, 23 (summer).

Declaration of War against the Americans Occupying the Land of the Two Holy Places (1996). English transcript of original Arabic text. Retrieved December 11, 2010, from http://www.pbs.org/newshour/terrorism/international/fatwa_1996.html

Denoeux, G. (2002). The forgotten swamp: Navigating political Islam. *Middle East Policy*, 9(2).

Devji, F. (2005). *Landscapes of the Jihad: Militancy, Morality and Modernity*. London, C. Hirst and Co.

Dilley, R. (ed.) (1999). *The Problem of Context*. New York and Oxford, Berghahn.

Djerejian, E. P. (1992). The US and the Middle East in a Changing World. *The DISAM Journal, summer*.

El-Hokayem, E. (2006). Hizbollah's enduring myth. *Arab Reform Bulletin*, November.

Emerson, S. (2002). *American Jihad: The Terrorists Living Among Us*. New York, The Free Press.

Ernst, C. W. (2004). *Following Muhammad: Rethinking Islam in the Contemporary World*. Chapel Hill, NC, University of North Carolina Press.

Esler, P. F. (1987). *Community and Gospel in Luke-Acts: The Social and Political Motivations of Lucan Theology*. Cambridge, Cambridge University Press.

Esler, P. F. (1998). *Galatians*. London, Routledge.

Esposito, J. L. (1995). *The Islamic Threat: Myth or Reality*. New York, Oxford University Press.

Euben, R. L. (1999). *Enemy in the Mirror: Islamic Fundamentalism and the Limits of Modern Rationalism*. Princeton, Princeton University Press.

Europol (2010). *EU Terrorism Situation and Trend Report 2010*. Brussels.

Evans, M. and Phillips, J. (2007). *Anger of the Dispossessed*. New Haven and London, Yale University Press.

Fabian, J. (1983). *Time and the Other: How Anthropology Makes Its Object*. New York, Columbia University Press.

Fadhlallah, M. H. (1995). Interview with Sayyed Muhammad Husayn Fadhlallah. *Journal of Palestine Studies*, 25(1).

Fakhry, M. (2004). *A History of Islamic Philosophy*. New York, Columbia University Press.

Fanon, F. (1988). *Toward the African Revolution* (H. Chevalier, Trans.) New York, Grove Press. (Original work published 1964.)

Fanon, F. (2001). *The Wretched of the Earth* (C. Farrington, Trans.) London, Penguin Classics. (Original work published 1961.)

Fernandez, B. (2001, September 22). US markets decline again. *The Philadelphia Inquirer*. Retrieved January 3, 2011, from http://www.accessmylibrary.com/article-1G1-120858112/u-s-markets-decline.html

Fetzer, J. S. and Soper, J. C. (2005). *Muslims and the State in Britain, France, and Germany*. Cambridge, Cambridge University Press.

Fisk, R. (2002). *Pity the Nation: The Abduction of Lebanon*. New York, Nation Books.

Fisk, R. (2007). *The Great War for Civilisation: The Conquest of the Middle East*. New York, Vintage Books.

Fradkin, H. (2008). The history and unwritten future of Salafism. *Current Trends in Islamist Ideology*, 6.

Fukuyama, F. (1992). *The End of History and the Last Man*. New York, Free Press.

Fuller, G. E. (2003). *The Future of Political Islam*. New York, Palgrave McMillan.

Ghadbian, N. (1997). *Democratization and the Islamist Challenge in the Arab World*. Boulder, CO, Westview Press.

Ghannouchi, R. (2000). Arab Secularism the Maghreb. In Tamimi, A. and Esposito, J. L. (eds) *Islam and Secularism in the Middle East*. New York, New York University Press.

Ghosh, B. (2008, September 20). Q&A: Bernard Lewis on Islam's crisis. *Time Online*. Retrieved January 3, 2011, from http://www.time.com/time/world/article/0,8599,1843104,00.html

Gledhill, J. (1994). *Power and its Disguises: Anthropological Perspectives on Politics.* London and Boulder, CO, Pluto Press.

Gold, D. (2006, March 5). Ties between al Qaeda and Hamas in Mideast are long and frequent/It shouldn't be any surprise that the two groups share ideology. *SFGate.* Retrieved December 11, from http://articles.sfgate.com/2006-03-05/opinion/17286102_1_hamas-posters-qaeda-new-hamas-government

Goodarzi, J. M. (2006). *Syria and Iran: Diplomatic Alliance and Power Politics in the Middle East.* London, I. B Tauris.

Goodwin, C. and Duranti, A. (eds) (1992). *Rethinking Context: Language as an Interactive Phenomenon.* Cambridge, Cambridge University Press.

Gray, J. (2003). *Al Qaeda and What it Means to be Modern.* New York, The New Press.

Gutiérrez, G. (1988). *A Theology of Liberation.* Maryknoll, NY, Orbis Books.

Haddad, S. (2010). Fatah al-Islam in Lebanon: Anatomy of a terrorist organization. *Studies in Conflict and Terrorism,* 33(6), 548–69.

Haddad, Y. (1983). Sayyid Qutb: Ideologue of Islamic Revival. In Esposito, J. (ed.) *Voices of Resurgent Islam.* Oxford, Oxford University Press.

Hadiz, V. R. (2004). The rise of neo-third worldism? The Indonesian trajectory and the consolidation of illiberal democracy. *Third World Quarterly,* 25(1).

Hafez, M. M. (2004). From marginalization to massacres: A political process of explanation of GIA violence in Algeria. In Wiktorowicz, Q. (ed.) *Islamic Activism: A Social Movement Theory Approach.* Bloomington, IN, Indiana University Press.

Hamas (1994, April 16). Rabin tries to cover his failing criminal policies. [Arabic original document].

Hamas (n.d.). *Mudhakarah ta'rifiyyah* ("Introductory Memorandum"). Arabic pamphlet.

Harb, M. and Leenders, R. (2005). Know thy enemy: Hizbullah, "terrorism" and the politics of perception. *Third World Quarterly,* 26(1), 173–97.

Harik-Palmer, J. (2004). *Hezbollah: The Changing Face of Terrorism.* London, IB Tauris.

Hegel, G. W. F. (1967). *Philosophy of Right* (T. M. Knox, Trans.). Oxford, Oxford University Press. (Originally published 1821.)

Hegel, G. W. F. (1977). *Phenomenology of the Spirit* (A. V. Miller, Trans.). Oxford, Oxford University Press. (Originally published 1807.)

Heristchi, C. (2004). The Islamist discourse of the FIS and the democratic experiment in Algeria. *Democratization,* 11(4), 111–32.

Hersh, S. (2005). *Chain of Command: The Road from 9/11 to Abu Ghraib.* New York, Harper Perennial.

Hezbollah (1997). *Kitab al-Senoi, 1995–1996 [Yearbook, 1995–1996].* Beirut.

Hijazi, A. (2009, August 16). *O Hamas! This is politics and progress through bloodshed and not brotherly strife.* [Arabic leaflet].

Hill, J. N. C. (2009). Challenging the failed state thesis: IMF and World Bank intervention and the Algerian civil war. *Civil Wars*, 11(1), 39–56.

Hirsi Ali, A. (2006). *The Caged Virgin: An Emancipation Proclamation for Women and Islam*. New York, Free Press.

Hoare, M. A. (2008, January 5). What do the figures of the Bosnian war-dead tell us? Bosnian Institute. Retrieved December 11, 2010, from http://www.bosnia.org.uk/news/news_body.cfm?newsid=2336

Hoffman, B. (2006a). *Combating Al Qaeda and the Militant Islamic Threat: Testimony presented to the House Armed Services Committee, Subcommittee on Terrorism, Unconventional Threats and Capabilities on February 16, 2006.* Washington, DC, RAND.

Hoffman, B. (2006b). *Islam and the West: Searching for Common Ground, The Terrorist Threat and the Counter-Terrorism Effort.* Testimony presented to the Senate Foreign Relations Committee on July 18, 2006. Washington, DC, RAND.

Hogg, M. A. and Abrams, D. (1988). *Social Identifications: A Social Psychology of Intergroup Relations and Group Processes.* London, Routledge.

Holloway, J. (1998). *Dignity's revolt.* Retrieved December 10, 2010, from http://libcom.org/library/dignitys-revolt-john-holloway

Hourani, A. (1983). *Arab Thought in the Liberal Age, 1798–1939.* Cambridge, Cambridge University Press.

Hroub, K. (2000). *Hamas: Political Thought and Practice.* Washington, DC, Institute of Palestine Studies.

Hughes, R. (1994). From radical mission to equivocal ambition: The expansion and manipulation of Algerian Islamism, 1979–1992. In Marty, M. and Appleby, R. S. (eds) *Accounting for Fundamentalisms: The Dynamic Character of Movements.* Chicago, University of Chicago Press.

Huntington, S. P. (1993a). The Clash of Civilizations? *Foreign Affairs*, 72(3), 22–49.

Huntington, S. P. (1993b). The West Unique, Not Universal. *Foreign Affairs*, 72(5), 29–46.

Hymes, D. (1972). Models of interaction of language and social life. In Gumperz, J. J. and Hymes, D. (eds) *Directions in Sociolinguistics.* New York, Holt, Rinehart and Winston.

Ingold, T. (ed.) (1994). *Companion Encyclopedia of Anthropology: Humanity, Culture and Social Life.* London, Routledge.

IntelCenter (2008). *Words of Ayman al-Zawahiri Vol 1.* Alexandria, VA, Tempest Publishing.

International Crisis Group (2002, November 18). *Old Games, New Rules: Conflict on the Israeli–Lebanon Border. Middle East Report No. 7.* Retrieved December 11, 2010, from http://www.crisisgroup.org/en/regions/middle-east-north-africa/israel-palestine/007-old-games-new-rules-conflict-on-the-israel-lebanon-border.aspx

International Crisis Group (2004, July 30). *Islamism, Violence and Reform in Algeria: Turning the Page (Islamism in North Africa III)*. *Middle East Report No. 29*. Retrieved December 11, 2010, from http://www.crisisgroup.org/en/regions/middle-east-north-africa/north-africa/algeria/029-islamism-violence-and-reform-in-algeria-turning-the-page.aspx

International Crisis Group (2009, February 19). *Nurturing Instability: Lebanon's Palestinian Refugee Camps*. *Middle East Report No. 84*. Retrieved December 11, 2010, from http://www.crisisgroup.org/en/regions/middle-east-north-africa/israel-palestine/084-nurturing-instability-lebanons-palestinian-refugee-camps.aspx

Israeli Ministry of Foreign Affairs (2006, July 12). *The Second Lebanon War (2006)*. Retrieved January 3, 2011, from http://www.mfa.gov.il/MFA/Terrorism-+Obstacle+to+Peace/Terrorism+from+Lebanon-+Hizbullah/Hizbullah+attack+in+northern+Israel+and+Israels+response+12-Jul-2006.htm

Jaber, H. (1997). *Hezbollah: Born With a Vengeance*. London, Fourth Estate.

Jalal, A. (2008). *Partisans of Allah: Jihad in South Asia*. Cambridge, MA and London, Harvard University Press.

Jibril, A. (1989, August 8–14). Statement by Comrade Ahmad Jibril, Secretary General of the Popular Front-General Command, on Radio al-Quds to the masses of our Palestinian people on the occasion of the intifada entering its third year. *Ila al-Amam*, 2018.

Jibril, A. (1993, October 21). Interview with Ahmad Jibril. *Al-Quds Palestinian Arab Radio*.

Jindau, A. (1986). *Fanon: In Search of the African Revolution*. London, Routledge and Kegan Paul.

Juergensmeyer, M. (1993). *The New Cold War? Religious Nationalism Confronts the Secular State*. Berkeley, CA, University of California Press.

Kafala, T. (2004, March 2). Analysis: Palestinian suicide attacks. *BBC News Online*. Retrieved December 11, 2010, from http://news.bbc.co.uk/2/hi/middle_east/3256858.stm

Karsh, E. (2006). *Islamic Imperialism: A History*. New Haven, CT, Yale University Press.

Keddie, N. (1983). *An Islamic Response to Imperialism: Political and Religious Writings of Sayyid Jamal ad-Din "al-Afghani"*. Berkeley, CA, University of California Press.

Keddie, N. (2008). Sayyid Jamal al-Din "al-Afghani". In Rahnema, A. (ed.) *Pioneers of Islamic Revival*. London, Zed Books.

Kedourie, E. (1992). *Politics in the Middle East*. Oxford, Oxford University Press.

Keenen, J. (2009). *The Dark Sahara: America's War on Terror in Sahara*. London, Pluto Press.

Kenney, J. T. (2006). *Muslim Rebels: Kharijites and the Politics of Extremism in Egypt.* Oxford, Oxford University Press.

Kepel, G. (2003). *Jihad: The Trial of Political Islam.* London, IB Tauris.

Kepel, G. (2004). *The War for Muslim Minds: Islam and the West.* Cambridge, MA, The Belknap Press of Harvard University Press.

Khomeini, R. (1989). Imam Khomeini's letter to Mikhail Gorbachev. Retrieved December 11, 2010, from http://www.ghadeer.org/english/imam/letter%20Imam/callto/callto2.html Krauthammer, C. (2002, March 27). Editorial. *New York Daily News.* Retrieved January 3, 2011, from http://avpv.tripod.com/suicide.html

Krämer, G. (1992). Liberalization and democracy in the Arab world. *Middle East Report,* 22(174).

Krämer, G. (1994). The integration of the integrists: A comparative study of Egypt, Jordan and Tunisia. In Salamé, G. (ed) *Democracy Without Democrats? The Renewal of Politics in the Muslim World.* London, IB Tauris and Company.

Langohr, V. (2001). Of Islamists and ballot boxes: Rethinking the relationship between Islamism and electoral politics. *International Journal of Middle East Studies,* 33, 591–610.

Lachkar, J. (2002). The Psychological Make-up of a Suicide Bomber. *Journal of Psychohistory,* 29(4), 349–67.

Laurence, J. and Strum, P. (eds) (2008). *Governments and Muslim Communities in the West: United States, United Kingdom, France and Germany.* Proceedings of a Conference sponsored by the Division of United States Studies, Woodrow Wilson International Center for Scholars, March 3–5, 2008. Washington, DC, Woodrow Wilson Center for Scholars.

Lawrence, B. B. (2010). Afterword: Competing genealogies of Muslim cosmopolitanism. In Ernst, C. W. and Martin, R. C. (eds) *Rethinking Islamic Studies: From Orientalism to Cosmopolitanism.* Columbia, SC, University of South Carolina Press.

Lawrence, T. E. (1997). *The Seven Pillars of Wisdom.* Ware, Hertfordshire, Wordsworth. (Originally published 1926.)

Leiken, R. S. (2005). Europe's Angry Muslims. *Foreign Affairs,* 84(4).

LeVine, M. (2008). *Heavy Metal Islam: Rock, Resistance, and the Struggle for the Soul of Islam.* New York, Three Rivers Press.

Lévi-Strauss, C. (1963). *Structural Anthropology* (C. Jacobson and B. Grundfest Schoepf, Trans.). New York, Basic Books.

Lévi-Strauss, C. (1966). *The Savage Mind.* Chicago, University of Chicago Press.

Lewis, B. (1996). Islam and liberal democracy: A historical overview. *Journal of Democracy,* 7(2).

Lewis, B. (2003). *The Crisis of Islam: Holy War and Unholy Terror.* New York, The Modern Library.

Lewis, B. (2004). *From Babel to Dragomans: Interpreting the Middle East*. Oxford, Oxford University Press.

Lia, B. (2008). *Architect of Global Jihad: The Life of Al-Qaida Strategist Abu Mus'ab al-Suri*. New York, Columbia University Press.

Löwy, M. (1973). *The Marxism of Che Guevara: Philosophy, Economic and Revolutionary Warfare*. Plymouth, Monthly Review Press.

Malinowski, B. (1935). *Coral Gardens and Their Magic, Vol. 1: The Description of Gardening*. London, Allen and Unwin.

Malinowski, B. (1993). The problem of meaning in primitive languages. In Maybin, J. (ed.) *Language and Literacy in Social Practice*, Clevedon, UK, Open University Press. (Originally published 1923.)

Malley, R. (1996). *The Call from Algeria: Third Worldism, Revolution, and the Turn to Islam*. Berkeley, CA, University of California Press.

Marrouchi, M. (2003). Introduction: Colonialism, Islamism, terrorism. *College Literature*, 310(1).

Martin, R. C. and Barzegar, A. (eds) (2010). *Islamism: Contested Perspectives on Political Islam*. Stanford, CA, Stanford University Press.

Marty, M. and Appelby, R. S. (eds) (1991–5). *Fundamentalisms Observed: The Fundamentalism Project (Vols. 1–5)*. Chicago, University of Chicago Press.

Marty, M. and Appleby, R. S. (eds) (1994). *Accounting for Fundamentalisms: The Dynamic Character of Movements*. Chicago, University of Chicago Press.

Marx, K. and Engels, F. (1962). *Marx and Engels: Selected Works, Vol. II*. Moscow, Foreign Language Press.

Masoud, T. (2008). Are they democrats? Does it Matter? *Journal of Democracy*, 19(3), 19–24.

McCarthy, R. (2006, January 26). We would share power, says exiled leader of Syrian group. *Guardian*. Retrieved January 3, 2011, from http://www.guardian.co.uk/world/2006/jan/26/syria.rorymccarthy

McGirk, T. (2007, June 14). Hamas' takeover of Gaza. *Time Magazine*. Retrieved December 11, 2010, from http://www.time.com/time/magazine/article/0,9171,1633072,00.html

Mekehennet, S. and Moss, M. (2007, March 16). In Lebanon a new face of jihad vows attacks on US. *New York Times*. Retrieved December 11, 2010, from http://www.nytimes.com/2007/03/16/world/middleeast/16jihad.html?pagewanted=1&_r=1

Merton, T. (1967). *Faith and Violence: Christian Teaching and Christian Violence*. Notre Dame, IN, Notre Dame University Press.

Metcalf, B. D. (2001). *'Traditionalist' Islamic Activism: Deoband, Tablighis, and Talibs*. Lecture presented at the Institute for the Study of Islam in the Modern World, Leiden University, November 23, 2001. Retrieved December 11, 2010, from http://essays.ssrc.org/sept11/essays/metcalf.htm

Migaux, P. (2008). The roots of Islamic radicalism. In Chaliand, G. and Blin, A. (eds) (2009). *A History of Terrorism: From Antiquity to Al Qaeda*. Berkeley, University of California Press.

Mirsepassi, A. (2002). *Intellectual Discourse and the Politics of Modernization: Negotiating Modernity in Iran*. New York, Cambridge University Press.

Mitchell, R. P. (1969). *The Society of the Muslim Brothers*. Oxford, Oxford University Press.

Moghaddam, F. M. (2008a). *How Globalization Spurs Terrorism*. Westport, CT, Praeger Security International.

Moghaddam, F. M. (2008b). *Multiculturalism and Intergroup Relations: Psychological Implications for Democracy in Context*. Washington, DC, American Psychological Association.

Moussalli, A. S. (1992). *Radical Islamic Fundamentalism: The Ideological and Political Discourse of Sayyid Qutb*. Beirut, American University of Beirut.

Murawiec, L. (2008). *The Mind of Jihad*. Cambridge, Cambridge University Press.

Nasr, V. (2007). *The Shia Revival: How Conflicts Within Islam Will Shape the Future*. New York, W. W. Norton.

Nasrallah, H. (2002). Address of the Secretary General on the ninth night of the month of Muharram. March 22. [Arabic audio file] Retrieved December 11, 2010, from http://audio.moqawama.org/details.php?cid=1&linkid=147

Nasrallah, H. (2004). Address of the Secretary General on the tenth day of Ashura in the holy month of Muharram. March 2. [Arabic audio file] Retrieved December 11, 2010, from http://audio.moqawama.org/details. php?cid=1&linkid=30

Nasrallah, H. (2004b). Address of the Secretary General of Hezbollah at a celebration of aid and support for the Iraqi people. May 18. [Arabic audio file] Retrieved December 11, 2010, from http://audio.moqawama.org/details.php?cid=1&linkid=34

Nasrallah, H. (2005). Address of the Secretary General at the official celebration of the girls of the Mahdi school. January 7. [Arabic audio file] Retrieved December 11, 2010, from http://audio.moqawama.org/details.php?cid=1&linkid=15

Nasrallah, H. (2006a). Address of the Secretary General on the occasion of expressing horror at the destruction of al-Hadi shrine February 23. [Arabic audio file] Retrieved December 11, 2010, from http://audio.moqawama.org/details.php?cid=1&linkid=350

Nasrallah, H. (2006b). Address of the Secretary General in commemoration of the children of the Prophet of God (pbuh). April 14. [Arabic audio file] Retrieved December 11, 2010, from http://audio.moqawama.org/details.php?cid=1&linkid=357

Nasrallah, H. (2006c). Full text of Hizbullah Secretary General, Sayyed Hassan Nasrallah's speech at the divine victory rally held in Beirut, September 22.

[Arabic audio file] Retrieved December 11, 2010, from http://english. moqawama.org/essaydetails.php?eid=709&cid=231

Nasrallah, H. (2007a). Interview with the Secretary General on "Talk of the Hour" on al-Manar Television. January 19. [Arabic audio file] Retrieved December 11, 2010, from http://audio.moqawama.org/details.php?cid= 1&linkid=381

Nasrallah, H. (2007). Address of the Secretary General on the night of the third day of holy Muharram. January 22. [Arabic audio file] Retrieved December 11, 2010, from http://audio.moqawama.org/details.php?cid=1& linkid=383

Nasrallah, H. (2008). Full text of H. E. Sayyed Nasrallah Press Conference: We are in a new period ~ Unconstitutional government must back down. May 8. Retrieved December 11, 2010, from http://english.moqawama.org/ essaydetails.php?eid=3450&cid=231

Nasrallah, H. (2011). Words of the General Secretary on Resistance and Liberation Day. May 25. [Arabic video file] Retrieved June 7, 2011, from http://www.almanar.com.lb/programs/videowatch.php?eid=7283&f=1

National Commission on Terrorist Attacks Upon the United States (2004). *The 9/11 Commission Report: Final Report of the National Commission on Terrorist Attacks Upon the United States*. New York, W. W. Norton and Company.

National Intelligence Council (2007, July). *National Intelligence Estimate: The Terrorist Threat to the US Homeland*. Washington, DC, Office of the Director of National Intelligence.

Nicholson, R. A. (1989). *The Mystics of Islam* (4th edn). London, Arkana. (Originally published 1914.)

Noe, N. (ed.) (2007). *Voice of Hezbollah: The Statements of Sayyed Hassan Nasrallah*. London, Verso.

Norton, A. R. (1987). *Amal and the Shi'a Struggle for the Soul of Lebanon*. Austin, TX, University of Texas Press.

Norton, A. R. (1995, January). The challenge of inclusion in the Middle East. *Current History*. Retrieved January 3, 2011, from http://www.hartford-hwp. com/archives/29/016.html

Nursery-Bray, P. (1980). Race and nation: Ideology in the thought of Frantz Fanon. *Journal of Modern African Studies*, 18(1).

O'Donovan, O. (2007). Political tradition, liberation and modernity. In Rowland, C. (ed.) *The Cambridge Companion to Liberation Theology*. Cambridge, Cambridge University Press.

Orwell, G. (1949). *1984*. London, Harcourt Brace and Company.

Paine, R. (ed.) (1981). *Politically Speaking*, St. John's, Canada, ISER Press.

Parekh, B. (2008). *European liberalism and the Muslim question (ISIM Papers No. 9)*. Amsterdam, Amsterdam University Press.

Patai, R. (2002). *The Arab Mind* (rev. edn) New York, Hatherleigh Press.

Peteet, J. (2005). *Landscapes of Hope, Landscapes of Despair: Place and Identity in a Palestinian Camp.* Philadelphia, PA, University of Pennsylvania Press.

Pew Research Center (2006, July 6). Muslims in Europe: Economic worries top concerns about religious and cultural identity. Retrieved December 11, 2010, from http://pewglobal.org/2006/07/06/muslims-in-europe-economic-worries-top-concerns-about-religious-and-cultural-identity/

Qassem, N. (2005). *Hizbullah: The Story from Within.* London, Saqi Books.

Qutb, S. (1970). *Social Justice in Islam.* Washington, DC, American Council of Learned Societies.

Qutb, S. (n.d.). *Milestones.* Damascus, Syria, Dar al-Ilm.

Rahnema, A. (2008). Introduction to 2nd edition: Contextualizing the pioneers of Islamic revival. In Rahnema, A. (ed.) *Pioneers of Islamic Revival.* London and New York, Zed Books.

Rajaee, F. (1983). *Islamic Values and World View: Khomeyni on Man, the State and International Politics.* Lanham, MD, University Press of America.

Ramadan, T. (2006). *With the Prophet Muhammad (Peace be upon him) 2/3 – Exile: Meaning and Teachings.* Retrieved December 11, 2010, from http://www.tariqramadan.com/spip.php?article701

Rapport, N. and Overing, J. (2000). *Social and Cultural Anthropology: The Key Concepts.* London, Routledge.

Roberts, H. (2004). From radical mission to equivocal ambition: The expansion and manipulation of Algerian Islamism, 1979–1992. In Marty, M. and Appleby, R. S. (eds) (1994) *Accounting for Fundamentalisms: The Dynamic Character of Movements.* Chicago and London, University of Chicago Press.

Roberts, H. (2007). *Demilitarizing Algeria: Carnegie Papers No. 86.* New York, The Carnegie Endowment for International Peace.

Robertson, N. and Cruickshank, P. (2009). New jihad code threatens Al Qaeda. *CNN Online.* Retrieved December 11, 2010, from http://www.cnn.com/2009/WORLD/africa/11/09/libya.jihadi.code/

Rodinson, M. (1988). *Europe and the Mystique of Islam.* London, IB Tauris.

Rollins, J. (2010). *Al Qaeda and Affiliates: Historical Perspective, Global Presence, and Implications for U.S. Policy.* Washington, DC, Congressional Research Service.

Roy, O. (2003). Islamisme et nationalisme. *Pouvoirs*, 104.

Roy, O. (2006). *Globalized Islam: The Search for a New Ummah.* New York, Columbia University Press.

Roy, O. (2007). *Secularism Confronts Islam.* New York, Columbia University Press.

Roy, O. (2009). Al-Qaeda in the West as a youth movement: The power of a narrative. In Emerson, M. (ed.) *Ethno-Religious Conflict in Europe: Typologies of Radicalization in Europe's Muslim Communities.* Brussels, Centre for European Policy Studies.

Ruedy, J. (1992). *Modern Algeria: The Origins and Development of a Nation.* Bloomington, IN, Indiana University Press.

Rushdie, S. (2005, August 7). The right time for an Islamic reformation. *Washington Post*. Retrieved December 11, 2010, from http://www.washingtonpost.com/wp-dyn/content/article/2005/08/05/AR20050805 01483.html

Sabet, A. (2008). *Islam and the Political: Theory, Governance and International Relations*. London, Pluto Press.

Said, E. (1979). *Orientalism*. New York, Vintage Books.

Said, E. (1993). *Culture and Imperialism: The T. S. Eliot Lectures at the University of Kent 1985*. New York, Knopf/Random House.

Said, E. (1996). *Representations of the Intellectual: The 1993 Reith Lectures*. New York, Vintage Books.

Sayigh, Y. (1999). *Armed Struggle and the Search for State: The Palestinian National Movement, 1949–1993*. Oxford, Oxford University Press.

Salamé, G. (ed.) (1994). *Democracy Without Democrats? The Renewal of Politics in the Muslim World*. London, IB Tauris and Company.

Sandoz, E. (ed.) (1998). *Political Sermons of the American Founding Era, 1730–1805, Vol. 1*. Indianapolis, IN, Liberty Fund.

Scharfstein, B. A. (1989). *The Dilemma of Context*. New York, New York University Press.

Schmid, A. P. and Jongman, A. J. et al. (1983). *Political Terrorism: A Research Guide to Concepts, Theories, Databases and Literature*. Amsterdam, North Holland Publishing.

Schwarzmantel, J. J. (2008). *Ideology and Politics*. Thousand Oaks, CA, Sage Publications.

Shakespeare, W. *Merchant of Venice*. In *The Works of William Shakespeare from the Text of the Rev. Alexander Dyce's 2nd Edition*, Vol I (Leipzig: Bernhard Tauchnitz, 1868).

Shariati, A. (2003). *Religion vs. Religion*. Chicago, ABC International Group.

Shiqaqi, F. (1997a). Al-qadiyah al-filastiniyah hiyah al-qadiyah a-markaziyah lil-harakah al-islamiyah...limadha? [The Palestinian problem is the central problem for the Islamic movement...why?]. In Sidahmad, Rifa't (ed.) *Al-'umal al-kamilah al-shahid al-doktor Fathi al-Shiqaqi: al-majalad al-awwal* [The Complete Works of the Martyr Doctor Fathi Shiqaqi: Part I]. Cairo, Markaz iafa li-l-dirasat wa-l-abhath. Originally published in *Majallah al-Mukhtar al-Islami*, 2(13), July 1980.

(1997b). Iran al-thawrah wal-dawlah [Iran, the revolution and the state]. In Sidahmad, Rifa't (ed.) *Al-'umal al-kamilah al-shahid al-doktor Fathi al-Shiqaqi: al-majalad al-awwal* [The Complete Works of the Martyr Doctor Fathi Shiqaqi: Part I]. Cairo, Markaz iafa li-l-dirasat wa-l-abhath. Originally published in *Majallah al-Mukhtar al-Islami*, 2(14), August 1980.

(1997c). Ma hiyah harakah al-jihad al-islami fi filastin? [What is the movement of Islamic jihad in Palestine?] In Sidahmad, Rifa't (ed.) *Al-'umal al-kamilah al-shahid al-doktor Fathi al-Shiqaqi: al-majalad al-awwal* [The Complete

Works of the Martyr Doctor Fathi Shiqaqi: Part I]. Cairo, Markaz iafa li-l-dirasat wa-l-abhath. Originally published in *Nusrah al-Mujahid – Filastin*, 146–9 (June-July 1992).

Siba'i, H. (2009, August 15). Hamas kills one who takes refuge in God's house: The martyrdom of Shaykh Dr. Abu Noor. [Arabic leaflet] Lebanon.

Sidahmed, A. and Ehteshami, A. (eds) (1996). *Islamic Fundamentalism*. Oxford, Westview Press.

Siddiqui, M. (2004). The doctrine of Hizb ut-Tahrir. In Baran, Z. (ed.) *The Challenge of Hizb ut-Tahrir: Deciphering and Combating Radical Islamist Ideology*. Washington, DC, The Nixon Center.

Soroush, A. (2000). *Reason, Freedom, and Democracy in Islam*. Oxford, Oxford University Press.

Stora, B. (2001). *Algeria*. Ithaca, NY, Cornell University Press.

Strindberg, A (2001). Interview with 'Imad al-'Alami. *Jane's Intelligence Review*, 13(11).

Strindberg, A. and Wärn, M. (2005). Realities of resistance: Hizballah, the Palestinian rejectionists, and al-Qa'ida compared. *Journal of Palestine Studies*, 34(3), 1–19.

Sturrock, J. (1979). *Structuralism and Since: From Lévi-Strauss to Derrida*. Oxford, Oxford University Press.

Tadelis, S. (1999). What's in a name? Reputation as a tradeable asset. *The American Economic Review*, 89(3).

Taher, A. (2008, June 8). Al-Qaeda: The cracks begin to show. *The Times Online*. Retrieved January 3, 2011, from http://www.timesonline.co.uk/tol/news/world/middle_east/article4087373.ece

Tajfel, H. (1972). La catégorisation sociale. In Moscovici, Serge (ed.) *Introduction à la Psychologie Sociale, Vol. 1*. Paris, Larousse.

Tajfel, H. (ed.) (1978). *Differentiation between Social Groups: Studies in the Social Psychology of Intergroup Relations*. London, The Academic Press.

Tajfel, H. and Turner, J. C. (1979). An integrative theory of intergroup conflict. In Austin, W. G. and Worchel, S. (eds) *The Social Psychology of Intergroup Relations*. Monterey, CA, Brooks-Cole.

Taji-Farouki, S. (2000). Islamists and the threat of jihad: Hizb al-Tahrir and al-Muhajiroun on Israel and the Jews. *Middle Eastern Studies*, 36(4).

Tamimi, A. (2001). *Rachid Ghannouchi: A Democrat Within Islamism*. Oxford, Oxford University Press.

Tashkiri, M. (1987). Towards a definition of terrorism. *Al-Tawhid*, 5(1). Retrieved December 11, 2010, from http://www.al-islam.org/al-tawhid/definition-terrorism.htm

Taylor, C. (1992). *The Sources of the Self: The Making of Modern Identity*. Cambridge, MA, Harvard University Press.

Thompson, W. C., Jr. (2002). *One Year Later: The Fiscal Impact of 9/11 on New York City*. New York, Comptroller of the City of New York.

Tibi, B. (2008). Why they can't be democratic. *Journal of Democracy*, 19(3).

Tripp, C. (1999). Sayyid Qutb. In Rahnema, Ali (ed.) *Pioneers of Islamic Revival.* London, Zed Books.

Tuastad, D. (2003). Neo-orientalism and the new barbarism thesis: Aspects of symbolic violence in the Middle East conflict(s). *Third World Quarterly*, 24(4).

Transcript of bin Laden's October interview (2002, February 5). CNN. com. Retrieved December 11, 2010, from http://edition.cnn.com/2002/WORLD/asiapcf/south/02/05/binladen.transcript/index.html

United Nations Human Rights Council (2006, November 23). Implementation of General Assembly resolution 60/251 of March 15, 2006 entitled "Human Rights Council Report of the Commission of Inquiry on Lebanon pursuant to Human Rights Council resolution S-2/1." New York, United Nations.

Usher, G. (1997). Hizballah, Syria, and the Lebanese elections. *Journal of Palestine Studies*, 26(2), 59–67.

Usher, G. (1999). *Dispatches from Palestine: The Rise and Fall of the Oslo Peace Process.* London, Pluto Press.

Vaisse, J. (2008). Muslims in Europe: A short introduction. *US-Europe Analysis Series.* Washington, DC, Brookings Institution/Center on the United States and Europe.

van Ham, P. (2001). The rise of the brand state: The postmodern politics of image and reputation. *Foreign Affairs*, 80(5).

Vertovek, S. and Peach, C. (eds) (1997). *Islam in Europe: The Politics of Religion and Community.* New York, Saint Martin's Press.

Voll, J. (1979). The Sudanese Mahdi: Frontier fundamentalist. *International Journal of Middle East Studies*, 10(2).

von der Mehden, F. R. (2008). Islam in Indonesia in the twenty-first century. In Esposito, J. L., Voll, J., and Bakar, O. (eds) *Asian Islam in the 21st Century.* Oxford, Oxford University Press.

Wadud, A. (2008). *Inside the Gender Jihad: Women's Reform in Islam.* Oxford, Oneworld.

Waterbury, J. (1994). Democracy without democrats?: The potential for political liberalization in the Middle East. In Salamé, G. (ed.) *Democracy Without Democrats? The Renewal of Politics in the Muslim World.* London, IB Tauris and Company.

Watt, W. M. (1961). *Muhammad: Prophet and Statesman.* Oxford, Oxford University Press.

Westoff, C. F. and Frejka, T. (2007). Religiousness and fertility among European Muslims. *Population and Development Review*, 33(4), 785–809.

Whitaker, B. (2004, May 24). Its best use is as a doorstop. *Guardian.* Retrieved December 11, 2010, from http://www.guardian.co.uk/world/2004/may/24/worlddispatch.usa

Whitbeck, J. (2002). The face of terror. *Arabies Trends*, 52.

White, G. and Taylor, S. (2001). Well-oiled regimes: Oil and uncertain transitions in Algeria and Nigeria. *Review of African Political Economy*, 89.

White, R. T. (1996). Revolutionary theory: Sociological dimensions of Fanon's sociologie d'une revolution. In Gordon, L. R., Sharpley-Whiting, T. D., and White, R. T. (eds) *Fanon: A Critical Reader*. Malden, MA, Blackwell.

White House (2006, September). *National Strategy for Combating Terrorism*.

Wickham, C. R. (2004). Interests, ideas, and Islamist outreach in Egypt. In Wiktorowicz, Q. (ed.) *Islamic Activism: A Social Movement Theory Approach*. Bloomington, IN, Indiana University Press.

Wiktorowicz, Q. (ed.) (2004). *Islamic Activism: A Social Movement Theory Approach*. Bloomington, IN, Indiana University Press, 2004)

Wiktorowicz, Q. (2005). *Radical Islam Rising: Muslim Extremism in the West*. Lanham, Rowman and Littlefield.

Willis, M. J. (2006). Containing radicalism through the political process in North Africa. *Mediterranean Politics*, 11(2).

Willis, M. (1996). *The Islamist Challenge in Algeria: A Political History*. New York, New York City University Press.

Wilson, S. (2007, June 30). With Hamas takeover, tough calls for Israel. *Washington Post*.

Wind, Y., Douglas, S. P., and Perlmutter, H. (1973). Guidelines for developing international marketing strategies. *The Journal of Marketing*, 37(2), 14–23.

Wright, R. (1992). Islam, democracy and the West. *Foreign Affairs*, 71(2), 131–45.

Ye'or, B. (2005). *Eurabia: The Euro–Arab Axis*. Madison, WI, Fairleigh Dickinson University Press.

Young, R. J. C. (2001). *Postcolonialism: An Historical Introduction*. Malden, MA, Blackwell.

Zisser, E. (2000). Hizballah: New course or continued warfare. *Middle East Review of International Affairs*, 4(3).

Zubaida, S (1989). *Islam, the People and the State: Political Ideas and Movements in the Middle East*. London, IB Tauris.

Index